OVER THE RAINBOW

MONEY, CLASS AND HOMOPHOBIA

SECOND EDITION

PRAISE FOR *OVER THE RAINBOW:*
MONEY, CLASS AND HOMOPHOBIA

'An extraordinary and original attack on homophobia —and an assertion of working-class unity in the struggle for sexual emancipation... the book, to my mind, remains unparalleled.'
—Leo Zeilig, author of *Philosopher of Third World Liberation: Frantz Fanon, Eddie the Kid*

'We all have a couple of key books in our lives that have really made us sit up and think. This was one of mine. It helped shape the way I thought about LGBT politics and my own sexuality. It is needed today even more than ever. I will also have to buy the new version because I gave away my battered, highlighted copy to a young, gay South African in 2003.'
—Dr Peter Dwyer, author of *African Struggles Today* and tutor in economics, Ruskin College, Oxford

'One of a few contemporary scholars going against the grain, continuing the groundbreaking effort to develop an understanding of how sexual identity features in and is shaped by capitalism.'
—Rosemary Hennessey in *Profit and Pleasure.*

'This important book addresses issues seldom discussed elsewhere. LGBT people have made great advances, but there are also real limitations. In particular, the commercial scene ... imposes values all too similar to those of their straight equivalents—the need to have the "right" body, wear the "right" clothes and so on. And that's much easier to achieve if you have the money. Field calls into question the simple assumption that we are all part of a "community" with the same interests.'
—Colin Wilson, author of *Gay Liberation and Socialism*

'I honestly cannot recommend this book enough... I believe that our movements—feminism, anti-racism, and environmentalism etc—need to be linked to a more comprehensive movement to transform society at its very roots. Nicola Field articulates that vision. She provides a long-awaited

analysis of the intersections of sexual and gender identity with class, as well as giving a superb immanent critique of the mainstream LGBT movement, which is dominated by bourgeois perspectives.... I'm dismayed, but not particularly surprised, that this book is so obscure. I am doing what I can to popularise it.'

—Gregory Esteven, Editor, *Monthly Review*

'What a fantastic book! Brilliant.'

—Marven Scott, *Marxist Internet Archive*

'I absolutely loved this one-woman tour de force exploring some elements of the facile politics at the centre of the LGBT movement in the 1980s and1990s. As someone who is not LGBT, feminist or Marxist I thought this book might not be for me but I didn't feel that for one minute. ...Nicola Field's main thesis is that much of the movement ignores the history of social struggle ... This separation from wider social issues creates a shallowness in the ability of the LGBT movement to give solidarity to others who are being systemically oppressed in other ways. Nicola Field's book is a broad and compelling theoretical observation... It speaks from the voice and body of someone who is getting their hands dirty. I admire her courage to confront huge, unholy cows of the movement ... This book is passionate, extremely intelligent and a delightful polemic of personal and political energy.'

—Chris Hart

'I am a teenage girl in South Carolina, in an ultra-conservative, predominantly republican-Fox News-watching area. I'm real into riot grrl music, and I've been sexually harassed verbally a lot... The other day I went into this used-book store, and wanted to read up on the gay movement, I came across your book and bought it, along with a Hole CD... It has touched my heart. I feel less alone as I read your book. Knowing that there are beautiful people like you makes me so happy. I picked up Over the Rainbow at just the right time. Today my aunt's friend was over, and she kept shoving her shit down my throat, so afterwards I came into my room and read a few sections of your book. It calmed me down. Thank you so much for your work.'

—Christy

OVER THE RAINBOW

MONEY, CLASS AND HOMOPHOBIA

NICOLA FIELD

FOREWORDS BY
ELLY BARNES, JONATHAN BLAKE
AND GETHIN ROBERTS

SECOND EDITION

Published by
Dog Horn Publishing
45 Monk Ings, Birstall, Batley WF17 9HU
United Kingdom
doghornpublishing.com

ISBN 978-1-907133-94-7

Cover design by
Ben Windsor

Typesetting by
Jonathan Penton

UK Distribution: Central Books
99 Wallis Road, London, E9 5LN, United Kingdom
orders@centralbooks.com
Phone:+44 (0) 845 458 9911
Fax: +44 (0) 845 458 9912

Overseas Distribution: Printondemand-worldwide.com
9 Culley Court
Orton Southgate
Peterborough
PE2 6XD
Telephone: 01733 237867
Facsimile: 01733 234309
Email: info@printondemand-worldwide.com

Contents

FOREWORDS

As a huge fan of the film *Pride* and the unifying work of LGSM, I was absolutely thrilled to be asked by Nicola Field to recommend *Over the Rainbow* in its new edition, especially as her class-based analysis of LGBT+ oppression is reminiscent of the political dimension in which, ten years ago, I first plucked up the courage at a meeting to express my concerns about LGBT+ kids' and teachers' experiences in school. It is this socialist perspective that remains fundamental to my approach with Educate & Celebrate in encouraging all schools and workplaces to join us on the journey to inclusion.

Nicola writes with astonishing clarity and focuses on issues which remain terrifyingly relevant in 2016, such as continuing LGBT+phobia, women's oppression, the imposed moral agenda from government and the media, the housing crisis, ideological attacks on state education and rising mental health concerns. Since *Over the Rainbow* was first published in 1995, Thatcher's Section 28 (which prohibited local authorities from 'promoting' or 'publishing' homosexual material) has been repealed. This should have given teachers in the UK the freedom to engage students in an LGBT+ inclusive curriculum. However, even with the subsequent arrival of LGBT History Month in 2005, the Equality Act of 2010, new government guidelines for schools, and marriage for everyone, we still, daily, have to change hearts and minds.

We are comfortable teaching about the struggle of women, ethnic minorities and disabled people in schools. However when I ask delegates 'what did you learn about the LGBT+ struggle when you were at school?' the answer is always 'nothing': and we wonder why there are high levels of homophobia, biphobia and transphobia? It is this level of invisibility that we must and can change through education to ensure all are treated equally and fairly by encouraging and modelling a more intersectional approach in the classroom. This would allow everyone to go forward with the knowledge but also the understanding required to play an active role in this ever-growing neoliberal climate, where state schools are forced to become free schools and academies, potentially giving way to private interests that take precedence over our social needs.

Children begin to discriminate by the age of seven, which is why I advocate an LGBT+ inclusive curriculum as soon as young people enter the education system through children's centres and nurseries. One deputy head, for instance, asserted that 'a lot of the parents' comments say they consider age-appropriate to be Key Stage 2 [seven+]'. This contradicts my research, which showed that reception and Key Stage 1-age pupils are more accepting and less affected by the use of terminology than we give them credit for. Therefore, we must start in Early Years Education to prevent future discrimination.

One key preventative method is to explore different family models, helping us to dispel the mythical and idealised heterosexual nuclear family, with its somewhat outdated gender roles and expectations, in order to give young people permission to recognise themselves and their own family units as special and unique. As a Year 6 class I worked with in 2015 said:

> 'Love has no right or wrong; you cannot change who you are; love has no limits; love is powerful no matter what; love has no labels.'

This powerful, potentially generational, process of positive change can then flow from our classrooms into the corridors, the playground and the street; and from there into the home and into our communities. This is why our student voice is vital to creating political and social change, by developing the need in young people to ask questions and by empowering them to create '*a society which reacts angrily to injustice and promptly sets about correcting it*' (Bauman, quoted in Giroux, 2004). A Year 11 student commented after our recent school showcase: '*I've never sat in a room full of people before who were all from different walks of life, ages, races, religions, genders and sexual orientations, all supporting and campaigning for the same thing. It made me proud to be part of a collective community which one day will change lives and opinions and will make this world a better place.*'

If we are to encourage promoting the ethos of the sponsor, how can we unify our values? '*In short, private interests trump social needs, and economic growth becomes more important than social justice*' (Giroux 2010 p.133.)We cannot achieve inclusion in a system based on inequality. In *Over the Rainbow*, Nicola makes an eloquent and heartfelt argument for the transformation of society, a view that I wholeheartedly share. Let's apply these arguments and create the beginnings of a cohesive community with people and social justice at its core.

Elly Barnes
CEO and founder of Educate & Celebrate
www.EducateAndCelebrate.org

It is a great pleasure to have been asked to write a few words for the second edition of *Over the Rainbow*.

I have known Nicola since the early days of Lesbians and Gays Support the Miners, and over many years and demonstrations. I am thrilled that this book is in print again; it's an important volume which shines a light on money, class and homophobia. As far as I am concerned there can never be enough discussion around these issues.

Nicola has always been a feisty individual with deeply held views, beliefs, principles and care for her fellow human beings.

She's always been tireless in her fight for those less advantaged and most vulnerable in our society.

I wish this revised edition of such a vital work every success.

Jonathan Blake
Original member of LGSM
London, April 2016

'The release of the film *Pride* in 2014 introduced a new generation of LGBT people not only to the story of Lesbians and Gays Support the Miners (LGSM) and the mining communities of the Neath, Dulais and Swansea valleys, but to the wider story of the 1984-85 Miners' Strike and the ongoing consequences of the defeat of the National Union of Mineworkers at that time. Many young people knew little or nothing about this story. Indeed, I remember being asked several times on the 2014 Pride in London march whether the LGSM banner (actually the film prop version) we carried was something to do with Turkish or Chilean miners – so completely had the memory of our once significant mining industry and powerful miners' union been eroded.

The idea that LGBT+ people can be part of a movement for radical social change has similarly been largely lost from popular perception. The radical ideals of the Stonewall Rioters, the Brixton Faeries and earlier movements for lesbian and gay rights associated with the British socialist-feminist Edward Carpenter; or the communist campaigner for Native American rights Harry Hay, appear to be largely replaced by a 'gay lifestyle' centred on recreational drugs, hedonism, fashion and same-sex wedding lists.

The Pride marches in the 1970s and 80s were a defiant protest as well as a celebration of our queerness. Now Pride is largely a marketing opportunity for corporate sponsors, shrouding themselves in a pink veil of 'diversity' to distract us from their opposition to trade unions and workers' rights, their evasion of taxes, their collusion with repressive regimes or their abuse of the environment. The whole squalid charade is orchestrated by wealthy and privileged LGBT+ business people accountable to no one but themselves and more concerned with the footfall for West End businesses than engaging with the lives of LGBT+ people outside their privileged circle.

The popular reaction to the film *Pride* was political. For the generation that had witnessed the tidal wave of opposition to Thatcher, who had been repulsed by her branding mining communities 'the enemy within' and her determination to starve those communities back to work, *Pride* was as much their story as ours. Activists from all communities, of all sexualities, identified with our story and were thrilled to see shared values and ideals celebrated on screen.

Young people who had no previous contact with trade unions or activism were moved to show solidarity, to ask which communities are now being marginalised and branded as 'the enemy within', to reclaim the principles that inspired LGBT+ activists and trade unionists involved in the UK Gay Liberation Front, Gay Left and many LGBT+ trade union groups who started to change our world in the 1970s and who inspired many of us in LGSM. I thought Stephen Beresford had very cleverly chosen 'Bread and Roses' for Bronwen Lewis to sing in the film to remind us of Rose Eiderman, the early 20th century American trade unionist and women's suffrage campaigner closely associated with that slogan. It turns out he just loved the song! But it remains true that LGBT+ people and working-class LGBT+ people in particular have always been part of progressive struggles around the world.

For many, the film offered an opportunity to advance these ideas and these values – not just in the UK but around the globe. In North America, from Montreal to Hawaii; in Belgium, France, Germany and the Netherlands; in Mexico,

Turkey and Denmark; in Warsaw and Palermo, Nicola, other original members of LGSM and I have been privileged to share LGSM's story, and increasingly, the stories of younger activists and trade unionists who are supporting refugees, housing activists, disability rights campaigners. They are speaking out against racism, Islamophobia and the demonisation of welfare recipients, and opposing the transfer of wealth from the poor to the rich under cover of the austerity agenda.

These reactions to the film were part of a much wider reaction against the neo-liberal agenda manifested in the mass popularity of Jeremy Corbyn and Bernie Sanders, the rise of industrial militancy and public support for striking doctors and other workers.

As disabled LGBT+ people face the withdrawal of essential benefits, as homelessness among queer youth rockets, as NHS managers dither over the provision of PrEP to prevent HIV infection and LGBT+ migrants face a desperately uncertain future, the need to address what went so wrong for the project of LGBT+ liberation is urgent and pressing.

The publishing of an updated version of Nicola's book which provides an essential starting point for this debate could not be more timely.

Gethin Roberts
Original member of LGSM
London, April 2016

Acknowledgments for the 2016 edition

Any shortcomings in the new material for this edition of *Over the Rainbow* are entirely my own but I owe a huge debt to the generous people who helped me with practical support, ideas and insights.

Marven Scott of the Marxist Internet Archive undertook the painstaking job of transcribing the original pages of the book, as only a comrade would.

For encouragement, honest advice, suggestions, reading and discussion, thanks are due to Roddy Slorach, Richard Bromhall, Laura Miles, Noel Halifax, Sally Campbell, Sam Fairbrother and Sheila McGregor.

Eileen Short edited the entire text with accuracy and understanding. Ben Windsor created the thrilling cover.

Elly Barnes, Jonathan Blake and Gethin Roberts kindly wrote insightful forewords.

Leo Zeilig, Anthony Arnove of Haymarket Press and Ramsey Kanaan of PM Press all encouraged the republication of *Over the Rainbow*, and made suggestions on how it could be achieved. In particular Paul Field (no relation, but I wish he was) gave moral support and helped me find the right words at critical moments.

Wonderful Anne Beech at Pluto Books made the process of reproducing the original book possible. Adam Lowe at Dog Horn Publishing took the brave step of offering to publish this new edition. His commitment has been steadfast. Charlotte Maxwell at Dog Horn has made light of publicity work.

Pamela Morton at the NUJ gave legal advice.

My fellow members of Lesbians and Gays Support the Miners and all our supporters were a source of ideas, energy and life-lessons. All the events I attended with them fed my imagination and my commitment to continuing to write about LGBT+ politics and class.

Colin Clews sent me clippings from his online archive *Gay in the 80s*.

Without all the people who contributed to the crowdfund, this book would not exist. They are:

Laura Miles, Al Garthwaite, Pascal Ansell, Rashida Islam, Lawrence Molloy, Djibril al-Ayad, Chloe Purcell, Jordan Rivera, Sue Caldwell, Sharon McDuell, Hilary Chuter, Ursla Hawthorne, Cathy Cross, Si McGurk, Sally Kincaid, Sara Todd, 'actoncurrer', Kate Mayer, Clare Cunningham, John Eccles, Stephen Beresford, Laura Salisbury, Michael Dance, Rahul Patel, Tim Evans, Phil Rowan, Roddy Slorach, Patrick Carmody, Catherine Grant, Lorraine Liyanage, Ben Field, Janyce Quigley, Jeff Cole, Petra Knickmeyer, Mark Dunk, Hope Lye, Can Yildiz, Phil Jones, Arthur Shaw, Peter Dwyer, Joanne Kelly, George McKay, Martin Adams, Janine Broderick, Esra Ozban, Diarmaid Kelliher, Cera Davies, Kate Douglas, Jade Evans, Sarah Cox, 'jhiacynt', Merlin Reader, Geoff Dexter, Catherine Booth, Samuel Solomon, George Binette, John Molyneux, Jill Kemp, Jonathan Blake.

Hilary Chuter is a staunch friend and walking mate; her loyalty has kept me going through happy and difficult times.

Geoff Dexter had the idea of getting *Over the Rainbow* republished. He has become a beloved friend and comrade whose political and creative brilliance never fail to inspire me. I dedicate this new edition to him.

NOTES ON
TERMINOLOGY AND PERSPECTIVE

Over the Rainbow: Money, Class and Homophobia, originally published by Pluto Books in 1995, was written at a time when the LGBT+ movement rarely embraced bisexuality and trans people. For that reason, the original text of the book, which remains intact in this edition, addresses trans issues only in passing. The chapter *Bisexuality*, however, represented a theoretical and political challenge to the lesbian and gay movement of the 1990s. My preferred present-day 'movement' term is LGBT+. However flawed, this 'label' offers common ground, openness and inclusivity. My usage includes the whole range of sexuality self-definitions, such as genderfluid, pansexual, demisexual, asexual, agender, intersex, queer and questioning, cis, non-cis and so on, with no exclusions.

'Queer' as an all-inclusive term is something I am slower to adopt. It has a dual connotation which is still evolving because history and language are still evolving. For my generation – I was born in 1960 – the term 'queer' was a horrible insult denoting abnormality, contamination, outsiderness and unnaturalness. And I am not alone in struggling to eradicate this association from my psyche. On the other hand 'queer' has been adopted by radical, younger activists and artists to carve out a counterculture which fosters new ideas about human expression, resistance and actualisation. So I remain open to embracing 'queer' until it becomes easier.

Overarching all the debates about terminology, however, is the principle of unity. For me the point is to think, argue and act together. That's why I prefer to stick to LGBT+ rather than add on all the initials to extend the acronym, as I believe the latter distracts its users from the real issue by focussing their efforts on deciding which letters should go into the acronym.

Terminology shifts and changes, but the need to unite and fight for human and sexual liberation remains paramount.

As a Londoner, I write from a UK-based perspective, but I hope the analysis is relevant or of interest to all who take part in the struggle for LGBT+ freedom, because we all live in a world dominated by capitalism and class. I hope that readers will find ways to adapt the material to their own circumstances, and seek their own examples to apply the book's principles.

Class is not just one in a range of intersecting oppressions. It is the fundamental structural condition in which we live, and the key social and economic mechanism upon which the capitalist system depends. Because I believe the central issue of divisions in the movement, commercialisation and the need for class unity remain the same as they did in 1995, I have decided to let the original text of the book stand, and simply added a new chapter. I believe there are lessons from its insights into the zeitgeist of 1990s LGBT+ history that we can relate to the current context. Therefore, neither Dog Horn Publishing nor I have changed a single word of it.

If I were writing this book today, there are undoubtedly some aspects I would write differently. I tended to subject the proponents of single-issue, cultural, direct-action and identity politics with the same searing critique that I applied to the gay businesspeople I interviewed for the book. In retrospect, I think I could have taken a friendlier approach to their activism and emphasised its value as well as its limitations. However, my respect for their commitment extends to a certainty that they can withstand a comradely challenge and a trust that they will accept my amends.

CHAPTER FOR THE 21ST CENTURY: *OVER THE RAINBOW* REVISITED

So much has changed in the UK and many other countries since I wrote *Over the Rainbow: Money, Class and Homophobia* (*OTR*). We have many more legal and institutional rights, a high level of positive media visibility, and the extraordinary and mixed blessing of same-sex marriage. The movement is much more inclusive. None of this seemed very possible or likely in the mid-1990s, so it would be reasonable to ask how the book might be relevant for the LGBT+ movement today. The answer readers have given me is that, in the brutal age of austerity and war, *OTR*'s appraisal of why there are splits and divisions in the movement, its critique of commercialisation of Pride marches and of identity politics, its analysis of the economic roots of LGBT+ oppression, and its call for resistance on the basis of working-class solidarity, are needed now more than ever. I am grateful to have the opportunity, in this introduction, to revisit the themes of the book, explore how it came to be written and describe the catalyst for its republication now in 2016. It is my hope that the book will resonate with those who want to uproot LGBT+ oppression rather than continue to simply grapple with it, and who are open to looking beyond the 'community' for the power to really change the world.

OTR contains an early account of Lesbians and Gays Support the Miners (LGSM), which I wrote without even acknowledging that I had been one of the group. It just didn't seem important at the time because the story of LGSM was little known, and my priority in 1994 was to critique attempts to build a unified political LGBT+ movement on the basis of a 'community' of shared sexual identity. I interviewed a number of gay businesspeople, showing how their interest in making profits and commercialising the movement meant they had very little in common with the majority of LGBT+ people. *OTR* tackled the way people thought about how to fight LGBT+ oppression in the 1990s, and used the story of LGSM to illustrate where the real power to build a new society lies. This story was virtually unknown until 2014. Then, thanks to the persistence and imagination of screenwriter Stephen Beresford, the powerful feature film *Pride* revealed the story to an unsuspecting worldwide audience. Today, I am able to write about how we may learn from LGSM and the politics of the 1980s by looking beyond the story told in that film, to reflect more deeply than I did in 1994 on the contradictory effect of the strike on the course of our history.

The *Pride* Effect

Anyone who has seen the film Pride knows about a historic day in June 1985 when coalminers from the Dulais valley in South Wales joined the Lesbian and Gay Pride parade in London, UK. The miners and their families were returning the solidarity and support they had received from London-based LGBT+ activists during their monumental 1984-85 industrial strike against the Conservative government, led by Margaret Thatcher. Thatcher's administration had hatched a secret plan to destroy the coal industry in Britain and cow the organised working class by crushing – with brute force – the country's most powerful and organised trade union: the National Union of Mineworkers (NUM). The miners, led by union president Arthur Scargill, responded to the threat of pit closures and mass unemployment by walking out on indefinite strike, without a ballot, and staying out for a whole year, in the face of extreme hardship, police violence and politically motivated media smears. Their courageous action was, and still is, an inspirational, salutary lesson to millions across the world. That joyous contingent on the Pride parade in 1985 was part of a seismic historical shakedown.

20

As depicted in the film *Pride*, we marched with our banners –Lesbians and Gays Support the Miners and Lesbians Against Pit Closures (LAPC)–from Hyde Park to the South Bank, where we gathered for the Pride party celebrations and to show our exhibition telling the story of LGSM and LAPC through photos, memorabilia and press clippings from the strike. Our exhibition stands were set up alongside the bright red van with a pink triangle on the side, bought for the Dulais Valley community with funds raised by LGSM. We sold solidarity badges, miners' lamps, our 'Pits and Perverts' t-shirts and tickets for our alternative post-Pride party at the London Lesbian and Gay Centre[1] in Cowcross Street. Siân James, a miner's wife who helped establish the Neath and Dulais Valley Support Group during the strike (and later became the first ever woman member of parliament for Swansea East), addressed the crowds that afternoon on a stage set up on the South Bank next to County Hall [2] to rapturous applause. She said it had been the 'best and friendliest' demonstration she had ever been on. Meeting gay people had a profound effect on the people of Dulais, she explained. 'When they first heard you were coming to town, older people in the village wanted to know what they should do. "Just act natural," we said. Now they ask, "When are those lovely people coming down again?"'. She promised that Dulais miners would be there to support gays, just as gays had been there when Dulais needed support. [3]

As *Pride* relates in its closing sequence, the Trades Union Congress (TUC)[4] in 1985 voted to formally adopt a policy on lesbian and gay rights and, the next year, the Labour Party followed suit. Attempts to get these proposals through had been made many times before, by LGBT+ members of public sector unions and by campaigning Labour Party members. What shifted it this time was the solid backing of the giant NUM [5], due to its members' experiences of community and class solidarity during the bitter, brave and extraordinary strike.

Striking miners and LGBT+ socialist activists were an unexpected subject for a mainstream movie but this film's warmth, humour and authenticity captured hearts and minds. We are often told that prejudice and ignorance take years, even generations, to break down, as shifts in attitudes take place slowly, rather like the gradual erosion of mountainous rock by wind and rain. The LGSM/LAPC story showed that, in the heat of class struggle, when we need to link arms and unite against the common enemy to defend our lives and our communities, prejudice and preconceptions can come tumbling down.

The response to *Pride* proved so powerful that the remaining original members of LGSM and LAPC re-formed for a year so that we could respond to the overwhelming number of international requests for speakers to address the tidal wave of enthusiasm. For those former members of LGSM and LAPC who came forward, our experience of the film's impact was a political and personal revelation. The timing was perfect; the film came out exactly thirty years after the strike and so became part of a raft of commemorative political events and initiatives. We witnessed an extraordinary live reaction unfold through screenings in schools, festivals, trade union events, cinemas, universities, community centres and meeting halls in London, New York, Montreal, Los Angeles, San Francisco, Amsterdam, Ankara, Istanbul, Warsaw, Moscow, Sydney, Birmingham, Bristol, Dublin, Newcastle and Manchester – to name but a few.

Social media networks sprang up to connect thousands of supporters around the world who wanted to link up to build solidarity, and to get involved in political campaigning in their own countries and communities. LGSM member Mike Jackson got hold of the replica LGSM banner from the *Pride* art department. We took it on picket lines and demonstrations, making collections and delivering financial solidarity and moral support to strikes and campaigns over austerity, racism, housing, privatisation, the Living Wage and other political/community issues. We reproduced our 'Pits and Perverts' t-shirts and posters, brought out new badges and were disconcerted to find ourselves accosted at merchandise stalls by people who wanted to have their picture taken with us. We raised money and awareness for the Terrence Higgins Trust's Red Ribbon support fund set up in memory of LGSM founder Mark Ashton, who died of HIV/ AIDS in 1987, aged 26.

We were also asked by the organisers of Pride in London to lead the parade in 2015. I will return to this later.

It was clear to me, amid the sometimes embarrassing media hype and celebrity fever surrounding LGSM, and from the debates I witnessed around the screenings and meetings, that the enthusiastic and emotional reaction to the film was an expression of a deep political hunger for an effective fightback against present-day oppression and exploitation. To everyone who remembered supporting the strike, and to young people born years after it ended, the story of LGSM offered a new symbol of unity, solidarity and defiance which went far beyond what many in the original group had anticipated. A new generation of young activists were seething with anger at attacks on their lives through conservatism, bigotry and heteronormativity (which in the 1980s we called 'compulsory heterosexuality'). They were facing the housing crisis, soaring rents, tuition fees, abolition of the Education Maintenance Allowance, zero-hours contracts, cuts in health and social care, welfare 'reform', racism, Islamophobia, immigration controls, and all the horrors of austerity, racism and imperialism. *Pride*'s story of a community under attack from a bigoted right-wing Tory government, and offering unconditional support to another beleaguered section of society, struck a chord with a new audience. If it could happen in 1984, could it happen now? If a force such as the NUM could be defeated, what did this mean for the future of collective struggle?

For some in the audiences who had experience of collective struggle and activism, in or outside trade unions, there was a feeling that social media and privatisation had lured the younger generations towards individualised and perhaps more passive approaches such as consumer boycotts and petition-signing. Due to the decreased level of strikes in the UK since the 1980s, and the half-hearted attempts of trade union leaders to challenge austerity, many young people in those audiences were questioning whether a strike like the miners' strike would be possible today, and how relevant trade unions are to young workers now. Listening to their heartfelt questions about the best ways to challenge austerity, I realised perhaps more acutely than before, the detrimental effect the defeat of the miners' strike had on working-class confidence. A sense that governments have unlimited power and can do what they like, however much it hurts ordinary people, is the new status quo seeping through the generations; the view that individuals only care about themselves and selfishness is an indelible human characteristic has become normative. I was also struck by a second legacy of the strike's defeat in the various forms of postmodern arguments that go something like this: if the pursuit of profit, regardless of human need, is an inevitable social dynamic, and if mass struggle is now impossible, then the brutality of capitalist economics can only be tackled at the level of personal defiance, individual solutions, the politics of shared identity, and localised community initiatives. In the LGBT+ movement, this often translates into focussing on the creation of 'queer space' or 'safe space' for a perceived LGBT+ 'community'. It's understandable, but it misses the fact that LGBT+ do not all belong to one community, and it won't change the world.

I believe that if we are to rid the world of sexual oppression and LGBT+phobia, we must go further and be much bolder. There is another legacy of the miners' strike to which we can turn. This is the tradition of learning lessons from the past, honestly and unflinchingly, seeing the mistakes made on our own side so that we may avoid the same mistakes again. This tradition makes us fiercer and clearer; it is the key to understanding that in fighting oppression and exploitation we have to be prepared to confront the forces and structure of the state in a revolutionary way. The real story behind *Pride* is a good place to start on this journey.

24

No Fairy Tale

Pride created a romantic comedy from LGSM, but it's vital not to romanticise the story or allow it to become a historical curiosity, nostalgia trip, or idealistic fairy tale. For me as a still-active socialist, revisiting the experience of LGSM has been a sharp reminder of how tough life was for LGBT+ people during the Thatcher period, and of the critical importance of the strike then and now.

Pride intimated that the TUC and Labour Party policies on sexuality rights were a direct result of or even 'payback' for the work of LGSM. In truth, a trade union can only change policy if enough members and branches agree. The new policy on lesbian and gay rights at the TUC in 1985 was only possible because of a **general** political development within the NUM's grassroots across the rural pit communities, along with political radicalisation and awareness of the power of industrial struggle amongst the multicultural and cosmopolitan populations of Britain's cities. South Wales-based NUM activist Dai Donovan (played by Paddy Considine in *Pride*) addressed a huge audience at LGSM's 'Pits and Perverts' strike fundraiser in Camden's Electric Ballroom in December 1984 [6], saying:

> *'You have worn our badge, "Coal Not Dole", and you know what harassment means, as we do. Now we will pin your badge on us, we will support you. It won't change overnight, but now 140,000 miners know that there are other causes and other problems. We know about blacks and gays and nuclear disarmament and we will never be the same... Victory to the old, victory to the sick, victory to lesbians and gays, and victory to the working class!'*

There may have been, as *Pride* dramatically depicts, homophobic opposition in South Wales to receiving solidarity from a lesbian and gay group. But LGSM experienced no tangible negativity either on the first visit to South Wales, or subsequently. Solidarity for the strike was a two-way process whose trajectory was highly contradictory in light of the eventual outcomes: defeat of the strike, alongside a highly raised level of political awareness and ideas across the British working class. This is a perfect example of the 'dialectic', fundamental to understanding any political situation at any time. It can be summed up as 'every cloud has a silver lining – and vice versa'. The defeat of the strike contained a silver lining of a generalised heightened political engagement and level of awareness of oppression. The strike itself was pure silver, surrounded by dark clouds of Tory intention and the TUC's timidity. So, how did this dual narrative play out?

Pride only obliquely articulated the reason for the strike: to stop mass pit closures, save jobs and preserve communities. An enormous volume of material now exists about the miners' strike and I want to focus here on the links between class struggle and fighting oppression and bigotry. But it's vital to understand that the Tories under Thatcher had dual tactical and ideological purposes in shutting the coal mines. They were determined to weaken the entire trade union movement and to privatise industries like coal, taken into public ownership by previous Labour administrations. Key militant trade union officials and representatives were victimised and sacked to neuter the resistance before the shut-downs and redundancies began. The Tories dismantled nationalised car manufacturing in 1979 and the steel industry in 1980. Civil servants who worked in intelligence at GCHQ were stripped of the right to strike in 1981. Train drivers were forced to accept inhumane shift rotas in 1982, the same year health workers' pay was cut. [7] All those workers fought, demonstrated and struck. The TUC stood by and allowed each union and each group of workers to be beaten. It came as little surprise when the miners were chosen for the next Tory battleground. Sheila McGregor, a socialist activist who helped organise political solidarity during the strike, summarises:

26

'The miners had defeated the ruling class twice, once in 1972 when their strike drove a coach and horses through the pay policy of the day, and then again in 1974 when Tory prime minister Ted Heath decided to call an election on who should run the country—and lost. The Tories never forgot and never forgave. They wanted to defeat the miners in open battle, so they prepared for a strike. As Thatcher's chancellor Nigel Lawson recalled the preparations, it was "just like re-arming to face the threat of Hitler in the late 1930s". One of Thatcher's ministers, Nicholas Ridley, was the architect of a strategy based on simple principles. Only take on one group of workers at a time to avoid solidarity between workers. Introduce anti-union laws … and allow for the fining of unions and the sequestration of funds. And change welfare legislation to deprive strikers and their families of social security support … they built up coal stocks, diversified the provision of power, organised pools of lorry drivers to move coal and established a National Reporting Centre at New Scotland Yard to coordinate police intervention. The police were given an additional 11,000 officers trained in riot control. Ian MacGregor, one of those behind the sacking of convenor Derek Robinson in 1979 from Longbridge, a key car plant in Birmingham, and then butcher of the steel industry in 1981, was appointed chair of the National Coal Board (NCB) in September 1983. The day after Thatcher was re-elected in 1983, she appointed Peter Walker, a veteran of the 1972 days, as Minister of Energy with the words, "We're going to have a miners' strike." So when battle was finally engaged with the shock announcement of the closure of Cortonwood colliery on 1 March 1984, the Tories were embarking on civil war. A special cabinet committee met twice weekly to ensure centralised coordination. A year later the Tories had won.'[8]

Pride didn't explain why the strike failed. The official reasons, provided by the TUC, government and media alike, is that the strike failed because Thatcher, the government and the forces of the state were just too strong for ordinary workers to overcome. (Riot police were joined by undercover operations and traffic control to stop miners and their supporters travelling to key picket lines; the courts fined and imprisoned strikers and supporters). In fact, the strike could have been won quickly, but for the failures and treachery of the trade union and Labour Party leaderships. As Sheila McGregor's article goes on to outline, secondary strike action could have provided the solidarity required to secure a decisive victory against the Tories.

Two lessons are particularly relevant to the LGSM story today. One is that in failing to co-ordinate secondary industrial action to support the strike against pit closures, the miners were left, tragically and unnecessarily, to fight alone. The second is that the government's seizure of NUM assets, and the failure of other union leaders, who feared sequestration and confrontation more than political defeat, to take the crucial secondary action, left striking miners and their communities absolutely reliant on activists organising locally. Trade union branches began to twin with mining villages to co-ordinate the transfer of provisions in order to combat starvation. A wider layer of political activists: black organisations, women's groups, lesbians and gays, students – people hated by Thatcher and who utterly opposed her divisive agenda of cuts, privatisation and bigotry, rose up to defend the miners. Millions mobilised and everyone took sides. In a concentrated and focussed way, as the people of Europe are today to counteract the EU's anti-refugee bigotry, working-class people in Britain and internationally took action in 1984-5 to keep the miners' strike afloat.

This fundraising effort was the trigger for LGSM, alongside many other community-based support groups. So the very existence of LGSM was contradictory. It arose out of a weakness and failure of the organised working class to respond fully to the attacks by the Thatcher administration. On the other hand, it was part of an outpouring of solidarity, organisation and commitment which raised the political levels of groups and campaigns fighting discrimination. It offered miners the chance to connect their fight with wider social issues, and civil rights campaigners and others the chance to find out where real power to resist lies within capitalist society. It created a fusion of political direction. The prominent political role of women in the strike – women who had never previously considered a role beyond domesticity – changed lives for many, and put a permanent stop to topless female models being featured in the NUM's newspaper, *The Miner*. The strike was a hotbed of ideas, a university of unity.

Pride hints at contemporary political tides within the LGBT+ movement. Jonathan's character is portrayed as a disillusioned radical activist from the Gay Liberation Front of the 1970s. The highly politicised atmosphere of 1980s London, and its lesbian and gay scene bristling with political and community experimentation, is forcefully expressed. The fact of a lesbian and gay miners support group was not in itself surprising, though it took socialists to make LGSM happen in the way it did. LGSM in London, the group featured in *Pride*, was part of a larger response to the miners' need for solidarity, as the attacks on the union escalated. Amongst LGBT+ communities, there were ten LGSM groups in the UK, and one in Dublin. London LGSM was founded by Mark Ashton – a leading activist in the Young Communist League – and Mike Jackson, also a committed socialist. They collected funds for the miners on Lesbian and Gay Pride in London in 1984 and called a meeting of other lesbian and gay socialists to launch a group which would organise solidarity, and spread the word of the importance and relevance of the strike to LGBT+ people in London.

That relevance was all about resisting 'divide and rule', a key tactic of governments, then and now. Urged on by political poison and media hysteria, people are pulled towards believing that the deprivations and difficulties they face are caused by other working-class people and marginalised groups.

The current scapegoats for this type of state-sanctioned hate in the UK are disabled people (framed as 'benefit scroungers'), refugees (dehumanised as 'migrants') and Muslims (portrayed as 'terrorists'). Back in the mid-1980s, LGBT+ people were perceived by the right as posing a challenge to the institution of the family. Given the option, it was feared, everyone might opt to choose a same-sex partner and cock a snook at heterosexual romantic love.

This was in the days when lesbians often lost the right to bring up their children, the police regularly staked out gay bars and clubs; when kissing your partner in the street could lead to prosecution, and LGBT+ people lost jobs because of their sexuality. The lawful age of consent for sex between consenting male adults 'in private' was 21, compared with 16 for heterosexual sex. Bereaved partners could be evicted from their homes by landlords, and homophobic families could prevent LGBT+ people from visiting their ill or dying partners. The idea of same-sex marriage belonged to the realms of Shakespearean fairytale fantasy. Policing varied from constant harassment to outright repression. There was no category for homophobic or transphobic hate crime, and LGBT+ people who experienced attacks because of their sexuality, and dared to report it, were more likely to face arrest for crimes against public decency themselves. Protests related to LGBT+ issues were attacked by the police, with marchers beaten and arrested. There were no openly LGBT+ police officers, only one openly gay Member of Parliament (Chris Smith), no LGBT+ soap characters. In April 1984 customs officers, citing legislation from 1876, raided Gay's the Word (the bookshop made famous in the film *Pride*), seized works by Oscar Wilde, Armistead Maupin, Tennessee Williams, Kate Millet and Jean-Paul Sartre – then charged the shop's directors and manager with conspiracy to import indecent or obscene material (the case was later thrown out). Thatcher's notorious Section 28, outlawing 'promotion of homosexuality' in schools, and the massive campaign to stop it, were yet to come.

The homophobic, right-wing Christian campaigner Mary Whitehouse was a household name for her anti-sex campaign against 'permissiveness' in the mass media. In 1987, following a screening of a film on HIV/AIDS, South Staffordshire council's Tory leader Bill Brownhill said:

'I should shoot them all... It is disgusting and diabolical. As a cure, I would put 90% of queers in the ruddy gas chambers. Are we going to keep letting these queers trade their filth up and down the country? ... some are even being knighted.'

The leader of the council's Labour Group, Jack Greenaway, echoed Brownhill's message, intoning: 'Every one of us here will agree with what has been said.' [9]

1987 also saw the firebombing of London's *Capital Gay* newspaper office. Tabloid headlines like 'GAS GAYS SAYS TORY: Answer to AIDS' and 'Lessons on gays "threat to life"' stoked up hatred and reinforced prejudice and bigotry.

Lesbian and gay people were subjected to a horrific barrage of politically co-ordinated media abuse. When right-wing tabloid *The Sun* dubbed HIV/AIDS the 'Gay Plague', it began a toxic tsunami of hysterical and panic-stricken media stories with headlines that included: 'Britain threatened by gay virus plague' (*Mail on Sunday*); 'Blood from gay donor puts 41 at AIDS risk' (*The Sun*); 'AIDS is the wrath of God, says vicar' (*The Sun*); 'March of the gay plague' (*News of the World*). [10]

In the final scene of *Pride*, a march organiser dismisses LGSM as 'too political'; this dramatises a real perennial tension within the LGBT+ movement. However, state repression and crude discrimination meant the movement of the mid-1980s had protest at its heart, even amongst those who would always have preferred a party.

Pride's negative portrayal of the initiative to set up Lesbians Against Pit Closures, however, is misplaced. I was part of this initiative, with others including Polly Vittorini and Wendy Caldon. For me it grew out of my first encounters in the LGSM group. My first LGSM meeting was a room full of men and just one other woman. Although I was then a somewhat inactive member of the Labour Party, here I found members of the Communist Party, Revolutionary Communist Party, and different sections of the Labour Party, all disagreeing with each other on finer points which I found quite bewildering. Many were already friends and initially I felt ill at ease. (This sense of being on the edge lessened as time went on, but never entirely went away.) Afterwards, the other woman at that meeting, Kate, a member of the Socialist Workers Party, came round to where I lived in Deptford. We decorated a bucket, went to a local gay club and collected some money – and that's how I learnt how to start building community solidarity for the miners.

Together with Kate and her partner Sally, I started to go to lots of lesbian-only nights up in town – Rackets, the Drill Hall, the Fallen Angel on Tuesdays, and the Bell on Wednesdays – places I was used to going to socially. I was quite nervous, thinking that people would be hostile because they'd judge the miners as sexist and homophobic, but actually there was a warm response and solidarity that I hadn't expected. Lots of women had come to London from areas similar to the mining communities, and they understood better than I did how devastating pit closures would be, socially and economically. This gave me confidence and inspiration to keep going. I met other women in these clubs who wanted to form a lesbian-only support group. I wasn't a separatist and believed in unity, so I had to reason it out tactically. LGSM members were already collecting in men-only venues where women couldn't go. The men couldn't come in the women's clubs, and many women chose not to go to mixed events, so forming a lesbian-only group could increase the amount of money collected. So I helped to form LAPC and was active in both groups. The separation, even now, can be interpreted as simultaneously both positive and negative: the way these weave together is how struggle against oppression and exploitation within and against the capitalist system develops. The shattering effect of the miners' defeat on the workers' movement, the heightened hatred and determination to keep fighting against Thatcher, and the resulting politicisation all fed into a new contradictory political climate, the context for *Over the Rainbow.*

Like many socialists who had supported the miners, I was demoralised by the defeat of the strike. I left the Labour Party; it had ceased to offer me any kind of inspiration and had betrayed my faith in its socialist principles. The policies passed by the TUC and Labour Party translated not into a fusion of class struggle and sexual politics, but a bureaucratisation of LGBT representation characterised by committees – I was on one of them!—working parties, training programmes and executive positions. They did good work examining the issue of equality in the workplace and the union, but it was divorced from economic and industrial issues. A large section of the movement for sexual liberation shifted away from class struggle. Like other LGBT+ socialists, although I understood the need to continue resisting Thatcher's assault on working-class life and organisation, for the rest of the 1980s I went with the movement into identity politics and its offspring: cultural production, direct action and single-issue campaigning.

It was through another political upsurge in 1990 that I realised there was another side to the left, a side that had learned the lessons of the Miners' Strike as it was happening and was still committed to fighting oppression on a class basis. It was when I moved out of identity politics into that revolutionary dimension that my perspective was transformed and it became possible for me to write about class and LGBT+ liberation.

Writing *Over the Rainbow*

I began to write *OTR* in 1993, when serious commercialisation and professionalisation of the movement began to take hold in the UK, though legal and social inequality persisted. The concept of the 'pink pound' was moving beyond the niche gay nightclubs, fetish clothing and specialist publishing, and into the mainstream. Alcohol, tobacco and clothing companies took out ads in the gay consumer press. Openly gay entrepreneurs opened up slick, bright, confident bars on main thoroughfares instead of the old-style windowless hostelries hidden in dark alleys. Law firms and financial services actively sought affluent gays to join their clientele. It was a kind of 'gentrification' of gay areas like London's Soho – simultaneously refreshing and socially exclusive. Some hailed the 'pink economy' as a new path to liberation. With its chapters on *Identity and the Lifestyle Market* and *Hostile Brothers, OTR* examined the values and trajectory of this market-led approach.

Bisexuality, intersexuality and trans issues were sidelined and largely ignored by the movement. Although bisexual, I felt under intense pressure to conform to something we would now call homonormativity, and wrote about the material reasons for this in the *Bisexuality* chapter, showing how the market needed a fixed clientele to expand the sale of 'gay identity'.

Many leading LGBT+ activists now felt that collective action, trade union struggle and class solidarity had decisively failed as a strategy. They thought socialism was finished and the transformation of society as a whole now impossible; LGBT+ people had to make alternative lifestyle choices and buy a way out of oppression, demanding civil rights on the basis of political lobbying and consumer choice.

The ideological impact of the miners' defeat led to a general reduction of trade union confidence. When strikes and industrial struggle did take place, the false separation between the fight for jobs, pay and conditions and the fight against oppression kept gaining ground. Unions hived off LGBT+ issues into the arena of 'equality' and the power of LGBT+ workplace activists became, ironically, less visible. This may have suited the few seeking a career in equalities policy and management. But it led many activists to seek the roots of oppression within people's heads and fight it only with ideas and PR, avoiding the thorny issues of that oppression's social and economic roots. *OTR* took up all these issues in the chapters on *Romance* and *Reform*.

At the same time, a right-wing backlash from politicians and the media promoted conservative family values through a reactionary campaign entitled 'Back to Basics'. The brainchild of Tory 'thinker' David Willetts and his policy document *Happy Families* [11], this promoted the heterosexual, married, nuclear family unit, and discouraged alternative family structures through unfriendly taxation and benefits restructuring, fuelling homophobia. I examined this in *OTR*'s chapter on *Family*.

The 1980s and 1990s thus saw lesbian and gay civil rights campaigning increasingly taken up by professional lobbyists, with commercial interests assuming more control within the movement. Members of the Gay Business Association were winning the argument that Pride marches should be more commercial. The annual protest moved further away from its radical roots in the Stonewall Riots of 1969 – when black and Latino trans prostitutes fought hand-to-hand against police harassment in Greenwich Village. The idea of completely changing society in order to get rid of the underlying causes of oppression fell off the agenda. Angling for reform was the only game in town.

There was active resistance and opposition to this 'respectable' approach. I knew where that radical energy came from, because I passed through the direct action and cultural activism emanating largely from direct-action groups like ACT UP, Outrage and Lesbian Avengers. These focussed on single issues and targets, not the wider political and social context and structure. LGBT+ writers and artists were busy creating alternative aesthetics based on a supposed shared 'sensibility'. The two sides of this reformist coin – 'respectable' professionalised lobbying versus minority, ultra-left, pop-up and individualised cultural activism – now dominated the movement which became consumed by internal arguments and infighting to gain ascendance and influence.

Over the Rainbow in many ways reflects my own life journey, experiences and political discoveries. I certainly wasn't born a revolutionary socialist. I grew up in the south of England in the 1960-70s in a family very similar to that of the character Joe in *Pride*. We lived in a three-bedroomed detached house in a cul-de-sac where husbands went out to work in suits and wives cooked and cleaned and kept everything respectable. I was continually told I wasn't 'normal'. Feelings I had that I might be lesbian or bisexual were absolutely terrifying. The words 'queer', 'homo' and 'lez' were bandied about as terms of abuse and ridicule, and being identified as sexually suspect was to be avoided at all costs. At school, a grammar school for girls in a Tory stronghold High Wycombe, same-sex love was mentioned only in Religious Studies. My teacher, a Church of England cleric, referred to a 'homosexual problem' which could only be 'cured' by religious willpower. Words like 'gay', 'feminist' and 'black', were part of a strange, unnatural world on television. I became the first person in my family to go to university (thanks to free tuition and a maintenance grant). There I met socialists, feminists, anti-racists and out gay people, had my first lesbian relationship, and gradually began to realise that the world was unfair and the right thing to do was to fight injustice. Taking part in the process of struggle and being exposed to new ideas got me into the resistance. Socialists showed me how different oppressions were connected and that we needed to support and campaign for each other. My first march was through the royal town of Windsor, demonstrating against hikes in tuition fees for overseas students.

I came out in the early 1980s when I joined a video project which went on to make a Channel 4 programme called

Framed Youth: Revenge of the Teenage Perverts. This film was a departure: it was made by young lesbians and gays, rather than professionals talking 'about' us. It was a painful time for me personally, as both my parents were absolutely horrified when I came out. They made it clear I was to hide my sexuality within the wider family or risk rejection. I returned to that experience when I came to write *OTR* ten years later. By that time, I had come to understand the ideological and economic role that the institution of the family plays in reinforcing and reproducing the rigid notions of gender expression and gender roles which underpin sexism and homophobia. Prejudiced ideas don't come from inside people's heads, they are learned through conditioning and nurtured by social structures and dominant cultural norms. People cling to them because they offer a false but much needed sense of belonging and safety; those who don't conform can face punishment, even exile. Writing the chapter on *Family* enabled me to make political sense of the outright rejection I had experienced as a young person.

In the 1980s the lesbian and gay movement gained momentum – and so did the Thatcher government. I joined the Labour Party and found members interested in working on oppression issues were on the fringes of the party. Homophobia was rife because the leadership felt that sexuality rights issues would put people off voting Labour. Later, writing *OTR*, I discovered a lot more about how the Labour Party accommodates both resistance and adaption to capitalism and oppression, and how this leads to principles being compromised and resistance being paralysed.

In March 1984, the Miners' Strike kicked off. A friend from the *Framed Youth* project, Jeff Cole, joined LGSM and said I should come along. *Over the Rainbow*'s final chapter, its most important statement about the link between class and sexual liberation, was set in motion at that moment. Entitled *Class Struggle*, it brought together as much material as I could find at the time about how people could use their collective power as workers (without whom nothing would get made or done, and no profits could be generated) to challenge and fight LGBT+ oppression. Alongside a story about transgender bus workers, the central story is as far as I know, the earliest first-hand record of LGSM published in a book.

After the Miners' Strike, I shared a house with Derek Hughes, a friend from LGSM who taught English in a secondary school, was active in the NUT trade union and worked hard to develop teaching around lesbian and gay issues as a member of the Gay Teachers Association. I learned so much from him. Derek and I and many of our friends were socialists who understood that fighting for LGBT+ liberation was part of fighting for a more equal society, but after the Miners' defeat, we were drawn into the confusions and inwardnesses of identity politics. We sometimes competed – often jokingly – to see who was 'more oppressed'; it reflected an underlying tension and political misunderstanding.

In 1986, working on a film about lesbian and gay employment rights, I met Sheila, a fellow filmmaker and artist who became my partner and introduced me to Gramsci. The original text of *OTR* is dedicated to her. When, like LGSM founder Mark Ashton and other friends, Derek died of HIV, Sheila and I were propelled into the world of HIV/AIDS campaigning. I joined the AIDS Coalition To Unleash Power (ACTUP), the UK incarnation of Lesbian Avengers, and the volunteer-driver team at my local HIV support centre in Brixton. Our cultural activism and direct action politics, described in the *Cultural Activism* chapter in *OTR*, was radical and hard-edged, but it had lost the class perspective that had been so important during the Miners' Strike.

Although we were passionate about our artistic work and our political causes, Sheila and I became frustrated by cultural activism. I had begun working for a community project that worked around issues of HIV prevention and drug use, and was acutely aware that poverty and class were underpinning the pandemic. Together Sheila and I started to find out about

Marxism and, eventually, after the Poll Tax Riots of 1990, and (recalling Kate from LGSM and my old socialist friends from university days) we started going to Socialist Workers Party meetings to try to make sense of what was happening around us.

It was this shift, this search for a political link between economics, dominant ideology and oppression, that, two years later, kickstarted me into writing *Over the Rainbow*. Until then I really thought that lesbian and gay oppression was due to uninformed and prejudiced people like my parents, or that it was so deeply ingrained through psychological conditioning that it could never be rooted out. I began to move out of that place of despair and cynicism and to recognise the limits of identity politics and single-issue campaigning. I started to understand how seeing the big picture and thinking through how to link issues together for solidarity and support was the key to getting the kind of society I wanted.

I began to learn the fundamental lesson that a society based on wealth inequality and exploitation needs scapegoats so working-class people will blame each other for the deprivation we suffer – the housing shortage, the cuts, the inadequate healthcare – and swallow the lie that there's not enough money for public services. Instead, I realised, we need to aim the blame at the top of society where the wealth and power reside. All the chapters in *OTR*, but especially those on *Romance*, *Police* and *Class Struggle*, express this fundamental dynamic.

The current movement: LGSM at Pride 2015

The story of LGSM dramatically symbolises the current polarisation of the LGBT+ movement. The film *Pride*'s seismic message of unconditional solidarity punched a big hole in the glossy facade of the current day LGBT+ movement, with its rampant commercialism and professional leaders.

The re-formed LGSM was invited by the Pride in London steering committee to lead the Pride parade in the UK capital on 27 June 2015. We called open meetings to begin planning our Solidarity Contingent on the march, with the stated intention of re-politicising the whole event, countering the prominence of corporate sponsors like Barclays and Starbucks with a message of working-class strength and solidarity. We invited anyone who wanted to fight LGBT+ oppression and build solidarity to march with us, whatever their sexuality. We were inundated with requests, and dozens of groups contacted us or turned up at our organising meetings. Ex-miners dusted off their old lodge banners and the Tredegar Town Band was booked to lead our contingent. Sian James MP, Stephen Beresford, and a host of actors and crew members from *Pride* pledged to be there. Anne Scargill and Betty Cook, former leaders of Women Against Pit Closures, the national organisation of solidarity and survival during the strike, arranged to join a coachload of school students coming down from Pontefract in the north of England. Unite members from Cardiff, Eurostar rail workers, GMB members from Leeds, lecturers from Leeds Beckett University, teachers from Lancaster and six other boroughs – all booked their transport. Disabled People Against Cuts joined in. Council workers in Barnet, north London, striking against outsourcing and library closures, decided to march with us. And, the crowning achievement, National Gallery workers engaged in an escalating industrial dispute against privatisation, decided to make 27 June a strike day, to march with LGSM at Pride in London and to lead our contingent to their picket line at Trafalgar Square. Everyone wanted to be in our Solidarity Contingent. We would be there in our thousands.

But this didn't fit with the business operators running Pride in London as a tourist attraction. If they had envisaged a nostalgia-laden historical re-enactment of the final scene in the film *Pride*, they hadn't reckoned on the spirit of solidarity being directed against the commercialisation of the Pride parade itself.

Principal backers Starbucks (who at the time didn't even pay the Living Wage to their coffee-shop workers) and Barclays Bank (which had propped up the Apartheid regime in South Africa until 1986 and has been investigated by the UK's Serious Fraud Office) were worried that their logo-festooned floats at the front of the march would be swamped by LGBT+ trade unionists and their supporters. The Pride Committee told us we would be allowed a maximum of 200 people in our contingent. LGSM members were not prepared to ditch supporters who had asked to march with us. We were relegated to march at the head of Bloc C, with the 'official' trade union bloc – the TUC being one of the main sponsors of Pride. It was a clear clash of interests: capital versus labour – and it sparked a furious public debate over the question: 'Whose Pride is it?'

A number of the teachers planning to bring their union banners to march with LGSM got together and wrote an open letter to the press arguing against the decision. They pointed out that the chair of the Pride in London board was Tory leader David Cameron's political head of broadcasting, and accused the board of trying to silence protest. Before sending the letter,[12] they circulated it to see if others might like to sign. A flood of senior trade union figures, student representatives, campaigners and left-wing politicians came forward to add their names. The ninety signatories included Jeremy Corbyn MP (before he became leader of the Labour Party), Natalie Bennett (then Green Party leader), and seven leaders of major trade unions, national executive and LGBT committee officers. Original LGSM members and other activists planning to march with us also signed.

The debacle of Pride 2015 clearly showed the contradictions and conflicts in the movement. The letter and campaign didn't change the decision of the organisers but it threw the debate into the public eye, and attracted even more people, especially teenagers who had gravitated to the LGSM banner the previous Saturday on a huge nation demonstration against austerity, to join the LGSM contingent. My most precious memory from Pride in London 2015 is a bunch of glittery, face-painted school students from south London. Though I had no idea what their sexualities were, it was the words they shouted that inspired me:

'L! G! B! T! FIGHT AGAINST AUSTERITY! L! G! S! M! FIGHT THE TORY SCUM AGAIN!'

The modern movement for LGBT+ liberation is still characterised by the same fundamental contradiction *OTR* addressed in the 1990s. This erupts from the mistaken but widespread idea that there is a discrete minority 'community' of people who are united by their LGBT+ identity. According to this idea, everyone in this supposed 'community' shares a common experience of oppression and a common interest in ending it, regardless of their class position within wider society. It maintains that only the sexual minority directly affected by LGBT+phobia, with a narrow cohort of allies, can effectively resist the oppression it faces.

The changes for LGBT+ people in the UK, the US and many other countries since the 1990s have been huge and positive. In addition to legal equality, hate crime against LGBT+ people is now taken more seriously. It is wonderful to see trans, bisexual and intersex people included in the movement. Most importantly, amongst many young people there is a progressive sense that sexuality and gender are non-binary or fluid, and a belief that LGBT+ lives should simply be defended and accepted as part of a multicultural society. Over the past twenty years, groups of workers such as teachers have helped to effect this change, taking part in an extraordinary revolution from below to tackle anti-LGBT+ bullying and isolation. Schools Out UK, originally the Gay Teachers Association, has driven this transformation. Educate and Celebrate is expanding LGBT+positive training and projects in primary and secondary schools nationally. These are substantial steps forward and they have been won by struggle from below.

While legal changes, greater equality, confidence and openness are absolutely welcome, we are very far away from LGBT+ liberation. Rejecting oppression means recognising that anyone can be oppressed and affected by oppression, whatever their class or social position. For the ruling class, what they gain from widespread social oppression of LGBT+ people and increasing disparity between rich and poor, outweighs the oppression they may undergo personally. For some middle-class LGBT+ people who live affluent lives, own comfortable homes in well-off areas, can get married with no money worries, and benefit from liberalisation through corporate positive-action policies, perhaps it feels like the struggle is over.

But for those on the sharp end of LGBT+phobia, the daily experience of prejudice and violence is very real. They also face austerity cuts, Islamophobia and racism, unemployment and zero-hours contracts, the housing crisis, debt, immigration laws, welfare reform and continuing trans-negative legal and healthcare discrimination. For them, liberation and even equality feel a long way off. The struggle for LGBT+ liberation is indivisible from the class antagonism society which underpins society and fuels oppression.

In November 2014, UK police reported rising levels of violent homophobic assaults and harassment offences, with 315 assaults reported in London alone from January to October that year. In Northern Ireland, homophobic crimes had been increasing year on year since 2007. Nevertheless, the vast majority of crimes remain hidden. Transgender identity hate crime is the least reported hate crime.[13] More than 75% of those experiencing homophobic hate crime do not report it to the police[14] and the government estimates there are 29,000 homophobic crimes every year in the UK.[15] Tory David Cameron may have introduced same-sex marriage but his vicious austerity programme disproportionately affects LGBT+ people through greater financial hardships from redundancies, pay cuts and changes to benefit rules.[16] The housing crisis means

LGBT+ experience more problems finding accommodation where they can feel safe. A reduction in sexual health and mental health services means LGBT+ needs are not being addressed, and the sense of being marginalised and invisible is increasing as specialist LGBT+ services disappear.[17] LGBT+ young people are more likely to find themselves homeless than their non-LGBT+ peers; are highly likely to have experienced familial rejection, abuse and violence; and comprise up to 24% of the youth homeless population.[18] Whilst homeless, they are significantly more likely to experience targeted violence, sexual exploitation, substance misuse, and physical and mental health problems than other homeless youth.[19] Services in all these areas are being cut drastically.

Reform has certainly not brought revolution. In fact, the austerity survey cited above mentions several times that respondents noticed how LGBT+ people were perceived as well-off beneficiaries of the 'Pink Pound' culture, so had little need of public services.

The idea that we can buy or vote or lobby our way out of oppression has proved, as *OTR* predicted, horribly mistaken. This is why I believe the key role in fighting LGBT+ oppression today must be played by the young: those with personal experiences of austerity, the least adaptation to institutionalised paralysis and professionalisation, and the most advanced ideas about human sexuality. They are the people for whom this book has primarily been republished.

Rampant commercialisation of Pride marches and painful splits in the movement require radical thinking and serious action. While fascist and neoliberal politics threaten us, new left-wing political protest forces across Europe and the US, such as Podemos and those inspired by Bernie Sanders – will continue to offer opportunities to build greater unity in the fight against oppression. We don't have to fight on our own and, I maintain, nor should we wish to if we are serious about eradicating oppression.

Much has changed since *OTR* was written, but the deep political contradictions the book describes persist. Has the LGBT+ movement been bought off? If we see legislative changes and equalities policies as ends in themselves, and a reason to put a brake on the fight for human sexual, social and political liberation, we may fall victim to our success. Being able to marry is not much use if you can't get a home or a job. It's great to have children born and brought up in LGBT+ families, but childcare costs and cuts in social care alike mean the burden of looking after the next generation is left to unpaid individuals – regardless of sexuality – struggling to balance their budgets, their time and their lives. In Britain, it is still not possible to legally define one's own gender. Intersex people are frequently forced to live as either female or male, while trans people have to fight for healthcare and self-determination. The commercialism *OTR* deplored was minuscule compared with today. We will be horribly exposed if we allow the voice of protest to be drowned out. We will never take our place in the forefront of the fightback against austerity if LGBT+ trade unionists are sidelined on committees and the question of oppression is separated from the urgent need for economic fightback. We let corporations which boast of their pro-LGBT+ stance off the hook if we ignore their failure to pay employees a living wage and decent contracts with full trade union rights. We will play a treacherous part in LGBT+ history if we do not fight for the rights of LGBT+ refugees in Britain, the US and on the frontiers of Fortress Europe, against being brutalised, humiliated, incarcerated, abandoned and deported.

But the young are not automatically drawn to class politics.

Just as in 1995, there is active resistance to the commercialisation, pinkwashing and exclusive professional networking which benefit some but not most LGBT+ people. Academic trends in queer theory, literary and film criticism, intersectionality and privilege theory are critiquing adaptations the movement has made to the market and institutionalisation, and the separation between LGBT+ oppression and other oppressions. They have, often brilliantly, uncovered and analysed the way oppression operates and manifests on different social and political levels. These trends of thought, which treat class as just one in a range of intersecting oppressions, underpin a radical movement of student and community LGBT+ activists who are rightly outraged by the material conditions in which they live and want to rise up and change things. The search for a political compass is continually developing, expressed in myriad imaginative and bold political gestures through community debates, direct action and interventionist stunts.

It's time to face the stark reality of how oppression functions to divide workers. One key issue is Islamophobia. Islamophobia is today's 'respectable' form of racism and is being used to create tension, fear and splits within the wider population, and to justify money being cut from public services and spent instead on imperialist war and 'anti-terror' measures domestically and internationally. David Cameron's Tory government and others, present themselves as championing equality by enacting equal marriage rights for same-sex couples. Across Europe and elsewhere, liberal-sounding Islamophobic rhetoric is used to stoke up hatred against refugees. Many of these 'migrants', we are told, would kill LGBT+ people and subjugate women if they had the chance – so we should keep them out. Tragically, some in the LGBT+ movement have fallen for this type of pinkwashing con-trick, where positive measures for LGBT+ people are used to promote attacks on other oppressed groups in society.

The cutting edge of LGBT+ political initiatives is pushing the limits of identity politics to highlight dangers facing refugees and the urgent need to counter racism, Islamophobia and austerity cuts. For instance, Lesbians and Gays Support the Migrants and LGBT+ People Against Islamophobia were set up in 2015 by the activists who came together around the re-formed LGSM. LGSMigrants states:

'As LGBTQ people we're being pitted against migrants, who we're told are a threat to gay rights. We refuse to see our sexualities used as weapons of border enforcement. Instead we will stand in solidarity with migrants in any way we can. As people that were once deemed illegal in the UK, we must stand in solidarity with the people currently facing persecution by the state and the media.'

LGBT+ Against Islamophobia issued an open statement in April 2016, underlining this point:

'We do not accept that the cause of LGBT+ rights should be used to divide the victims of prejudice and inequality against one another. Specifically we are absolutely opposed to the use of LGBT+ rights to justify Islamophobia. The representation of Islam as more homophobic than any other religion is false and amounts to an excuse for racism... The Tory Government is in disarray, from the NHS to education, from tax avoidance rip-offs to benefit cuts. In order to force through austerity they try to use racism to divide us.'

The statement goes on to draw a parallel between the Cameron administration's 'Prevent' strategy, which encourages teachers to spy on children as young as three years old in order to identify 'potential terrorists', and Thatcher's Section 28.

These initiatives will not appeal to all LGBT+ people on the basis of morality, equality or civil liberties. They are cutting through the pink ribbons of corporate LGBT+ posturing and shining a light on the dark reality of the capitalist system. The original LGSM group did not win the support of all LGBT+ people, far from it; the Miners' Strike divided the queer nation as much as it divided Britain as a whole. Many middle-class gays thought Thatcher was wonderful. How far the new initiatives will withstand attacks from within the LGBT+ 'community' remains to be seen. They will need strong class politics in the times ahead;

without it, many resort to moralism. Internal splits, sectarianism, fingerpointing and smearing are tragic characteristics of those who rely on identity politics to fight oppression. Tragically, many fall away from activism, exhausted by the impossibility of building unity across opposing class interests.

LGBT+ people are in a good position to understand what it feels like to be demonised as a threat to 'normal' society and western civilisation. We were the migrants of the 1980s, 'outsiders' in our own country. We need to step up for the scapegoats of today, just as LGSM stepped up for the miners – our fellow 'enemies within' – in 1984.

Over the Rainbow: Into the Future

There are many new areas to explore in the twenty-first century. The role of the market in social development has been laid bare for all to see, as marriage and parenthood commercial services have come to dominate LGBT+ lifestyle journalism and advertising. *OTR* was written when there was much less information about LGBT+ involvement in class struggle. There is a strong 'red thread' of class struggle in LGBT+ history. It needs to be teased out and understood in the context of anti-capitalism.

The new generations' embrace of non-binary sexuality, mutability and gender fluidity is consistent with scientific and anthropological discoveries. It is time to interrogate the concept of sexual minorities *per se* to examine how far it assists the fight for liberation and equality, and how far it may be holding us back. Current-day identity politics are largely formed around three main trends of thought: privilege theory, intersectionality and queer theory. Their limits require testing. Moreover, they are not monolithic trends. They include many variants, with differing degrees of unity, differentiation, inward-looking and fragmentation. Moralism and no-platforming can lead to some of the most catastrophic distractions, turning activists' attention away from the real enemy and onto their fellows.

Internationalism in our movement also needs to be clarified and refined by understanding the history and role of imperialism. While the majority of western states have liberalised laws on sexual orientation, LGBT+ people face heightened persecution in many countries. How can we effectively support those people and resist the oppression they face, whilst not aligning ourselves with racist narratives about 'backward cultures', nor appearing to ignore the real terrors LGBT+ people face on a daily basis from repressive regimes and vicious sectarianism?

The institution of the family has been transformed by the increase in LGBT+ marriage and parenting rights. There has been a huge increase in the numbers of same-sex couples setting up family units. It is right to celebrate the changes, but it is also vital to ask whether this development is a challenge to the capitalist system or an assimilation into it. Are same-sex parent-couples simply an extension of the standard mode of reproduction and home life which workers are compelled to adopt?

These and many more questions remain to be addressed and I aim to continue my work in this area. Meanwhile, my greatest hope is that readers will enjoy this book and use the ideas it offers to create solidarity and to develop clarity at a time when we have much to lose, but a world to win.

Notes

1   The centre closed in 1991
2   Thatcher abolished the Greater London Council in 1986 and the County Hall building is now a private hotel, art gallery and tourist attraction.
3   *Capital Gay* July 5 1985
4   The UK's trade union federation

5   As I wrote these words in December 2015, the last deep coal mine in the UK, Kellingley Colliery in Yorkshire, which at its peak employed 16,000 workers, closed for the last time.

6   *All Out! Dancing in Dulais: Lesbians and Gays Support the Miners*, LGSM/Converse Pictures 1986

7   For a full account of the background and history of the Miners' strike and Thatcher's tactics, I would direct readers to the remarkable documentary film *Still the Enemy Within*, (2014) produced by Mike Simons and directed by Owen Gower, and the book *The Great Strike: The Miners' Strike of 1984-5 and its Lessons*, by Mike Simons and Alex Callinicos, (Bookmarks 1985).

8   Sheila McGregor, *Socialist Review*, March 2014 (389)

9   *In the Pink,* January

10 Colin Clews's survey of media homophobia in 1985-86 can be found on his website www.gayinthe80s.com

11 Centre for Policy Studies, 1991

12 The full text of the letter with selected signatories can be read at http://www.theguardian.com/world/2015/jun/12/corporations-spoil-the-spirit-of-pride-london

13 Corcoran, Lader and Smith, *Hate Crime, England and Wales, 2014/15*, Home Office Statistical Bulletin 05/15.

14 Guasp, Gammon, Ellison, *Homophobic Hate Crime: The Gay British Crime Survey* 2013, Stonewall

15 Corcoran, Lader and Smith Op. cit.

16 *Implications of Austerity for LGBT People and Services*, NatCen Social Research/Unison, 2013

17 Ibid.

18 *LGBT Youth Homelessness,* Albert Kennedy Trust, 2015

19 Ibid.

OVER THE RAINBOW
MONEY, CLASS AND HOMOPHOBIA
(1995)
NICOLA FIELD

Nicola Field
*Over The Rainbow –
Money, Class and Homophobia*
Pluto Press, London, Connecticut 1995

First published 1995 by Pluto Press 345 Archway Road,
London N6 5AA and 140 Commerce Street, East Haven,
Connecticut 06512, USA

To Sheila Gillie

ACKNOWLEDGMENTS FOR
THE 1995 EDITION

The following people gave their time and expertise and helped me to find documents, press cuttings, facts and figures: Roberta Wedge of the London Bisexual Group, Alison Rowan of *Bifrost*, Ian Taylor of *Socialist Worker*, David Allison of Outrage! Sherry Wolf of the International Socialists in New York, Anya Palmer of Stonewall, Vicky Powell of the *Pink Paper*, Delia Hirons of the Terrence Higgins Trust.

The 'Hostile Brothers' themselves also gave up their time to air their views on the potential political power of pink money: Ivan Massow (Ivan Massow Associates), Gordon Lewis (the Village bars), Michael Mason {*Capital Gay*), Kim Watson (*Pink Paper*), Gary Henshaw (Kudos) and Mike McCann (Clone Zone).

Paud Hegarty, Jim McSweeney and Jane de Silva of Gay's the Word bookshop all provided information and inspiration.

For help, support, contacts, discussions and arguments along the way, thanks go to: Noel Halifax, Regan Kilpin, John Shemeld, James Blewett, Janet Noble, Lesley Hilling, Jackie Burke, Chris Boot, Ceiren Bell, Katy Swan, Anita Heavens, Caroline Natzler, Roger Barton, Pauline Haynes, Jane Lewis, Mark Brown, Steve Hack, John Lindsay, John McKay and Duncan Blackie.

The following people read sections of the text and made invaluable comments: Mary Phillips ('Family'), Jo Eadie ('Bisexuality'), Gareth Jenkins ('Cultural Activism').

Sheila Gillie and John Shemeld deserve special thanks for reading the whole thing, (in Sheila's case over and over again!), giving their comments and their encouragement. I am also grateful for the affectionate help of M & H who bailed me out of debt at a crucial time and allowed me to get on with finishing the book.

This book would not have been attempted without the galvanising influence and patience of Anne Beech at Pluto Press.

INTRODUCTION: SEIZING THE TIME

The 1990s have seen an extraordinary polarisation over the politics of lesbian and gay liberation.

There has been a feverish explosion of lesbian and gay commercial visibility. The pink pound and dollar are gaining increasing credibility and influence in the marketplace. A new generation of magazines, books, bars, cafes, shops and clubs, catering for an upmarket clientele, has been growing up in cities across the UK, the US and Australia. What's on sale is a designer gay lifestyle and an off-the-peg social identity. London has outstripped Amsterdam and Berlin to become the gay capital of Europe, offering a dazzling array of nightlife venues as well as clutches of sophisticated cafes to while away the hours between bouts of shopping and personal beautification. Advertising and marketing journals extol the benefits of targeting the pink spend, a seemingly bottomless oasis in the midst of world recession. The media offer a sparse but heady mix of debate, drama, documentary and deliberation, projecting the gay lifestyle to the forefront of alternative culture. For liberal journalists and programme-makers, 'gay' is a fashion item, bringing with it a touch of sophistication and street credibility. It seems everyone— from police officers to Shakespearean actors—is coming out of the closet and into the public eye.

The hype is inevitably going political. Gay entrepreneurs have emerged as spokespeople for lesbians and gays, bringing glamorous news of financial and commercial successes. All this, we are told, will bring great joy and benefit to the community as a whole. Apparently, lesbian and gay people are being welcomed, little by little, into the powerful heart of society. For those who are investing in the pink economy as a political focus, gay oppression really seems to be falling away.

Meanwhile, however, 'family values' are on the rise and morality is gaining ascendancy. The rise of ultra-right fascist organisations, unchecked by states or governments, is precipitating an atmosphere of terror amongst gays and black people. Violent homophobic attacks are on the increase. Lesbians and gays are still losing custody of their children because their sexuality is regarded as making them 'unfit' parents. Many public housing tenants lose their homes when their partners die because their relationships are still not recognised.

Despite softly-softly guidelines, gay people are systematically harassed and entrapped by police. Homosexual men—and occasionally women—continue to be arrested, convicted and imprisoned for consensual sexual relationships. Homophobic ideas and attitudes, both blatant and subtle, continue to pour into people's homes and heads via the mass media. The handful of information and support services for lesbian and gay people have been more or less wiped out as local government dumps action on equality in the wake of draconian public spending cuts. There is still no effective treatment for HIV infection, let alone a cure, yet government funding for AIDS care and research dwindles year by year. The majority of people who have homosexual feelings are not even out. In short, the everyday lives of most lesbians and gays have not noticeably benefited from the burgeoning strength of pink money.

What does the organised gay movement make of this apparently contradictory state of affairs? Tragically, the response is fragmented. Reform, lobbying and radical action groups seem split over how to move forward. Some advocate building a movement through the cultivation of influential public figures and the organisation of glitzy publicity events. They concentrate on political lobbying and manoeuvring in the corridors of power. Many, though, are frustrated by the exclusiveness of this approach and favour direct action. They want to fight homophobia through head-on confrontation and their approach defies the deal-making strategies of the assimilationists. Others, however, yearning for unity, insist that effective gay politics must involve both kinds of activity. They support the lobbyists' efforts and applaud the street antics of the direct action packs. But are these two approaches really the only options available? Are we really doomed to watching sporadic street stunts interspersed with letter- writing campaigns and everything held together by a continual in-fight over who has the most support and street credibility?

Arguments over gay oppression and how to fight it have been rumbling and raging ever since the very beginnings of the modern gay movement. Chuck Rowland was a founder of the US gay rights organisation Mattachine, which led the movement in the 1950s. He describes a disagreement at a Mattachine convention which could equally be applied to the movement today:

> *To most of the people who attended that convention, the only way we were ever going to get along in society was by being nice, quiet, polite little boys that our maiden aunts would have approved of. We were not going to get along in the world by going out and flaunting our homosexuality. There were people of goodwill, who would help us, but we could not do anything naughty like having picket signs or parades. Only communists would do things like that.[1]*

This pattern was going strong in the late 1960s. Barbara Gittings was active in the lesbian-organised Daughters of Bilitis (DOB) which started out with a progressive agenda and was then taken over by conservative lobbyists. The conservative activists did not experience the everyday harassment faced by most working-class gays and so resented attempts by left-wingers to make the organisation more radical:

> *The police went into the bar and more or less picked out women at random and put them in paddy wagons ... The*

women spent a night at the police station and they were
outraged. They wanted to do something. The obvious vehicle
was the existing chapter of the DOB [in Philadelphia].
But they found they could hardly blow their noses without
permission from national headquarters of DOB, which was
all caught up in a big election for the board . . . So they
broke off from DOB, ended the chapter and founded a new
organisation for both men and women, called Homophile
Action League, that was dedicated to political action.[2]

A similar tale can be told about the UK, with disagreements and splits over political strategies, most of which revolved around the liberal Campaign for Homosexual Equality and the radical, left- led Gay Liberation Front. Today, the names of the players have changed. Lobbyists are found in the US National Lesbian and Gay Task Force and at the UK Stonewall Group. Radical in-your-face street activity is organised by queer coteries ACT UP, Queer Nation, Outrage! and the Lesbian Avengers. The arguments, though, remain pretty much the same. The gay press is filled with articles and letters amplifying the debate and provides endless fora for reiterating the same old discussions.

Some commentators wonder if this fragmentation is endemic to the lesbian and gay communities. It is tempting to suspect that the in-fighting, back-biting and endless criticism is there because lesbians and gay men are, let's face it, somewhat prone to bitchiness, jealousy and self-destruction. It has also been suggested that the splits are all down to self-oppression and an inability to respect 'our' own achievements. In a feature entitled 'Are We Eating Our Own?' US lesbian journalist Cynthia Scott exclaims:

I am alarmed at how internalised homophobia continues
to pervert our vision and dictate that, sooner or later any
gay man or lesbian who achieves success and visibility in
the larger community will become a target within his or her
own community.[3]

However, while the splits cross international boundaries and the disagreements mutter on, one thing unites all the gay leaderships.

Every one of the community and political spokespeople, whatever their political and organisational preferences, adheres to the notion that lesbians and gays are linked by an overriding common interest: their sexuality. They all believe that lesbians and gays, whatever their social class or level of income, whether they own a bar or work in the kitchen, all experience gay oppression in the same way. That working-class and poor gays are less likely to be out, less able to find safety off the streets and more likely to be criminalised or sacked because of their sexuality, is a constant thorn in the side of gay reform organisations. The facts upset their fundamental belief that all lesbians and gay men have the same interests in getting rid of gay oppression.

The effect of this artificial, imposed unity is to lay the foundations of serious *disunity*. There is now a high level of cynicism and demoralisation. The absence of class as an organisational basis means many feel isolated and vulnerable. Activists often do little more than devote themselves to building a haven-like ghetto in which they can foster the illusion of safety and community. The idea that it is only lesbians and gays who can do anything about their oppression is reiterated over and over in ever-diminishing gatherings. As US Lesbian Avenger and novelist Sarah Schulman claims: 'Nobody cares about us except us, that's the fact of the matter.'[4] This idea feels like a lifebelt but has the effect of a millstone. The community, such as it is, is plagued by an acute lack of direction and cohesion.

Mass communications are perceived as an all-powerful anti-gay force, as an expression of widespread homophobia. Many left-wing gays have taken refuge in counter-culture to concentrate on changing the world by reforming the media. These radical reformists work hard to shake off the grotesque ideological construction of the homosexual as a predatory and lust-crazed pervert and paedophile. The 1990s-style sex-positive aesthetic puts a finger up at the mainstream cultural establishment and seeks to re-eroticise representations of gay sexuality within the independent arts and media sectors. Its undercurrent—'we're here, we're queer, get used to it!'—defies sexual repression but ultimately fails to ignite the fuse between material reality and the power of imagination. The images pour out, the coverage shifts a little, but the facts of life for ordinary lesbians and gays don't really change. The *effects* of gay oppression become clearer and clearer. However, its root *causes* remain submerged in mystery and rhetoric.

The idea of uniting on the basis of class has often been distorted. Class is frequently used in identity politics as a basis for self-definition rather than collective political action. The term 'working class' has been used as a vehicle for tedious self-inquiry and a futile search for individual social or cultural roots. It has also been a convenient weapon in the war between competing oppressions which has resulted from the 'movementism' of the 1970s and 1980s. Rather than describing an economic and material relationship—which is what work and production are all about—'working class' has been bandied about in an attempt to gain political currency on a political left almost shredded by notions of autonomy and separatism. The use of 'class' in this sense fits neatly with vacuous notions of class as a state of consciousness. In Britain, for instance, where this book has been written, there is a strong tradition of class division, as delineated by accent, breeding, education and style. In reality, class is not caused or determined by these factors, but merely expressed by them. The 'stiff upper lip' is a sign of upper-class conditioning, not the cause of class itself. Having been brought up on dripping or grits is an effect of class oppression, not a badge of working-class identity.

It is crucial that the gay movement wakes up to the reality of class as a factor in gay oppression because the tide is turning fast. The splits and arguments in the gay movement reflect a growing sense of desperation. This desperation is one of the results of widespread and increasing pressure on the poor to make them poorer. The demoralisation of the 1980s is building up into a militant class revolt in the 1990s. Working-class communities are organising to defend hospitals, schools, colleges and welfare services. Housing, unemployment, health and transport are becoming key political issues. Lesbian and gay activists need to be taking a leading role in this class struggle, ensuring that issues of equality achieve the prominence they deserve in the rank and file workers' organisations now springing up. The exchange of new ideas about socialism and about the urgent need to change the world are magnificent opportunities. They represent a real chance to take forward all arguments and ideas about universal sexual liberation.

Notes

1   Chuck Rowland, 'The Organiser', in Eric Marcus, *Making History: The Struggle for Lesbian and Gay Rights,* Harper Collins, New York, 1992, p. 34.
2   Barbara Gittings and Kay Lahusen, 'The Rabble Rousers', in Marcus, *Making History*, p. 125.
3   *The Advocate* 13 August, 1992.
4   *She-Bang*, no. 4, summer 1993.

2. FAMILY

Perhaps most bitter to industrial man is the divisiveness which permeates relationships with those most dear, and the enmity between husbands and wives, parents and children.[1]

—Eleanor Burke Leacock

When, at the age of 22, I 'came out' and told my parents that I was a lesbian, I was not really prepared for their reaction. My mother said that she wasn't sure that she wanted to be my mother anymore. My father, in a letter, declared he found the whole subject nauseating and has refused to discuss it ever since. At the time I deeply regretted having said anything and my advice to other young lesbians and gays was 'Don't bother telling them, it really isn't worth the trouble.' What hurt most of all, apart from the threats of rejection, was the no-win situation inflicted on me by my parents through their moral teaching. Like most kids I had been taught that telling lies was wrong, that hiding things was dishonest and secretive. In the spirit of openness and honesty I felt honour-bound to tell them the truth and harbour no guilty, sneaky secrets. Not only that but I was excited by my new-found life and identity and wanted to tell my mum and dad.

Their horrified outrage was wounding. The idea that perhaps, as an adult, I might be making an informed, independent decision was evidently unthinkable. Once again the pattern had caught me out. Whatever I said or did, I would never win the approval and respect of my parents.

Awkward Questions

I tell the above story, not because I believe it to be necessarily representative or typical, but because my experience of coming out to my parents was a starting point in coming to understand the painful conflicts of family relationships and how they are connected to the fundamental problems about the way our society is organised. Facing up to the apparent injustice of their response and the illogic of their prejudices meant that I had to work out where their attitudes had come from. Why could they not just accept me for who I was? Why was my being gay such a shock and disappointment to them? Why were they too ashamed and embarrassed to talk about sexuality? Family relationships are supposed to be close and loving, and we are encouraged to look to our parents and other relatives for support in times of trouble and stress. Why then, at an important point in my life, when I was making difficult decisions and discoveries, did I not receive that love and support? It reminded me of times when I was small and slaps and smacks were administered 'for my own good'. In both cases, the image was of a loving parent intentionally inflicting pain. Overwhelmingly, this felt like a contradiction with which I was not allowed to argue. This contradiction, to a lesser or greater degree, is faced by virtually all children growing up within our society.

The institution of the family is at the centre of our social, political and economic system. It is where, as very young children, we learn about our place in the world and our rights to express, assert and defend ourselves.

Over 99 per cent of Britain's children live with one or both of their parents. Under 1 per cent are in the care of local authorities. Even here the family plays a major role. Half of the children in care are in residential homes run by local authorities or voluntary organisations. The remainder live in families: with their parent(s), guardians or, increasingly, with foster parents.[2]

A great deal of social value and weight is placed upon parents' ability to balance the responsibilities of nurturing and caring with discipline and authority. As children we look for comfort, reassurance and emotional warmth from the same source that controls us through regulation and punishment. 'Good' parenting is supposed to provide children with a coherent and consistent set of codes through which we learn to recognise, and live within, the boundaries of acceptability. In reality, the pressures and responsibilities of parenthood— which include the provision of physical necessities such as food, warmth and shelter—mean that parents are weighed down by a double imperative which is both moral and material. They must care and provide. They must also control and train. They must go out to work, but be ever-present in the home. No wonder that, under such pressures, parents are not always consistent. No wonder that, for many of us, the experience of childhood is often isolating, alienating and confusing. To make matters worse, this experience is at odds with socially accepted images of children as innocent and protected. We are all taught that children are safest and most loved within the home.

Institutions like the media, the government, schools and many workplaces promote homophobia as powerfully as they promote the family. None of us escapes being touched by these influences. When we consider how consistently homophobic ideas are peddled, it is hardly surprising that many parents are horrified when they hear that their son or daughter is gay. Their impression, gained from years of mass media consumption, may well be that homosexuals are lust-crazed perverts unable to control their unnatural desires. Cinema and television have, over decades, portrayed lesbians and gays as child abusers, man/woman haters, having no future, lonely, prey to prejudice and violence, weak, dishonest and pathetic.

Even today, alongside a flourishing gay media, it is still possible to find many instances of homosexuals being treated as figures of fun and objects of contempt. Along with this vicious anti-gay propaganda goes a virtual denial of lesbian and gay existence. In all aspects of our lives which are socialised—like health care and education, benefits and welfare—gay relationships and sexual desire are virtually ignored, as though this will make them all go away. Gay and lesbian activists, and their supporters, have worked hard to expose these slurs and injustices in the years since the formation of the modern gay movement. We now know how to recognise homophobia and anti-gay propaganda, however subtle. However, the skills of deconstruction and textual analysis tell us very little about why homophobia is there in the first place. What interest can institutions have in trying to influence our sexual choices? What do they gain from making people afraid of homosexuality in themselves and others? Why is love between people of the same sex perceived as such a terrible threat?

Clearly my experience of coming out is not unique. Many lesbians and gays have met with varying degrees of moral outrage from their families. Very little research has been carried out into the complex set of social attitudes surrounding homosexuality, but in 1984 the London Gay Teenage Group published *Something To Tell You*—the results of a city-wide survey amongst lesbians and gays under 21. The survey showed that almost one in five young lesbian and gay people attempt suicide because of the pressures, harassment and prejudice they face. The study also shows that the vast majority of parents greet the news that their son or daughter is homosexual with horror, confusion and anger. Many young people are thrown out of the family home and ostracised. It's a far cry from the traditional reaction of proud mothers and fathers when they hear of their offsprings' impending engagements, marriages or babies.

In order to create a society where sexual and social relationships are freely chosen and uncluttered by 'traditional' expectations, we need to begin to understand the role of the family in society today. We also need to learn important lessons from history—about the development of 'gay politics'—and about the events that have caused real and dramatic changes in the way people perceive themselves and their relationships.

An Open Prison?

What is the family and why is it always the subject of so much political concern and controversy? Surely family life is private? Why, then, are politicians and social 'experts' always talking about it in parliament and the newspapers? Why are cabinet ministers brought down by their extra-marital affairs? Why are politicians so keen to be photographed surrounded by spouse and kids? If sexual relationships are private and personal, why are weddings so loud, showy and expensive, preserved for posterity in photographs and on videotape? What does all this have to do with loving, supportive relationships between individual human beings?

For the individual, there is really no escape from the family. Even if we try to 'opt out' or join a commune we will still be surrounded, affected and influenced by 'family values'. Whether we are talking about the nuclear family—with its 'norm' of biological mother, father and 2.2 children—or extended families—with influential aunts, uncles and cousins—the family image and its web of social and power relations dominate the lives of everyone. Even those of us who have grown up outside families, in institutions and 'alternative lifestyles', cannot fail to be affected by the overwhelming social message that families are 'good' and 'normal'. Everything—from housing and transport to welfare provision and insurance—is based on the assumption that most people live, or aspire to live, within the structure of the family. Advertising, one of the principle forms of communication, reflects this assumption everywhere. The images of advertising promise happiness, success and normality in the context of the family. The products themselves are sold as accessories to happy family life. In other words, our happiness is said to be tied up in the family itself and its ability to purchase the accoutrements of efficiency, cleanliness, beauty and normality.

This barrage of propaganda is not convincing. Most of us know the reality of housework is a million miles away from the sanitised images used to promote cleaning products. Women know that the idealised female body—thin, white, devoid of fluids and odours and used to sell anything from shampoo to cars—does not exist. Representatives of ultra-masculinity in alcohol adverts effectively throw down the gauntlet to ordinary men who are struggling to reconcile the dominant roles expected of them with their real feelings of confusion and insecurity. These grotesque narratives and unreal fantasies play an important role in a dangerous game. They perpetuate myths which haunt and patrol sexual and social relationships between men and women; if you are a woman you must be coy, intuitive and enigmatic; if you are a man you need to be confident, daring and protective. In order to have any value in the world you must be sexually attractive to the other sex. They tell us that sex is, in and of itself, the endlessly confusing ritual played out at the centre of family life; anarchic and chaotic but codified, sanctioned and given meaning by the institution of marriage. This version of heterosexual love and sex towers above us all. It tells us that the differences between men and women are ones of consciousness and nature; timeless and inescapable.

Surely the Family Is Good?

We are taught that to be in a family is good and natural and that family ties are the most stable, loving and unselfish relationships we will have in our lives. For most of us, this lesson flies into the face of our own experiences of brutality, alienation and confusion within the family. But so powerful is pro-family propaganda that we tend to deny our knowledge of family life, with all its pain and disappointment, believing that we are isolated cases, or that our parents' behaviour is 'normal' because we don't know any different. The family, far from being a haven and a retreat from the outside world, is actually a very dangerous place, both physically and mentally.

Children face particular risks. Despite right-wing rhetoric about a decline in 'family values' and standards of behaviour since the 'permissiveness' of the 1960s, figures show that throughout this century children have been targets of violence and cruelty from adults within their families. Since it was founded in Britain 100 years ago, the National Society for the Prevention of Cruelty to Children has taken steps to protect over 9 million children suffering abuse and neglect.[3] Further studies show that boys are more likely to be physically abused (what is often termed 'corporal punishment') while girls are more likely to suffer sexual abuse.[4] The vast majority of child sexual abuse is carried out by close family members. That abuse is integrated into the fabric of family life is illustrated by a 1992 study which noted that, 'Many acts of abuse begin as attempts to discipline children and there is a fine line between firm discipline and abuse. In some families aggression is an inevitable part of family life.'[5]

Studies in the 1980s showed that over 100 children die in the UK each year as a direct result of physical abuse and neglect.[6] As X-rays began to be more widely used in the 1950s, cases of untreated multiple bone fractures (which had healed by themselves) and other serious injuries began to emerge. By 1962 many physicians were in no doubt that many of these injuries had been intentionally inflicted by parents.[7] Nevertheless, countless cases of suspected child abuse have been neglected because of professionals' unwillingness to acknowledge the potential dangers of family life.[8]

Violence against women is also a significant part of family life. Some 70 per cent of violence against women takes place within the domestic environment.[9] The traditional roles of housewife and mother, far from being instinctive or natural, appear to be highly problematic for many women:

Married women ... report about 20 per cent more depression than single women and three times the rate of severe neurosis. Married women have more nervous breakdowns, nervousness, heart palpitations and inertia. Still other afflictions disproportionately plague married women: insomnia, trembling hands, dizzy spells, nightmares, hypochondria, passivity, agoraphobia and other phobias, unhappiness with their physical appearance and overwhelming feelings of guilt and shame.[10] Women now form 50 per cent of the workforce in the western world. Many of them are juggling low-paid, high-stress jobs with domestic responsibilities. When seeking help for health problems, women often find that the material causes of their symptoms (stress, overwork, worry about money, isolation) are overlooked in favour of more pathological solutions. These medicalised opinions treat women as individuals whose problems stem from internal inadequacies. Many are prescribed psychotropic drugs to enable users to endure the pressures that triggered the depression in the first place. Diazepam (Valium) has been found particularly effective in helping women accept the stresses and strains of everyday life, and to 'maintain themselves in roles that they find difficult or intolerable'.[11]

The fact that the vast majority of work within the home is done by women, including care of children and elderly or disabled relatives, means that on a superficial level the family appears to offer men some benefits:

The mental health data, chronicled in dozens of studies that have looked at marital differences in the last forty years, are consistent and overwhelming: the suicide rate of single men is twice as high as that of married men. Single men suffer from nearly twice as many severe neurotic symptoms and are far more susceptible to nervous breakdowns, depression, even nightmares... bachelors are far more likely to be morose, passive and phobic than married men.[12]

However, sociological studies also show high levels of psychological aggression and hostility in marriage which can be initiated or inflicted by either partner. It appears that monogamy, in the form we associate with heterosexual marriage and family life, engenders behaviour and insecurities which are hard to equate with notions of loving couples who care for and trust one another. Documented types of aggression and hostility include: efforts to monitor and control the other partner's activities, humiliation/degradation, efforts to denigrate or ridicule, threats of physical violence, damage to personal property, accusations of infidelity, attempts at financial domination, refusal to provide emotional support, efforts to downplay the extent or impact of abuse through questioning the partner's perceptions, feelings or sanity.[13]

Of course, there are some people who have positive experiences of family life and the evidence put forward here is not intended to deny those experiences. Nevertheless, the propaganda surrounding us throughout our lives, that family life is the norm and that families with problems are 'dysfunctional' (and therefore in need of professional intervention), is dangerous and misleading. Beneath the pervasive gloss of romance which dominates our perceptions of marital and family relationships, lies a reality of frustration, fear and despair. Unless we understand that the family offers no safe haven from the harsh outside world, and that it is in fact a powerful weapon *within* the world, we will continue to blame one another—parents, children, lovers and partners—for the pain and suffering we undergo. It is necessary therefore to discover who in society benefits from the perpetuation of family life and whose interests will be served by a radical critical appraisal of its social and political function.

Surely the Family Is Natural?

The modern family came into existence around the time of the

Industrial Revolution. At the end of the eighteenth century England began to change from a predominantly agricultural society to a pre-dominantly industrial society.[14] Technology transformed all areas of production and revolutionised people's participation in work. The establishment of huge industrial centres led millions of people to leave the grinding poverty of rural life for work in mills and factories. When the industrial bosses found they needed more workers they literally forced people to move from the land to the city. Workers had no choice but to uproot and go to the towns in order to try to survive. This mass migration was accompanied by a huge population explosion. Within a period of only 50 years, the lives of ordinary people were changed beyond recognition and a new social class emerged: the industrial working class. Changes as fundamental as those described above had a huge impact on people and their relationships. Sexual behaviour began to be subject to new kinds of regulation: the criminal law on prostitution, policing and the workhouse. Most important during the Victorian period was the rise of the ideal of the nuclear family unit where the husband/father worked outside the home and the wife/mother combined the running of the home with a life of leisure. For most working-class families such an arrangement was, literally, a fantasy. They desperately needed the wages of as many members of the family as possible. Both women and children carried out arduous and dangerous work in factories and mills. However, pro-family propaganda, which was just as vitriolic and moralistic as it is today, was needed to inhibit the demand for expensive welfare services. The ruling class needed the family to continue to bear the brunt of caring work so that it could keep its costs down and its profits up.

For some workers, wage labour heralded an improvement in their material conditions. Many peasants had lived in the very depths of poverty with no civil, political or property rights. For millions, though, wage labour signalled the beginning of a life of horrifying toil and danger in death-trap factories. Many gains were won by workers organising together over decades for improvements in their working conditions. One gain, however, has come to be recognised as a barrier to working-class unity.

Although women's lives had been dominated by childrearing in feudal times, the growth of industrialisation was a turning point in the nature of women's oppression. Factory work offered women a level of independence and self-sufficiency they had not experienced before. Marriage and childbearing were no longer the only options open to girls. Consequently, crude and dangerous forms of contraception and abortion began to be widely practised. This presented problems for those who wanted future supplies of wage labourers. Who would look after the young children? How could a child's parentage be established when workers were not bothering to marry? What would the sexual practices of a mass of unmarried people all living and working closely together lead to? And what was to be done during periods when there were more workers than jobs? (Capitalism had already begun to show its cyclic nature: boom-recession-slump).

The expensive solution would have been to provide flexible housing and universal health care. The cheap solution was to make women responsible for child care, and the home was the cheapest way of ensuring the orderly reproduction of the workforce. When women were encouraged to go into the home and stop competing with men for jobs, the wages of men rose and there were some improvements in health and safety conditions. At first this seemed like a massive improvement because it meant that women and children did not have to work outside the home. But the appalling drudgery of housework, combined with the inevitable necessity of carrying out paid work from the home (such as laundry and needlework), meant that women had really been thrown out of the frying pan and into the fire.

As a result of these changes, women who were obliged to work outside the home received lower pay than men. Men began to regard women workers as a threat—a cheap workforce that would undercut them and take their jobs away. This discrepancy effectively pitted men and women against one another when fighting for better wages, rather than uniting them against their common exploiter. This was compounded by the social effects of making men the 'head of the household', engineering a gender-division of labour based on prejudice, competitiveness and artificial status. Moreover, the eventual institution of children's rights, whilst protecting the very young from the worst dangers of working life, was accompanied by a flood of cultural sentimentality over the new concept of 'childhood'. Far from becoming people with rights over their own bodies, children were framed as holy innocents needing constant protection. The new charitable educational and welfare institutions treated them as untrained savages in need of correction and discipline.

All of these developments have a strong resonance today. They have also generated some strange contradictions. Many lesbian and gay activists assert that the family is privileged in society and gets more support from the state. On one level this is true, since parents can get limited tax allowance and child benefits. However, lesbian and gay couples on unemployment benefit and income support actually get more because the state won't recognise gay relationships. This contribution to lesbian and gay invisibility in society is really based on money. The state, as a tool of the ruling class, does not want to foot the bill for lesbian and gay equality because it would ultimately cost too much.

Class Control and the Myth of Heterosexual Privilege

Contemporary lesbian and gay activists base their political agenda on the belief that all heterosexuals are privileged in comparison with homosexuals. However, gay oppression and state persecution of same-sex relationships are, in reality, components of wider sexual repression. Homophobia is tied up with women's oppression through dominant ideas about family life. Central to these ideas is the question of control. The material basis of the family and its role in class society is at the root of all sexual oppression. All forms of sexual freedom are curtailed, controlled and punished, if not by law and taxation then by social taboos and cultural disapproval. The right of all people to control over their bodies and free expression of their sexualities is wholly subordinated to the imperative of controlling the working class. Sexual mores change, yet particular forms of sexual expression continue to remain the focus of disapproval and fear, because they strike at the heart of the institution of the family. Ideas surrounding the family can transform, loosen up and adapt to changing social and economic patterns of work, but the oppression of women and the repression of homosexuality remain priorities for regulation. Whilst it is acknowledged that same-sex relationships (from life-partnerships to clandestine sexual encounters) exist, resources are devoted to making sure that they remain marginalised, sensed as transgressive and held completely incongruous with 'normal' family life. The position of women and homosexuals within class society is rooted in concern about family life and social order.

The state and its charitable helpmates serve to protect the interests of capital, partially through the distribution of welfare in a 'moral context' which delineates sanctioned sex from taboo sex. Whilst homosexuality has historically remained a taboo, this does not mean that heterosexuality per *se* *is* uniformly sanctioned.

Since the Industrial Revolution, a tidal wave of 'advice' for working class families has flooded western culture. The aim of this advice is to build a moral context for people's lives and to persuade workers to organise their lives to fit into this context. Lesbian, gay, bisexual and straight workers, young and old, are subject to this moral restraint and social control. Battalions of medical, social and psychological 'experts' have marched through virtually all aspects of working-class people's 'private' lives, dispensing guidelines on sex and housework, making the family work better, hold together more securely, produce better-behaved children and need less financial and practical support.

The 1920s was a time of immense industrial development. Concerns about the social effects of this expansion also took on new forms and concepts. Marie Stopes, a middle-class pioneer of sex education and contraception, formulated a practical and moral solution to the social problems of a society undergoing such transformations. Her contribution was to relocate family values in a 'scientific' context which permitted the hitherto taboo practices of contraception and admitted the existence of marital sex for pleasure. She believed that the Victorian habits of denying female sexual pleasure and surrounding all sexual activity in mystery and ignorance were the cause of mass unwanted pregnancies and family breakdown. Her mission was to create a language of sex which would, she hoped, eradicate sexual ignorance and provide a framework for essential moral indoctrination. Her motives were wholly class-conscious, as can be seen in her advice to teachers on dealing with naughty children given to 'vulgarity and nastiness of speech':

> *Sheer dirtiness of mind will seldom be given much chance to be injurious in an ordinary class of nice-minded, healthy British children, whether boys or girls, but if, as sometimes happens in large slums or city districts, a considerable proportion of children have been nurtured in the gutter the vulgarity of diction may spread to all.*[15]

Eugenics, or the theory of 'race hygiene', aims to shape human reproduction around the question of 'breeding'. It has its roots in class control. Eugenic thought is at its most influential in contemporary European and US debate over abortion and reproductive rights. Eugenicists question the social implications of single women, lesbians, poor women, black women and women with disabilities having children. Their underlying assumption is that such women are not capable of successful parenting and that being poor, or disabled (or whatever) implies fault or imperfection inherent in the women themselves.

Eugenics is also at the heart of programmes of mass sterilisation and injected contraception in the Third World where false concepts such as 'overpopulation' are put forward to account for poverty and famine rather than global economic policy and the pursuit of profit. Proponents of this 'science' describe society as a farm, where the breeding of livestock is crucial to the quality of the farm's efficiency. The family plays an important role in eugenics because it provides a focus for social classification. You define who you are by the kind of family you come from. Eugenicists worry about the ruling class qualities of leadership, authority, reputation and honour being eroded by the infiltration of weaker strains from people of lower classes. They are equally alarmed by the prospect of working-class people moving into positions of relative power, or aspiring to greater autonomy and status:

> *All must agree that many men fail to win high wages because they are weak, sickly, foolish, ill-tempered, drunken, careless, or dishonest ... The smaller families now being produced by those doing well-paid work leave more vacancies ... and to fill them more persons are available because of the diminished death-rate amongst the poor ... We are faced with a new and formidable condition of things[16]*

Eugenic solutions lie in stopping the very poor from having more than one or two children and by applying punitive taxation to large families. More extreme measures include compulsory sterilisation and legalised euthanasia for people with mental and physical disabilities (which, for some theorists, include homosexuality). These ideas were used to justify the mass murder programmes of Nazi Germany where racism and anti-semitism also provided convenient scapegoats for appalling poverty during the depths of capitalist recession. Winston Churchill was attracted to such solutions, as are the extreme-right and fascist elements of today. The influential Marie Stopes took a pragmatic and liberal view of social change and eugenic dangers. Her solution lay in education. Like the conservatives and moralists of today, she did not attempt to criticise the material conditions of poverty and deprivation but provided a model of damage limitation through proposed moral teaching by schools and parents. The teacher's role was to control pupil development through careful segregation and constant surveillance, while parents had the responsibility for instilling appropriate moral values. Her concerns are clearly grounded in the preservation of private wealth. She is determined to keep the material costs of social welfare to a minimum:

> *If dogs should be mated carefully to produce valuable puppies, should not human beings be mated as carefully in the interest of their children? Directly the question of human inheritance and its importance to the race arises, some explicit information about the dangers of departing from the accepted code of morality can be given.*[17]

She goes on to tell a cautionary tale of a young man 'from a line of good parentage' who flouted the moral law by impregnating a 'feeble-minded' woman. The resulting child then had many children, 'feeble-mindedness being very prolific', with the following calamitous consequences:

> *of this one illegitimate son's four hundred and eighty descendants only forty-six were normal; one hundred and forty-three were feeble-minded; very many of them were immoral or criminal in a variety of ways and very many of them were drunkards. The cost to the state in money, in all sorts of incidental ways, involved in curbing, punishing*

and caring for these wastrels was immense.[18]

Here we can see early examples of how crime levels, prison over-crowding and social spending are blamed on sexual 'immorality' and single parents, rather than poverty and poor housing. Stopes develops her argument by referring to the values instilled by sports and team games where selfish and reprehensible acts 'are not done' because they result in an unfair burden being placed on one's fellow players. Today's accusations from the right wing that the poor, disabled, old and unemployed are scroungers and a burden to society can be placed in a similar context.

Sexual relations continued to be an object of concern after the Second World War. The sexologist Kenneth Walker, writing in the 1950s, reflected the values of socialised education and medicine when he announced that differences in social class between potential marriage partners were less important than differences in educational background. He believed that engaged couples need to share similar views on religion and similar tastes in books, films and social pursuits. However, his views on mixed-race marriages are firmly grounded in a sophisticated eugenic argument which off-loads his authoritative racism onto what he sees as the incorrigible ignorance and prejudice of wider society:

> *To a member of the so-called Aryan race ... the marriage of a white man to a negress and still more a white woman to a negro, is utterly abhorrent and we have to accept the fact that this instinctive revulsion, on both sides, exists and that it is very deep-seated. No intellectual argument is capable of removing it for it is in the blood and beyond the range of reason . . . It is quite true that half-breeds are usually ill-adjusted people, but this is not due to inherited deficiencies but to the great difficulties which half-breed children encounter from the start.*[19]

Advice to women and men on sustaining marriage relationships and healthy, 'normal' families has centred around the constant redefinition of sex roles and the gender-division of labour in the home. Whilst advice has changed with changing social conditions, the overwhelming importance of maintaining a stable family unit and providing children with the necessities of physical and psychological health have remained paramount. Tory Edwina Currie's advice, to women in the north of England in the late 1980s, to improve their children's health by serving up fewer fried potatoes, comes from a long line of bourgeois intervention in the lives of the working- class household. Much of this advice is directed towards women in an attempt to fit them, generation after generation, into carrying out the privatised functions of the family: cooking, cleaning, nursing, mending and so on. The International departmental Committee of Physical Deterioration reported in 1904 on the educational needs of women:

> *At thirteen years of age the majority of these women would have begun to work in a factory, to handle their own earnings, to mix with a large number of people with all the excitement and gossip of factory life ... After marriage ... it is hardly probable that they would willingly relinquish this life to undertake work of which they are in so large measure ignorant and which is robbed of all that is to them pleasant and exciting. Until as girls they have been taught to find a pleasure in domestic work ... it is useless to expect them to relinquish factory life.[20]*

Since the beginning of the twentieth century many social changes have been brought about by the battles for women's equal rights and women's entry into the work force. However, the contradiction between conservative ideology (which says that women's place is in the home and that's where they will be happiest) and the reality of women's experiences of housework continues to dominate thinking about gender and labour. In the 1970s, as part of a movement which attempted to formulate a scientific analysis of the value of housework in capitalist economics, socialist feminists grappled with the intolerable pain and stress of privatised family life. Whilst they tended to concentrate on the *separation* rather than the *connection* between 'men's work' outside the home and women's work inside the home, they enabled a greater understanding of the material conditions of housework. These kinds of insights indicate the common links between gender and sexual oppression and point to the common interests of those fighting for gay liberation and women's liberation. Sheila Rowbotham comments:

> *If care were truly social, there would be no need for defensive homes as castles, tenderness would not be connected with submission, nor love with possession... The family under capitalism carries intolerable weight: all the rags and bones and bits of old iron the capitalist commodity can't use. Within the family women are carrying the preposterous contradiction of love in a loveless world...[21]*

She goes on to draw the links between freedom from reproductive labour and sexual freedom:

> *For the first time in history it is possible for women to choose when they become pregnant. This with the panic about population explosion means that the persistent connection between sex and procreation, and the fear in male-dominated society of female sexual pleasure, and often of any sexual act which is not likely to produce children, lose their force to contain women—and men. The implications of these for both women's liberation and gay liberation are apparent.[22]*

Alongside the age-old, feverish preoccupation with sexual

morality and the importance of gender-training, conservative sexologists and moralists offer endless advice on early detection of homosexual inclinations as well as directives on how to deal with or 'cure' homosexuality. Kenneth Walker speaks again:

> *During the early years of the war a youth, then still in his twenties, was brought to see me by his parents, in the hope that I would do something to help him... Now there are many types of homosexuals, some of whom are curable and others incurable, and in my opinion this boy belonged to the latter class... I no longer see any hope for this man for he is now a neurotic who has lost all respect for himself and is able to face his fellow men only after priming himself with alcohol.[23]*

In his influential 1971 women's health guide *Everywoman*, Derek Llewellyn-Jones warns of the dangers of misguided parenting and the potential for preventing many cases of homosexuality:

> *Ultimately the sexual inclinations of the child are determined by the attitudes of its parents, and some parents unwittingly encourage homosexuality in their children... Children reared in families which have only one parent, which are disturbed by distortions in the relationships of the parents to each other or to the child, or whose sexual attitudes are repressive or ignorant, are particularly vulnerable.[24]*

The political uprisings of 1960s America, which spawned the ideas of modern women's and black liberation and the gay movement, were followed by a backlash of pro-family propaganda which included a whole new generation of child-rearing advice books.

Titles like *Power to the Parents!* (1972), *Raising a Responsible Child* (1971), and *Dare to Discipline* (1972) began to crowd the fading copies of Spock and Ribble on suburban library shelves. Commonly they began with a little synopsis of the failure of permissiveness, with reference, in varying degrees of explicitness, to the resultant dope addicts, homosexuals and revolutionaries.[25]

Regulation of sexuality and family life down the century also gives us a clue as to the direction liberationists must take in the process of building this new kind of society. Frederick Engels, colleague and comrade of Karl Marx, described in 1884 the bourgeois ideal of family life, and hinted at the Catch-22 situation of working-class women who either can't or don't want to live on a husband's wages:

With the patriarchal family management lost its public character. It no longer concerned society. It became a private service; the wife became the head servant, excluded from all participation in social production...if she wants to take part in public production and earn independently, she cannot carry out her family duties... The modern individual family is founded upon the open or concealed domestic slavery of the wife, and modern society is a mass composed of these individual families as its molecules.[26]

This is how the working-class woman is the subject of 'expert' concern over her family functions. If she does not fulfil her privatised role then demands will have to be made upon the state. She has to be indoctrinated with the ideals of the bourgeois family so that if her household functions are not completed satisfactorily she and her family will perceive it as being her own fault, a failure in playing out her social role, rather than the result of inadequate state provision. Moreover, nursing homes and public nurseries are given bad press. Propaganda tells us that the people in such places receive less sincere care than they would from their relatives, thus enticing us, through guilt, to make fewer demands for full-time nursing and child care and expend more energy trying to cope in impossible situations.

The actual bourgeois family, of course, is not subject to such regulation and control because it is able to buy child care, private health insurance or domestic cleaners, without recourse to state support. The middle-class lifestyle may occasionally stretch the conventions of 'traditional' family life but as economic units their families do not threaten the profits of the ruling class.

The working class simply does not have the resources to live up to the family values that are rammed down its throat and so it presents a constant threat to the rule of capitalist order. Demands for an adequate free health care system, for nurseries to be kept open and for schools to be well-maintained are not isolated protests for individual communities. They represent a significant fightback against a system which makes workers and the poorest and most vulnerable people in society pay for its grossly wasteful economic priorities. It is *workers* who have a material interest in the abolition of the family, whatever their sexual orientation.

The Moral High Ground

Keeping the family more or less intact has been a social policy priority for governments of all parties this century. So integral is the institution of the family to the running of capitalism that all attempts to keep money moving, make production profitable and be competitive are underpinned by constantly changing laws affecting families. Over the past few years we have seen all the major western political parties battling over the title 'The Party of the Family'.

Centre-left parties, to which the majority of the working class and 'minority' oppressed groups look for support and representation, offer a rhetoric of social welfare. Their leaderships promise social policies which will enable the family to function more effectively. Marginal improvements in state backup will be paid for by a minuscule redistribution of wealth.

In contrast, right-wing conservative parties have an uncomplicated commitment to bolstering the rich and entrenching the privatisation of the family. This is because the 'party of property' is also, by definition, the organisation of the ruling class. The managers, bosses and proprietors employ our labour, own our homes and the land they are built on, and take the vast majority of the wealth we work so hard to produce. Conservative politicians organise on their behalf. They therefore have an uncomplicated investment in social control and the political manipulation of the family. However, in order to win working-class support they have to encourage and appear to protect the pervasive ideal of 'normal' family life. This is despite the fact that they are well aware of the 'normal' family's non-existence because they are the ones employing women on poverty wages to clean their offices and slave in their sweatshops.

Campaigning for the Moral Context - The British Conservative Government in the 1990s

In 1993 John Major's government launched a 'Back to Basics' campaign: a programme of massive public spending cuts across all government departments concerned with social policy: education, social security, health, housing, the environment and employment. Workers were asked to pay for the £50 billion national deficit brought about by the disastrous economic tactics of the 1980s. The moral pronouncements and judgements being used to justify these savage spending cuts are chilling continuations of the moral guidelines dispensed by 'experts' over the past 150 years. And like the early capitalist moralities, present-day pronouncements are just as obsessed with people's sexualities and the importance of keeping families under control. In December 1993 John Patten, secretary of state for education, issued guidelines on changes in the arrangement for sex education in schools. Sex education was to be taken out of the science curriculum and put into a separate 'moral context'. His circular said the law would now require that, 'all sex education must encourage young people to have regard to moral considerations and the value of family life'.[27]

At a press conference Patten made clear that this meant insisting that heterosexuality was preferable to homosexuality. Later on that same day the Health Secretary Virginia Bottomley was questioned on national television about Patten's statements and challenged to refute his moralistic judgement on homosexuality. Her reply was a perfect description of the role of family values in capitalist society and the idolisation of the 'traditional' family as a way of diverting people's anger from the inadequacy of basic and necessary services. She emphasised that monogamy, marriage, fidelity and heterosexuality were 'goals to aim for' rather than rules to be followed to the letter. The subtext is that if you really cannot reach these high ideals then you must simply strive to get as near to them as possible. Sexual freedom, therefore, is sacrificed to social and class control *through sexual morality*, or exhortations to be 'better'.

Patten's proposal revealed a clear understanding of the class implications of family life, rebutting theories that the family is breaking down with the assertion that 'the family is still at the core of society—the cement holding us all together'.[28] Moreover, the family is placed at the centre of social discipline, being 'the primary setting of the establishment, maintenance, development and transmission of values. It provides a basic sense of belonging and an essential reference point for children.'[29] Like Marie Stopes, Patten sought to assign the blame for crime and social insubordination (which have always existed in societies based on class and private property) to poor parenting and lack of discipline in schools. This enabled him to offer repression, control and punishment as an appropriate remedy rather than improved conditions for people to live and work in.

The themes of morality and discipline were developed by Prime Minister John Major. The universal introduction of school uniform, regimented lines of desks, detention punishments and team sports were put forward by him as elements of 'good order' necessary to the efficient running of schools. This draconian plan links in with some far-right Tories who say that schools should use discipline like the armed forces. They suggest that redundant ex-servicemen should be encouraged to bring their expertise and control into schools by being recruited as teachers. Major also talked about a new era of 'the fourth R' in which pupils would learn the difference between right and wrong through the imposition of moral values in the classroom.[30]

The 'Back to Basics' agenda, like all imposed moral crusades, was a covert campaign to safeguard the position and private prosperity of the rich. Its theoretical basis was in a pamphlet called *Happy Families* published in 1991 by the British right-wing think-tank, the Centre for Policy Studies (CPS), an organisation with influence and connections right across the international conservative political agenda. Written by David Willetts, the Director of Studies at the GPS, the pamphlet proposes making private childcare more attractive and larger families less attractive by changing the law on benefits and taxation.

Willetts does not shrink from presenting a radical right-wing moral and theoretical basis for his proposals. He resorts to a woolly spirituality in order to prove that families are eternal and natural: 'The family, meaning a married couple with their children, has survived because it meets human needs; it embodies a "latent" wisdom.'[31] At the same time he offers the material reason for his historically inaccurate claims: 'The party of the property should be the party of the family ...'

Willetts also manages to gloss over the primary role of the family in the production of cheap labour with the following convoluted and ludicrous arguments which attempt to define human emotions as commodities which can be marketed:

It could be argued that the idea of the family as an essentially private emotional affair is itself a consequence of the triumph

89

of free markets. Since it is the essence of such free markets (the argument runs) that our interests as consumers should prevail over our interests as producers, then why does that not apply here? Instead of seeing a family as the producer of a set of social services, we should see our role within it as consumers of emotional and private satisfaction.[32]

Willetts never allows financial considerations to go out of sight. He describes the increase in children being born outside marriage as being 'like a run on a bank and we cannot tell where it may lead'. He also addresses the need for the family to provide primary elements of class control through authority and discipline. It is, after all, within the family that we first discover our social class and our role within society. Willetts makes the link between private and public methods of punishment and reform:

The exercise of authority is not a dry run for fascist dictatorship. The truth is that it is only through experiencing discipline within the family that children learn to exercise the virtue of self- discipline in their adult lives. And if we lack self-control... then discipline and constraints have to be external instead.[33]

A Record of Reality

The hypocrisy of politicians' claims to support 'family values' is well known through the publicised corruption and sexual affairs of those in public life. Whilst preaching monogamy, fidelity, marriage and the evils of single parenting and homosexuality to the rest of us, these rich and powerful individuals behave quite differently in their private lives. The real meaning of their obsession with family values, though, is far more sinister than a few individual cases of gross personal hypocrisy. Political parties and governments across the world have consistently attacked working-class people, wrecking their family relationships and devastating their standard of living through unemployment, wage and benefit cuts, the decimation of social and health care services and inadequate provision for public housing.

The idea that heterosexual people are uniformly privileged in comparison with lesbians and gays is unsustainable in the context of class society. The movement of wealth throughout the 1980s has been away from the poor and into the pockets of the rich. In 1988-89 around one fifth of the population in the UK was living in poverty, more than twice the number of 1979. During that ten year period 'the poorest tenth of the population saw their real income (after housing costs) fall by 6%...while the richest tenth enjoyed a staggering rise of 46%'.[34]

This growing polarisation between the poor and the rich was starkly illustrated just before Christmas 1993 when income tax increases, the imposition of VAT on domestic fuel, cuts in unemployment benefit for the under 25s, threatened council rent rises and a cut in student grants were matched by huge wealth boosts for the rich. Banks in the City of London handed out hundreds of £1 million bonuses to dealers. Sick pay payments to cover employees' illness were scrapped, foreshadowing sackings for those with high sickness records. Secret Customs and Excise reports revealed that businesses avoid paying £6,000 million in VAT each year—'that's VAT we have paid out but which never gets passed on to the government. The Tories have written off £333,000 in this way EVERY DAY since their election in 1979.'[35]

In 1989, 30 per cent of all children were living in or on the margins of poverty, as compared with 19 per cent in 1979.[36] In 1993, in the Liddle ward of the London Borough of Southwark, 57 per cent of children were reported as living in non-wage-earning households.[37]

Because of discrimination, black people and women are proportionally more likely to be unemployed or in low-paid work with bad conditions such as health and safety risks and shift work. People who have come from abroad to live in Britain are often denied full or any access to welfare services, thus reinforcing the racist notion that black people in Britain are 'outsiders' or foreigners. This has been made worse by the Tories' ever-more stringent laws on immigration, justified by propaganda that people from abroad are the cause of poverty in Britain.[38]

Women, because of their enforced role as mothers, carers and providers, shoulder much of the brunt of poverty. The annual British Social Attitudes Survey showed that in 1991 the vast majority of domestic labour—including looking after children—was done by women.[39] Today, 62 per cent of adults receiving income support are women.[40] Because many women are in low-paid and often part-time work, they have few employment rights and are cheaper to dismiss. For the same reasons, their income often falls below the National Insurance contribution rate, forcing them onto non-contributory and means-tested benefits.[41] The Tories' Child Support Agency, set up in 1993, has the power to deduct 20 per cent in personal benefit from women who refuse to co-operate with the pursuit of maintenance from absent fathers.

Poverty and discrimination have a devastating effect on people's physical and mental health. Feelings of powerlessness, isolation, of being a failure and of constant worry about money are familiar to many people today, regardless of their sexuality. Parents worry about being able to feed, clothe and shelter their children, let alone buy them Christmas and birthday presents. New clothes, visits to the hairdresser and going out are luxuries many people cannot afford. Many families live in damp, cold, substandard housing, with horrific effects on their health. Depression, insomnia and aggression are all related to repetitive, low-paid work and unemployment.

It is not difficult to see that 'the party of the family' is, whatever its political and national home, committed to creating conditions which bring about deep divisions between groups of people in society. Right-wing governments in Europe and the US have attempted to off-load the blame for, and the costs of, their mistakes onto vulnerable groups in society: the unemployed, people on disability benefits, single mothers, immigrants, travellers and lesbians and gay men. The sexist, racist and homophobic arguments they put forward to justify their attacks are intended to alienate support for those groups and prevent them from being able to organise any kind of fightback. Government measures have also had a serious effect on the mental and physical well-being of working people and their families, causing rows, breakdowns, assaults and even murders. Lesbians, gays, bisexuals and straights: all are in it together.

There Is No Such Thing

Margaret Thatcher, as prime minister, once stated: 'There is no such thing as society. There are only individuals'. Her intention, of course, was to deflate arguments for more socialised welfare services and appeal to voters who, appalled by the apparent social breakdown around them, were all too ready to respond enthusiastically to calls for more individualism and more privatisation. Her rallying call was for the elevation of the family, the 'reinstatement' of family values as the guiding principles of civilisation. Quite wrongly, she implied that there were no meaningful relationships outside of the family for working-class people.

Our response is that, on the contrary, it is the idealised family that does not exist. People are of course tied together by many things: love, desire, dependency and friendship. The mythical family, whilst a powerful force for control and political manoeuvring, is an abstract concept which hovers over our daily lives and infiltrates our activities and thoughts. In the sense of being a real basis for human development, it is impracticable and impossible. Its rules are broken all the time by people determined to struggle and survive and be themselves.

By understanding this, we can begin to see that heterosexuality itself is not privileged in society. Rather, certain limited and contorted forms of heterosexuality are permitted, sanctioned and encouraged. Gender roles at work, play and in sex are promoted throughout every aspect of our society and culture. These roles inhibit and distort men's and women's identities and actions as well as their relationships. Jealousy, fear, machismo and femininity are all products of sexuality under capitalism, where desire and property have become deeply tangled and confused.

The idea of the family as a protective haven is a myth, the family unit cannot provide the haven it promises. On the contrary, we can never isolate ourselves from social and political relationships in the world. The places we choose to hide are always inseparably connected to the real world. It is not the failure, or the breakdown, of the family which causes our alienation, but the ever disappointed hopes instilled in us as children. These hopes are false dreams of being cocooned and of belonging. Our real chance of community lies in the future, not in the past.

Notes

1   Introduction to Frederick Engels, *The Origins of the Family, Private Property and the State*, Lawrence and Wishart, London, 1972.

2   Hilary Graham, *Women, Health and the Family.* Harvester Wheatsheaf, London, 1984.

3   White and Wollett, F*amilies: A Context for Development*, Falmer Press, London, 1992.

4   Ibid.

5   Ibid.

6   Brown et al., *Early Predictions and Prevention of Child Abuse*, Wiley, Chichester, 1988.

7 Kemp etal., *Journal of the American Medical Association* no. 181, 1962.

8 Richard J Gelles, 'Family Violence' in *Family Violence, Prevention and Treatment*, ed. Hampton et al., Sage, California, 1993.

9 *Womankind International Report*, November 1993.

10 Susan Faludi, *Backlash: The Undeclared War Against Women*, Verso, London, 1992, p. 56.

11 Cooperstock and Lennard, 'Some Social Meanings of Tranquilliser Use' in *Sociology of Health and Illness* 1979 1, 3: pp. 331-47.

12 Susan Faludi, *Backlash*, p. 35.

13 Murphy and Cascardi 'Psychological Aggression and Abuse in Marriage', in Hampton (ed.), *Family Violence*.

14 For a detailed account of this period see Lindsey German, *Sex Class and Socialism*, Bookmarks, London, 1989.

15 Marie Stopes, *Sex and the Young*, Putnam, London, 1926, p. 23.

16 Major Leonard Darwin, *What is Eugenics?*, Watts and Co., London, 1928, p. 65.

17 Marie Stopes, *Sex and the Young*.

18 Ibid., p. 114

19 Kenneth Walker, *Love, Marriage and the Family*, Odhams, London, 1957.

20 Quoted in Gill Blunden, 'Our Women are Expected to Become', in *The Sexual Dynamics of History*, ed. London Feminist History Group, Pluto Press, London, 1983, p. 89.

21 Sheila Rowbotham *Woman's Consciousness, Man's World*, Pelican, London, 1973, p. 77.

22 Ibid.

23 Kenneth Walker, *Love, Marriage and the Family*, p. 314.

24 Derek Llewellyn-Jones, *Everywoman*, Faber, London, 1971, pp. 78-9.

25 Barbara Ehrlich and Deirdre English *For Her Own Good: 150 Years of Advice to Women*, Pluto Press, London, 1979, p. 237.

26 Frederick Engels, *The Origins of the Family*, Lawrence and Wishart, London, 1972, p. 137.

27 Education Act 1993, Circular X/94 issued by the Department for Education, April 1993.

28 Ibid.

29 Ibid.

30 *Guardian*, 1 January 1994.

31 David Willetts, *Happy Families?* CPS, London, 1991.

32 Ibid.

33 Ibid.

34 Carey Oppenheim, *Poverty: The Facts*, Child Poverty Action Group, London, 1993, p. 1.

35 *Socialist Worker*, 11 December 1993.

36 Derived from Social Security Committee, Second Report, *Low Income Statistics: Low Income Families 1979-89*, HMSO, London, 1993.

37 'The Poverty Profile: Indicators of Poverty and Deprivation in Southwark', Southwark Council, London, 1993.

38 Carey Oppenheim, *Poverty: The Facts*, p. 120.

39 K. Kiernan, 'Men and Women at Work and at Home', in R Jowell *et al*, (eds), *British Social Attitudes*, 9th Report, 1992/93, Dartmouth, 1992.

40 Carey Oppenheim, *Poverty: The Facts*, p. 33.

41 Ibid.

3. ROMANCE

Those who try to break from the family norm, as gays do, suffer prejudice and discrimination as a result. Indeed, many gay relationships end up reproducing traditional sex roles.[1]

—Lindsey German

What is love? We all want it, but why? The word conjures up a sense of loyalty, affection, respect, caring. To be loved implies some sort of security. To love is to be capable of high and noble sentiment. Love can also mean control, jealousy, protectiveness and obsession. It can mean danger. It is often associated with pain and fear. Love can involve desire, longing, passion, need. Love can be greed, use and abuse. To love, according to the *Shorter Oxford English Dictionary*, means: 'to hold dear, to be unwilling to part with (life, honour etc.), to be devoted or addicted to, to take pleasure in the existence of, to tend to thrive in, to be accustomed, to caress or embrace affectionately'. We think of love as a human emotion which is also a spiritual energy, constant and unchanging across history and culture. We are fascinated by its complexity and we revel in its simplicity. It's a huge joke and it's deadly serious. If you love, you also hate.

Love is nearly always thought of as a private emotion, an exchange between individuals or a surge of feeling contained within a person's mind or body. At the same time society recognises the public significance of love through representation and regulation. The image of the white, heterosexual family is a symbol of national social order. Young people are understood to be naturally consumed with the need to make sexual contact with the opposite sex. Education and youth welfare are organised around this assumption. There are laws which decide who is allowed to have sex with whom (including when and where), public opinions expressed about the boundaries of acceptable behaviour and endless cultural debates about the languages we use to talk about sex and love. Sex scandals involving highly placed politicians are shot through with confusion over whether the private behaviour of public figures is a public issue. A public lavatory cubicle is a private place when a person is urinating in it but a public place when they masturbate or have sex there. Public housing becomes private when two people have sex in a bedroom, but public when three people are involved. The structures of social control are blatantly inconsistent, illogical and hypocritical. One might think that such a confused set of social mores would inevitably collapse into unregulated anarchy. Instead, laws close in more tightly and proscriptive prejudices become more entrenched.

To understand this contradiction we need to understand how concepts of 'public' and 'private' do not refer, as they purport, to clearly separate aspects of our lives. They are not descriptions of social order, but methods of enforcing social control. Labelling something 'public' (whether it's an industry, a chunk of wealth or a person's speech) places it in common ownership and makes it, to varying extents, accountable. Calling something 'private' shields it from scrutiny, protects it from access. To privatise is to close the doors on a space which creates its own regulations and boundaries of practice. But that which is private and that which is public intersect. The economy of the nation is public. The money in your pocket is private. Yet the money in your pocket came to be there because of the way the nation's economy is managed. Thus: money, people, behaviour, information can move from public to private according to what is expedient at any given time.

Justifications for these shifting contradictions and transformations are given through ideology. The political codes and principles handed down to us through education, religion, the media and law enforcement make these contradictions seem reasonable and consistent—turning them into 'common sense'.

But these explanations are a fantasy designed to make us doubt the evidence of our own eyes and overlook the lessons of our own experience. Thus all the confused feelings surrounding our personal relationships, our duties to our relatives, our sense of nationality, our responsibilities to our children and our sexual energies are subsumed by and reduced into a meaningless concept called 'love'. Love is paraded, peddled and processed through the marketplace by means of romance. The ideology of romance overrides contradictions and simplifies overwhelming complexities. Romance is there to blur the past, and fudge over the real contradictions of the present, in order to control the future. Romance is captivating because it appears to be simultaneously secure and dangerous, cosy and rebellious, conservative and adventurous.

The bourgeois gay movement has drawn on romance in its determination to carve out a space for itself within the system. Romantic gay sensibility has attempted to create an alternative gay family, forging proto-family relationships through the establishment of a haven 'community' wherein individuals will find recognition and roles to play. This development is mirrored by the romantic gay demand for space and voice within the outside world. Not only is this apparent in the domain of public politics, where representation, speech and visibility are paramount in order to prove existence, but also in the arena of commerce. The innovation of a 'new way' of doing business— through gay commerce, within the pink economy—fits nicely into a rosy picture of radical change without the inconvenience and discomfort of complete revolution.

This chapter is about exposing the ideology of romance and its links to gay oppression. It will show how romantic ideas lie at the heart of confused contemporary notions about truth, the individual, the nation and commercial enterprise. It will show how these notions feed into and are taken up by the ideologies of the conservative moralists and the far right. It will then point to the elements of romance which dominate 'alternative' gay and lesbian culture, again centering discussion on the principle sites of romantic thought: truth, the individual, the nation and commercial enterprise. Such a model of personal liberation will be shown to resound in the defences built around the gay community—constantly defining and reasserting who belongs to 'them' and who belongs to 'us'. This section will continue the argument that gay oppression cannot be fought on a separate battleground from the central war against class oppression.

Seduction and Suffocation

All personal relationships are influenced by changing social codes and values. Conventions (marriage, housework, bread-winning, child care) surrounding sex between women and men clearly operate as tools to divide and control. Heterosexuality, as defined by these conventions, is a complex institution which not only scapegoats and alienates people who have same-sex relationships, but continually polices love and sex between people of different genders. Romance, far from being a fluffy, harmless heart-shaped cushion on which lovers dally is actually an ideological weapon which serves to regulate, sweeten and pacify. Romance cloaks the connection between 'private' areas of our lives and the ruthless arena of the marketplace. Romanticisation of love and sex is linked by a network of propaganda, myth and regulation to the lies which surround us about money, normality and social order.

Romance is a mythological framework on which we pin our hopes and desires and feelings because we have no other way to explain a sense of emptiness and frustration. The romanticisation of human emotion is a story of control and seduction. It bestows a spiritual blessing on the institutions of heterosexuality and the family, encasing them within a mysterious fickle Nature where the relations between power and profit, pain and pleasure are preordained *and* subject to pure chance. Mirroring this process, lesbian and gay culture pretends that homosexual love too is a pinnacle of self-hood, the means by which individuals can escape a harsh, outer reality. The commercial gay scene is regarded as the place where this romance can be achieved.

It is little wonder—given the sickening injustices, horrendous brutalities and continual drudgeries of everyday life—that people seek respite in families, private homes and closed communities. Into these apparent havens are poured all our hopes of time, space and freedom: time to be with the people we love, space where we can feel safe and relaxed, freedom to develop and express ourselves. Lesbian and gay relationships are not immune to the pervasive influences of this environment. Whilst homosexual behaviour is marginalised and punished, and gay culture is developed in protest and resistance against this persecution, the political and commercial gay scene we know today displays many of the hallmarks of romanticisation.

For lesbian and gay people, commercial venues like clubs and cafes are an alternative version of the haven fantasy. Criminalised for showing affection on the streets and in public spaces, lesbians and gays are forced to gather around the focal point of a gay social scene. Inside these venues there is an illusion of safety, of being one of a kind, of being part of a community, instead of an isolated and vulnerable individual on the street. Although these venues are a necessity whilst gay oppression persists, they do not really provide a haven from the injustices of capitalism. Their main function is to offer a temporary screen from the homophobia rampant elsewhere in our lives. They *appear* as concrete extensions of our hope of a society which is not threatening or stressful. However, they do not operate outside the structures which form the foundations of gay oppression.

The system as a whole feeds on our hopes of an end to stress and repression by reinventing fantasies of their fulfilment through a process of expenditure and accumulation (we spend, the rich accumulate). Purchasing power, we are told, will bring us freedom through the liberty to buy the things which will release our inner selves. For instance, cars will make us independent, fast, stylish and sexy whilst sanitary towels and tampons will open the door to a dazzling social life. Mortgages will give us spacious, sunlit rooms where our creativity will burst forth and flourish. Microwave meals and kitchen gadgets will free us from unnecessary housework so that we can sprawl, our loved ones surrounding us, in front of the TV, or wander gracefully across paradisal green fields at dusk. Gay markets, aiming for the single male with no kids, offer an equally hollow alternative. Haircuts, clothes, shoes, designer beers, opera compilations, custom-made cappuccinos, exclusive interior decor—all are marketed to a fantasy of 'gay taste' which is in reality simply a middle-class lifestyle. However good they make you feel (if you can afford them) these accoutrements and accessories do nothing to challenge the material basis of homophobia and discrimination.

While rows erupt, tears flow, roofs leak, nightclubs disappoint and cars continually break down, the fantasies play on and somehow we feel it's our fault that our lives just don't quite match up. Gay or straight, bisexual or celibate, what we all have in common is the desire to escape from society as it is with its rotten unfairnesses and perplexing contradictions. Reality, our own experience, is a blot on the idealised landscape. A baby's cries interrupt our dreams, the clock on the wall screams the start of the next shift, a gas bill drops uninvited onto the doormat, our social plans are thrown into disarray by ill-health or fatigue. But still we return to our fantasies because they are our only hope, our sole reward for sufferings and toil. Via their romance, we pretend to escape into the realms of privacy and pleasure.

Hopes and dreams also surround our attitudes towards love and sex so that these aspects of our lives are drawn into the material marketplace with its fantasy world of climaxes and fulfilment. The image we are sold is a travesty of a representation of human passion and affection. Even sex itself is an absurd event—usually a pseudo-cataclysmic act of penetration and transformation. A man and a woman fuck—penis in vagina (no hands)—to achieve so-called full intercourse. They 'went all the way', resolved all confusions, overcame obstacles, created heterosexualised order out of chaos. But where is the erotic trepidation of desire, the attraction of sameness as well as opposites, the excitement of sex in all its forms and expressions? These are rarely glimpsed, if ever, in mainstream culture. Restricted narratives replaying sterile versions of heterosexuality carry on endlessly around us. They filter through television, magazines and films. They are the reference points of social and legal institutions which document and regulate sexuality by the de-recognition of any type of behaviour which is not an extremely narrow form of 'normalised' heterosexuality.

Love, we are told, comes from the heart and cannot be rationalised. It is irresistible. We catch someone's eye across a crowded room, clasp hands in public places and gaze into one another's eyes across the dinner table. Love conquers all, it survives all hardships, it is on a higher plane than the material world. It will eradicate all loneliness and fill our lives with sexual and emotional fulfilment as we grow monogamously together, our passion maturing and our intimacy deepening. It has a *moral* value in that we will be made good and kind and unselfish, willing to carry out any deed or task to provide or care for the one we love. It will survive loss, separation, harsh words and inadequacy. If our love is true, it will endure.

Romance also surrounds our role as workers in a class system. It offers a confusion of ideas about inevitability and unstoppable forces, as Paul Foot illustrates:

The recession, it was said, started somewhere else. It was like the weather—like a depression which had mysteriously started somewhere over Greenland, and had swept from there to Britain and the rest of the world ... Politicians who pretend they are in charge of every other aspect of human society insist that as far as the most important issue is concerned, the economic well- being of the citizens they aspire to represent, they are not in charge at all. They resort to biblical metaphors, to the parable of the seven lean years and the seven fat years, and blame poor old God for all the disasters which encompass us.[2]

If lovers can be 'made for one another' then it seems feasible that workers were born to sell their labour for a meagre wage. From this religious logic comes the belief that, by chance, we are born to create wealth for a ruling class, which, equally by chance, is burdened with the responsibility to rule, control and get richer. Who benefits from such religious beliefs is self-evident. The fact that individuals on their own cannot change society is clouded by notions of class mobility where, supposedly taking charge of her/his destiny, a person can 'better' themselves in society by means of their own efforts. The apparent contradiction between being able to help yourself and being swept along by the forces of nature are resolved by the overriding purpose of capitalist ideology (whether that reaches us through government policy or commercial advertising): to prevent workers from identifying and fighting back against the real causes of their oppression and hardships.

Enterprise and the Nation

The moral right-wing, with its sanctimonious ranting against homosexuality and single parents, sees the romantic struggle against 'immorality' and 'abnormality' as heroic and patriotic.

How long can normal families go on taking the strain for other people's 'alternative lifestyles'? Conservative Family Campaign is not a single-issue group, because there are so many issues which impinge on the family, from divorce and taxation to the promotion of the occult in children's comics and the banning of Christian material from the airwaves. The odds are stacked against the family. The forces we confront are daunting. However, like Gideon's army, we put our trust in the Lord and look to his strong right arm for victory. Please help us to help the family. We remember the words of the author of Proverbs 14:34: RIGHTEOUSNESS EXALTETH THE NATION.[3]

This ultra-conservative position, which is echoed in 'moral majority' fundamentalist propaganda in the US, manages to harness the nation-state itself to a whole set of moral values about relationships, sexual behaviour and childhood experience. It reveals the close connections between economics and ruling class interests in the sexual lives of ordinary people. These moral values themselves are upheld as simultaneously timeless *and* civilised, natural *and* indoctrinated. By linking sexuality to patriotism, the groups which own and control wealth can create a lynch-pin for individuals to attach themselves to a system which oppresses them. Thus, however insignificant they are conditioned to see themselves, morality offers a way of contributing to national order through private and personal regulation. By living right, by living clean, we can do our bit for the nation. On behalf of the ruling class, morality raises morale and defuses discontent.

UK proponents of national chauvinism paint an extraordinary picture of quintessential English life which, to the vast majority of ordinary British people, is totally meaningless. British Tory John Redwood, who in 1993 led a right-wing ministerial campaign to withhold state benefits from single parents (whom he described as having 'done life the wrong way') later shared his musings on ideal country village life. His 'vision' is a continuation of the dangerously deluded chauvinistic fantasies propounded by romantic moralists of all nationalities: 'the maypole music of rural English communities. The sound of leather on willow or the clip-clop of horses' hooves on the metal bridle ways of the village centre.'[4]

British conservative pro-censorship campaigner Mary Whitehouse (who has carried her message to other countries, including the US and Australia) demonstrates a parallel obsession with the decline of the nation:

Here in Britain, the 1939-45 war had left us weary. During the 1950s, we watched our Empire slipping away and, with it, our identity on the world stage... Throughout the 1960s Britain was punch drunk. On the one hand, a continual stream of advocacy in favour of premarital sex, abortion on demand, homosexuality. On the other, abuse of the monarchy, moral values, law and order and religion.[5]

Conservative, moralistic viewpoints which point to homosexuality as a symptom of social degeneracy and to the redemptive qualities of patriotism and religion as a key to community rehabilitation, are often obsessed with a fantasy of bygone days. They see the present as the result of a recent history of decline, of the blurring and confusion of bedrock values. They locate these 'good' values within a mythical past where everybody knew their place, where the nation was confident and powerful, where licentious civilisation had not yet eroded a natural order based on morality, self-restraint, racial purity, natural selection and spiritual obedience. The continual social and political upheavals of human history (famines, wars, revolutions, uprisings and repression) are conveniently forgotten, blotted out, in the creation of a nostalgic fantasy on which to construct a programme of blame, punishment and alienation. The aim: to build a model of social control which appears attractive, secure and familiar. To seduce, entrap, bring into line. Whitehouse's arguments illustrate a romantic association of 'freedom' with market forces, nationhood, property and egotistical expression.

Lesbian and gay people are often portrayed as unpatriotic, not only because their sexual behaviour is deemed by conservatives (of all political persuasions) to be letting the side down, bringing down the country's moral standards, but also because they are assumed to be unable and unwilling to reproduce the next generation of soldiers and workers. The patriotic argument against homosexuality is a smokescreen for the real fears of the ruling class and its lackeys in the media and social institutions. It is used to try and prevent people from recognising that nationality represents no real material common bond. It is used to stop us looking for common interests which have nothing to do with nationality and everything to do with fighting back as a class.

Patriotism is one of the ultimate forms of romanticism, the highest pinnacle of loyalty and courage being to die for one's country. The reality is that soldiers and civilians die in wars to further the interests of competing sections of the ruling class as they vie for control over land, labour and resources. In this context it is clear that romance and morality go hand in hand to preserve and bolster the systems of private property and class exploitation which are at the root of our everyday experiences. Wilfred Owen, the poet who fought and died in the trenches during the First World War, is claimed today as a gay historical figure because of his loving relationships with other men. He wrote of the hypocrisy of wartime propaganda, ripping apart a patriotic slogan which claimed that it is 'sweet and noble to die for one's country':

If in some smothering dream you too could pace
Behind the wagon that we flung him in,
And watch his white eyes writhing in his face,
His hanging face, like a devil's sick of sin;
If you could hear, at every jolt, the blood
Come gargling from the froth-corrupted lungs,
Obscene as cancer, bitter as the cud
Of vile, incurable sore on innocent tongues, -
My friend, you would not tell with such high zest
To children ardent for some desperate glory,
The old Lie: Dulce et Decorum est
Pro Patria Mori.[6]

Also during the First World War, in 1915, an article was published in *Atlantic Monthly*, entitled 'The African Roots of War'. Written by black American socialist W.E.B. Du Bois, it explained how Germany, Britain and their respective allies were, contrary to the propaganda, actually fighting over the natural resources of the African continent: gold, diamonds, oil, cocoa, rubber and ivory. He compared social movements for democracy in America and Western Europe with the increasing subjugation of the people and lands of Africa and pointed to the danger of the white industrial working classes of imperialist nations believing that they could benefit from the plundering of black people's lives and resources. Du Bois could see that war provided a way for capitalism to link its objectives to the aspirations of its exploited classes so as to distract workers' attention from the crimes and atrocities of imperialism. Racist ideas were of course a necessary weapon in the operation to carve up Africa. And because American working-class people were needed to enter the carnage of the war, patriotic ideas had to be whipped up without delay.

Du Bois saw the ingenuity of capitalism in uniting exploiter and exploited—creating a safety valve for explosive class conflict. 'It is no longer simply the merchant prince, or the aristocratic monopoly, or even the employing class, that is exploiting the world: it is the nation, a new democratic nation composed of united capital and labour.' The United States fitted that idea of Du Bois. American capitalism needed international rivalry—and periodic war—to create an artificial community of interest between rich and poor, supplanting the genuine community of interest among the poor that showed itself in periodic movements. How conscious of this were individual entrepreneurs and statesmen? That is hard to know. But their actions, even if half-conscious, instinctive drives to survive, matched such a scheme. And in 1917 this demanded a national consensus for war.[7]

As we look at the meaning and function of patriotic rhetoric, it becomes clearer how and why lesbian and gay oppression is an essential component in the network of lies, distortions and fear-mongering which underpins national geographical, social and economic boundaries. Many of the weaknesses of the gay movement derive from a political unwillingness to separate from the powerful propaganda of romance. Gay romanticism is about specialness, an identity based on being victimised, being oppressed and marginalised, ennobled through suffering. Sexual orientation has come to mean more than just an erotic preference, a desire for same-gender sex. To be gay or lesbian in the 1990s implies the ownership of a particular sensibility, a sense of otherness, of being 'different'. Gay sensibility is about having felt the pangs of forbidden love and the fear of isolation and then moved into a new consciousness of pride, of membership of a community of one's 'own kind'. The increasing commercialisation of gay life has led to the promotion of the idea of 'them and us', a gay community held together by a shared sexuality, regardless of differing class interests and varying social relationships. This shared sexuality has developed into a cultural code for shared consumer taste, a predilection for certain forms of art, decor, clothing, food and drink. This concept of separateness has a two-fold political repercussion. First, it means that there is a clear-cut gay market demarcation, ever-ready for penetration by a business class (made up of gay or straight individuals) wishing to capture the pink money. Second, it has led to a straitening and reduction of the vision of gay liberation into a lukewarm set of meagre single-issue demands which reflect the very few common interests of a fictional cross-class 'community'.

Lesbians and gays come together because they are oppressed, persecuted, made invisible by the pro-family propaganda of mainstream culture and society. The persistent criminalisation of gay sexuality, where gay sex and public displays of affection are regulated by draconian laws, means that gay clubs and pubs are a necessity. They are virtually the only places where lesbians and gays can relax enough to hold hands, cuddle or kiss. But the idea that all lesbians and gays are bound together by a common sexual orientation which unites across differences of class, is a dangerous myth. It lies at the root of the perennial splits and divisions within the gay movement. It is the explanation for underlying discontent with those who set themselves up as community leaders or spokespeople. It is the reason why no one can ever agree on a common agenda for gay equality. It is the driving force behind the idea that being gay is defined by the way you spend your money.

Individuals who are out within the gay 'community' are regarded as having revealed the essential truth about themselves. Liberation is therefore understood as a process experienced by an individual, through their personal feeling of release after denouement. Most importantly, it is seen as an end in itself, releasing the individual into a transformed world or bestowing upon the individual a new-found identity. Obviously, in a society where normalised heterosexuality and the family are pushed as the only valid expression of sexuality, individual 'coming out' is more or less the only way to reject dominant values and   live as an out gay person. However, the vast majority of working class people who experience lesbian or gay feelings cannot go through this individualised process because they do not have the necessary levels of independence, support and confidence to do so. Their class oppression is overwhelmingly the most powerful censoring and silencing influence in their lives. The 'truth' of working-class sexual oppression is not about to be resolved by revelations of individuals' sexual preferences. Coming out needs to be a collective experience, not just for the people who wish to reveal themselves as lesbian, gay or bisexual but also for the whole of society in liberating itself from the *causes* of sexual oppression.

Totalitarianism: One Step Further

In fascist and other totalitarian societies moral restraint is even more severe than in so-called democratic countries. Rudolf Klare, legal adviser to Hitler during the 1930s when the National Socialist (Nazi) Party came to power, drew up a list of legal definitions of homosexual behaviour by which suspects could be identified. (The Nazis had recriminalised male homosexuality upon assuming power.) The list of homosexual acts included 'simple contemplation of desired object'.[8] In Nazi Germany one famous case saw a man convicted for watching two people having sex in a park. Another saw a woman arrested for wearing man's clothing.

Jung Chang wrote in her autobiography of the censure she experienced in relation to her sexuality as a young Chinese student under the dictatorship of Chairman Mao:

> *Our political meetings now included an examination of how we were observing 'the disciplines in foreign contact'. It was stated that I had violated these because my eyes looked 'too interested,' I 'smiled too often,' and when I did so I opened my mouth 'too wide'. I was also criticised for using hand gestures: we women students were supposed to keep our hands under the table and sit motionless.*

Censure of women who expressed their sexuality was tied in with the morality of Chinese nationalism:

> *Much of Chinese society still expected its women to hold themselves in a sedate manner, lower their eyelids in response to men's stares, and restrict their smile to a faint curve of the lips which did not expose their teeth. They were not meant to use hand gestures at all. If they contravened any of these canons of behaviour they would be considered 'flirtatious'.*[9]

Fascism feeds on the most extreme forms of romantic natinal chauvinism, where people desperate for some explanation of their poverty and hardship turn to a fantasy of order and simplicity as a solution to their problems. Fascists look for weak or easy targets to blame ('foreigners', lesbians and gays, disabled people) rather than the real causes of deprivation and discrimination. They therefore displace the material causes of suffering and hardship onto vulnerable groups in society, fostering division and weakening the working class. They see the core of national identity within an idealised picture of idyllic rural life rather than in the everyday experiences of workers who have materially created the nation and its wealth.

Fascism, an extreme form of capitalism, is the outcome of economic crisis and appears to offer a way out of the never-ending cycle of boom, recession, slump and recovery. Like the fanatical ravings of Redwood and Whitehouse, romantic ideas in pulp fiction and TV mini-series find a chilling echo in ultra-right literature on sex and the family. Conservative propaganda about crime, punishment and military discipline finds its logical extension in Nazi plans for authoritarian states. In 1928 Rudolf Klare received a canvassing letter from a homosexual law reform activist asking for the Nazi party's views on the decriminalisation of male homosexual acts. At this time the Nazis were working to gain credibility as a respectable political party. Klare wrote back:

> *It is not necessary that you and I live, but it is necessary that the German people live. And it can only live if it can fight, for life means fighting. And it can only fight if it maintains its masculinity. And it can only maintain its masculinity if it exercises discipline, especially in matters of love. Free love and deviance are undisciplined. Therefore we reject you, as we reject anything which hurts our people. Anyone who even thinks of homosexual love is our enemy...Might makes right.*[10]

The fascist British National Party (BNP) states clearly its policy on gender-conditioning:

Much of the rampant feminism of our times is due to the general decline among the White Race of real manhood. The real man brings out the best in woman, where manhood is in short supply, woman begins to try and ape man... School teachers should have it drummed into them at all teacher training colleges that they must use all the influence within their power to combat any sign of effeminate tendencies within boys, just as they must encourage to the utmost the development of femininity in girls.[11]

As outlined in a 1993 election manifesto, BNP policy includes dismantling the welfare state, bringing back compulsory national service, the abolition of the trade unions and the deportation of all immigrants, black people and Jews. The National Health Service is described as a 'Multinational Disease Industry' and the BNP aims to ration health care, only treating sick and injured people according to 'individual merit' so as to 'breed healthy British natives'. Party leader John Tyndall's avowed 'doctrine' is Hitler's *Mein Kampf* which set out the dictator's plans for mass murder of Jews, homosexuals, gypsies, disabled people and others. These plans became a nightmare reality in the genocide of the Holocaust. Present-day Nazis claim the Holocaust never really happened. Clearly, the fear and hatred of homosexuality is part of a whole picture of repression, terror, racism and blanket censorship.

Alienation

In so-called democratic countries most people participate in important decision-making by putting a cross on a piece of paper every five years. Elected representatives thereby decide on the conditions of our lives from health and safety at work to hospital care, leisure facilities and sexual matters like access to family planning or abortion and lesbian and gay equality. Accountability does not really function on any meaningful level at all.

This mass alienation means that peoples' experiences are constantly turned into a set of banal and regimented personal responses. For instance, mass sackings become a collection of individual decisions to take redundancy rather than a collective determination to fight for jobs. Attitudes to homosexuality are seen as the private views of individuals rather than a political and cultural confusion about the nature of sexuality. These responses then become part of a complex set of behavioural codes with artificial social boundaries. For instance, some men do not like the idea of their women partners earning more than they do. This is explained in terms of innate masculine pride which has to be pandered to in order to maintain social order. In fact it is the ideological basis for keeping women's wages unequal and thereby keeping down wage levels for women *and* men, as US socialist Sharon Smith explains:

Whenever capitalists can threaten to replace one group of workers with another, poorly paid, group of workers, neither group benefits... In the US women's wages tend to hover between 60 and 70 percent of men's. But this has the net effect of depressing men's wages, for they are made constantly aware that, if their own wage demands aim too high, they can be replaced with cheaper women workers.[12]

The separation of sex from material reality continues with an idea that 'real' relationships are not concerned with money, that there is no economic exchange within true love. Romance insinuates that a true lover will not have sex with someone because s/he wants financial reward or because s/he wishes to financially protect (and therefore control) the other person. Sex which takes place with direct exchange of money is labelled 'prostitution' as though it is qualitatively and quantitively different from all other sexual experiences. But prostitution is only one example of the way sexuality is distorted under capitalism. Sex between people of the same sex is used to define and therefore create a group of people who can absorb blame for perceived social disorder.

The Romantic Origins of Lesbian and Gay Identity

Is there such a thing as a gay community? 'Yes. Our starting point is a shared sexuality and a shared oppression.'[13]

At the very heart of all thought and activity in the modern lesbian and gay movement is the concept of *identity*. This idea of shared identity across classes is no more real than the nationalistic concept of shared national interest across classes. Nevertheless, the entire edifice of gay political culture is based upon unity through sexuality and a common experience of oppression. Gay identity specifically consists in being sidelined, ignored, criminalised, made invisible in mainstream society. It is seen as being shared by a specific group of people who have a mutual and *exclusive* interest in getting rid of gay oppression. The developing gay commercial scene offers apparent havens (venues, events, publications) for gay self- expression. What is contained in these havens amounts to the components of gay identity, *sold as the essence of what it is to be lesbian or gay in modern society*. In that these clubs, magazines, events are targeted at a gay market, they provide the focus for lesbians and gay men to lead apparently separate lives from heterosexual people. We come to believe that gay and straight people are essentially different from one another, with separate social and sexual experiences and aspirations. This 'specialness' contains the ideas that gay people are particularly sensitive (as a result of suffering persecution) and sexually explorative (as a result of not being formally sexually 'educated') . This section aims to show where these ideas have come from and the elements of romanticisation contained in the concepts of lesbian and gay identity.

Capitalist history shrink-wraps events and social relationships, packaging them into superficial and repetitive stories about ruling class personages (kings and queens, prime ministers, declarations of war and key speeches). This romanticisation is extended, rather than countered, by the history of gay sensibility. To look for evidence of a common thread of experience, based on sexual preference, through the past, present and future, is akin to chauvinistic rhetoric about 'being British' (stiff upper lip, sense of fair play, sympathy for the underdog) or 'being an American' (land of the free, true grit, pioneering spirit). Both of these patriotic delusions, in the true tradition of romance, blur and distort a gruesome track record of imperialism, murder, repression, slavery and vicious class oppression. This is because they are ideology: part of the awesome weaponry of social control.

The idea that sexuality can be explained in terms of orientation comes from social and scientific developments in the latter half of the nineteenth century. These originate in the work of two German reformists: Karl Heinrich Ulrichs and Magnus Hirschfeld. Their writings and research led them to call for the repeal of Paragraph 175, the Prussian law which criminalised male homosexuality. Through them, homosexuality ceased to be regarded as a type of unnatural behaviour and came to be seen as the characteristic of a group or sub-species within society.

Ulrichs began in 1864 to publish a series of pamphlets about 'uranian' love—or love between men, showing the extent of discrimination against uranians and arguing forcefully for an end to oppression and prejudice. As his ideas developed he asserted that uranians were men and women belonging to a 'third sex', biologically different from the majority of society. They could be detected through their behaviour and their tastes in activities, uranian girls preferring boys' games, uranian boys preferring traditionally feminine activities like knitting. He argued that uranians had existed throughout history and in all societies, born that way and ultimately unchanging. Same-gender sexual acts were not, as was the dominant view of the time, activities any person might choose to participate in if they were sufficiently depraved, but the particular characteristics of an oppressed minority. Since they were born that way they should not be said to have committed a crime by acting on their nature. Ulrichs's writings were banned on the grounds that they undermined marriage and the family.

Ulrichs's ideas, though, were not the brainchild of a maverick thinker out of touch with the norms of his own society. Times were changing and his writings were a reflection of changing concerns within emergent industrial capitalism. Germany was establishing itself as a highly industrialised nation. The development of the modern family and the social and moral codes surrounding sex and reproduction, together with the appalling living and working conditions of most of the labour force, meant that people were beginning to organise around issues of common interest. Workers' organisations, political parties, and a feminist movement began to coordinate a culture of resistance. There was also a flowering of all kinds of 'New Age' interests such as vegetarianism, natural healing, mysticism and nudism. It was in this context in 1897 that Dr Magnus Hirschfeld, a pioneer in the new science of sexology, founded his Berlin centre for sexual research: the Scientific Humanitarian Committee (SHC). Established with the aim of bringing about enlightenment on matters of sexuality and the legalisation of gay sex, the SHC continued its research and campaigning work until it was forcibly closed down after the Nazi party came to power.

Hirschfeld developed the theory of the Third Sex through interviewing and observing thousands of people who did not conform to the conventional stereotypes of masculinity, femininity and heterosexuality. He believed strongly that homosexuals (as they had now begun to be called) were physiologically and psychologically different from heterosexuals, to varying degrees. Hence people who had sex with both women and men could be seen as a variant of the Third Sex. Again, the argument that people were born like that and that they could not be changed by legal restraint or punishment was at the centre of Hirschfeld's sexological theory. The theory of the Third Sex was the inspiration behind the first organised homosexual rights movement which gained considerable ground at the beginning of the twentieth century. He was an idealist, in the sense that he believed you could change society by the introduction of enlightened ideas. He mistook a symptom of oppression in society for its cause and believed that a rational, convincing case would surely put an end to backward ideas, superstitions and prejudices. Hirschfeld failed to recognise the connection between gay oppression and the material and economic organisation of the society he lived in. Although Paragraph 175 was repealed in 1929, the Nazis came to power in 1933 and homosexuals were recriminalised, many of them rounded up during raids on private clubs and homes. Thousands perished alongside Jews, Gypsies, socialists and others.

Hirschfeld's romanticism leaves a cultural legacy which has remained influential to this day. His idea that homosexuals were a particular group of people with their own characteristic way of life has stayed at the centre of political campaigning around issues of sexual liberation and lesbian and gay equality. Being lesbian or gay is now more or less a prerequisite for inclusion in the perceived lesbian and gay rights movement. Hirschfeld's reforming agenda has defined a set of criteria for defining lesbian and gay sex and identity and created a space for the development of gay sensibility, a gay way of looking at the world, a gay consciousness. The notion of an essential 'difference' between gay and straight holds an important position in contemporary gay culture, feeding into the romantic construction of a *race apart*, or a *queer breed*. It is this idea which lies behind the politics of queer and the establishment or recognition of a Queer Nation, a parallel dimension which pretends to operate outside the margins of society. In effect, the Queer Nation is a virtual reality kingdom.

Hirschfeld was not the last proponent of scientific 'evidence' for theories of essential difference. In 1991 gay neuroscientist Simon LeVay developed his own theory that a part of the brain called the hypothalamus was smaller in gay men than in heterosexual men.[14] His research was based on dissecting the brains of men 'presumed gay' who had died of AIDS, but his findings were dubiously received mainly because the size of the hypothalamus can change as a result of sexual behaviour and illness. LeVay's claims were followed in 1993 by the publication of US cancer researcher Dean Hamer's research into the possibility of there being a 'gay gene', detectable before birth.[15] Mark Brown, commenting on the sensation surrounding press reports of these research projects, points to the material motivation of apparently neutral media and scientific interest in sexual identity:

It became increasingly clear that the work of the likes of Hamer and LeVay are given a high media profile not as a result of any outstanding scientific merit but due to the relations their claims have to the enduring argument about the 'cause' of homosexuality. That is to say without homophobia such 'findings' would be irrelevant, and, in fact, such research would never have been undertaken.[16]

Both LeVay's and Hamer's findings reached interested ears amongst gay 'community leaders'. Peter Tatchell of the reformist campaigning group Outrage! argued that while there was a danger that suspected 'gay foetuses' might be aborted, science might well offer parents a chance to choose gay offspring. Richard Kirker of the Lesbian and Gay Christian Movement echoed Hirschfeld's view that science had proved that discrimination was unjustified because gay sexuality is 'natural', inborn or God-given. None of the findings addressed the question of lesbians or the challenge of bisexuality to the 'fixed sexuality' tradition—and few gay commentators saw fit to point out these discrepancies.

Leadership, Class and Confusion
in the Queer Nation

The 'agenda' of the politics of identity has, in true romantic tradition, blurred and distorted the material roots of gay oppression. By ignoring class, community leaders and spokespeople effectively sidestep the real reason for discrimination against lesbian and gays, opting instead for a single issue—'gay rights'—which they divorce from the wider context of class struggle. This single issue has become the rhetorical property of prominent gay rights campaigners who use their influence within the established gay media to batter on the door of the establishment, demanding to be let in. Many of them are obsessed with the idea that they are excluded from the system and talk woolly strategies for being included. Larry Kramer, the US writer and activist renowned for his continual explosions of anger at gay oppression and government inactivity over AIDS research, is constantly found raging at the fact that gay men like himself are not getting their fair share of the capitalist cake:

> *One reason that keeps my anger going constantly and for so long is that I'm just so angry that we're not getting our rightful due in any area, be it politics or AIDS research funding or in the* New York Times *or in Hollywood and it's just wrong and it makes me very angry.*[17]

Whilst his anger is evidently justified, Kramer limits his demands to the selective admittance of a few gay men into the political arena, the allocation of sections of multinational pharmaceutical budgets to AIDS research and the inclusion of gay stories and images in current affairs and Hollywood films. He doesn't talk about the fallacy of democracy in the western world, the necessity for health care on the basis of need rather than profit, the control of information by international news agencies and the role of Hollywood in defusing social unrest. His primary interest is in the single issues of gay rights and AIDS funding without any deeper analysis of class society and the potential role and interest of the working class in overthrowing the status quo. Connecting his reformist emotionalism to an image of gay people as suffering victims, Kramer is responsible for a number of cultural outpourings which, by being 'angry', appear to be radical whilst in fact conveying a deeply romanticised message.

Edward King, founder member of the UK health education agency Gay Men Fighting AIDS, adopts a similar approach to intervention in the AIDS crisis:

> *We demand respect for the enormous blow that we have suffered as a community, and the courage we have shown in fighting AIDS. We have been progressively written out of the history of the epidemic, and our pioneering work has been ignored.*[18]

Again we see heroism, martyrdom and victim-status being politicised as part of a naive radicalism. The tragic truth is that AIDS, like all human disease, is primarily a symptom of class society. No government has ever admitted responsibility for what amounts to genocidal neglect and acknowledged the courageous role of sexual outcasts in preventing sexually transmitted diseases. King's colleague Peter Scott went further to say, 'Look what's happened to so-called equal opportunities in the AIDS field. Nobody ever mentions gay men. Isn't it time we started demanding that 60-80% of the jobs should go to gay men?'[19]

Scott is talking here about professional management positions; his vision is of a layer of professional gays, appointed on account of their supposed shared sensibility with a sexual minority population. When glossy New York magazine *OUT* previewed the May 1993 lesbian and gay civil rights March on Washington, it asked 53 prominent celebrities the question:

what do gay men and lesbians want? The answers varied from revolutionary to frivolous. Shot through many responses was a strong sense of 'them' and 'us', a siege or national mentality and a desire to gain institutional power. Cheryl Clarke, poet, said 'Institutionalise lesbian-feminist leadership.' Susie Bright, author and sexpert, called for 'Queer joint chiefs of staff.' Sandra Lowe, Director of the New York Governor's Office of Lesbian and Gay Concerns, asked for the right 'to attain full citizenship and full humanity in this society under the Constitution of the United States'. Peri Jude Radecic of the National Lesbian and Gay Task Force voiced an ambition 'To be part of the governing coalition of this country.' Ann Northrop, of the Gay and Lesbian Emergency Media Project, asked for 'A lesbian president of the United States.'

Some respondents to the questionnaire blatantly privatised the meaning of gay rights, reducing the concept of liberation to an individual financial, emotional or spiritual state. Andrew Sullivan, editor of the *New Republic*, announced 'We want to be recognised as human beings made in the image of God.' Sarah Schulman, author, dreamed of 'Universal mind expansion, retribution and peace.' Barney Frank, US Representative, Massachusetts, was of the opinion that 'Gays want what every other citizen wants, to pursue his or her business without oppression or being harassed', while fashion designer Isaac Mizrahi gushed 'Gays and lesbians want archetypes, fabulous shining examples. They want to be able to go to the movies and figure out how to lead their lives.'

Many contributing to the feature, however, especially those not at the head of lobbying and commercial gay institutions, envisaged material gains that had nothing to do with entrepreneurial, nationalistic romanticism. They called for such things as free health care, universal housing, money for AIDS research, a cure for breast cancer, an end to the 'scientific' search for the cause of homosexuality. One expressed a frustration with the lesbian and gay community's apparent need 'to talk constantly about sexual identity'.

Because reformist demands do not acknowledge or analyse the experiences of the majority of lesbians and gays the statements of prominent gay community leaders frequently provoke discontent. Ordinary lesbians and gays who face day-to-day harassment and pressure at work, housing problems and money worries, become impatient with the self-indulgences of the gay media-cliques. Moreover, the continual suppression of wider issues in the drive to separate gay liberation from the need to change the system as a whole, leads to a difficulty in articulating this impatience. The anger and frustration—the need to get to the bottom of gay oppression, root it out and have done with it for good—circulate in a vacuum, finding no outlet or platform either within reformist gay organisations or in the gay media. Time and again new organisations are set up, proclaiming a broader approach to gay equality, and time and again they either founder or are subsumed into the single-issue bind.

Playwright Oscar Watson, writing in the newsletter of the Edward Carpenter Community (named after the turn-of-the-century Utopian gay socialist) bemoans the racial divisions in the commercialised, predominantly white, gay male scene and waxes hopeful about the future of gay identity:

> *Ultimately, I search for a Gay cultural identity which encompasses the differences in our community. I dream of a sense of nationhood and history which accepts and builds on the contribution of the individual which adds to the collective power of the community. Divide and rule is the oldest trick in the book and we fall for it every time.*[20]

Watson points to racist ideas as being divisive, as they clearly are, and realises that political strength can only be built collectively by people working together. However, his solution for overcoming division does not in any way recognise the fact that both gay oppression and racist ideas are there to divide working-class people and prevent them from organising in their common interests. He asks his white gay male readers to 'go out and make friends with Black Gay men ... and invite their new friends to join them on an interesting alternative holiday'.[21] (He is referring to the regular men-only holidays run by the Edward Carpenter Community at Lauriston Hall in Scotland.) Whilst pleading for unity and political change, Watson simultaneously promotes an individualised, lifestyle solution which shuffles back into separatism and the vain desire for a safe gay haven.

The Future of the Nation

Some lesbians and gays, especially those involved in the media, see the politics of queer as a way of uniting people of all sexualities who want to fight for sexual liberation. Others see the term '**queer**' simply as a shorter and more pugilistic way to say 'lesbian and gay'. In relation to romantic ideas about 'community' and common interests, few queer devotees can agree on a common political agenda for sexual liberation across class. Extraordinary confusions arise around working out who is 'us' and who is 'them'. For instance, filmmaker Inge Blackman sees solutions in language: 'Naming is powerful. Black people and gay people constantly renaming ourselves is a way to shift power from whites and hets respectively.'[22]

Harriet Wistrich, a member of Justice for Women, can't bring herself to align even with gay men: 'I don't use that term (queer). I associate it with gay men and I'm dubious about reclaiming derogatory terms. The "queer agenda", as you call it, isn't my struggle. I put my feminism before my lesbianism.'[23]

'Queer dyke cultural activist' Tessa Boffin seizes on queer as a way of resolving the inadequacies of sexual labelling and as a way of showing anger and defiance in the face of oppression: 'I never identified with the word lesbian because it seemed quite medical ... Queer was one of the ways of identifying with a mixed movement and challenging both separatism and misogyny at the same time.'[24]

Unfortunately queer is largely an alternative form of sexual labelling and its politics far from clear cut about whom it includes and excludes. It does nothing to relocate sexual liberation within the politics of class. This is the quandary of gay romanticism and the contradiction of seeking social change without changing the class system. You are special; you are the same. You are just as good; you are better. You alone can understand your oppression; the rest of the world should understand. You need to form a self-reliant community; you want to be incorporated into the mainstream. You need to separate, you need to integrate. You want to protect; you want to take a risk. You want massive social change but you don't want to tamper with the class system. You want gay liberation but you don't want to look at the causes of gay oppression.

The gay business class (highly developed in the US and on the rise in the UK) uses an open rhetoric of liberation and self-expression through commercial strength and consumer power. It offers a version of gay freedom which is based on the visibility and power of gay markets. Whilst most gay people have no illusions about the aim of any commercial enterprise—gay or straight or just making money—the frustration, anger and sense of political vacuum means that sometimes business appears to be the only way to develop, the only way of attaining bargaining power. The positive, thrusting confidence of the gay marketeers appears to make a refreshing change from the familiar reiteration of suffering, persecution and passive victimhood:

The higher-than-average disposable income of gays and lesbians makes them an attractive target for marketers. Yet advertisers invariably shy away from targeting them because they do not wish to be identified with them. Can the advertising industry continue to ignore a group that forms an estimated 10% of the buying public?[25]

Capitalist ideology continually aims to make workers see their role in society as consumers of products rather than producers of wealth and commodities, necessities and pleasures. The politics of gay power through consumer power are no different. Most lesbians and gays are obviously not high earners and yet the corporate identity being pushed is one of well-heeled individuals with taste and money. The implication is that the gays who will make it into the millennium with impunity will be those who can afford to buy into the trappings of corporate gay sensibility. The substitution of one set of romantic ideas for another, under the guise of radical or liberal intervention, does not constitute social change. We need to bring about an environment where all consensual sex can be freely enjoyed without fear of censure, persecution or intrusion. Romance is a barrier, not a channel.

The Future of the Nation

1   Lindsey German *Sex, Class and Socialism*, Bookmarks, London, 1989, p. 43.
2   Paul Foot *Why You Should Join the Socialists!* Bookmarks, London, 1993, p. 12.
3   Conservative Family Campaign promotional brochure,— *The Family Needs Friends*.
4   John Redwood, *The Global Marketplace: Capitalism and its Future*, Harper Collins, London, 1994.
5   Mary Whitehouse, *Whatever Happened to Sex?* Wayland, Hove, 1977.
6   Wilfred Owen 'Dulce et Decorum Est' in *War Poems and Others* ed. Dominic Hibbert, Chatto & Windus, London, 1973.
7   Howard Zinn, *A People's History of the United States*,

Longman, New York, 1980, pp. 354.

8 Richard Plant, *The Pink Triangle*, Mainstream, London, 1986, p. 113

9 Jung Chang *Wild Swans: Three Daughters of China,* Flamingo, London, 1993, p. 648-9.

10 James Steakley, *The Homosexual Emancipation Movement in Germany,* Ayer, New York, 1986, p. 84.

11 From the 1993 British National Party election manifesto, as reported in *Socialist Worker*, 13 November 1993.

12 Sharon Smith, 'Mistaken Identity', *International Socialism*, 62, spring 1994.

13 Alison Gregory, editor of the *Pink Paper*, interviewed in *Gay Times*, January 1994.

14 Simon LeVay, *The Sexual Brain*, MIT, 1993.

15 Dean Hamer, 'A linkage between DNA Markers on the X Chromosome and Male Sexual Orientation', *Science*, vol. 261, 16 July 1993.

16 Mark Brown, 'Genetic Liberation Front?' *Rouge* 14, 1993.

17 Larry Kramer speaking on 'Out in America' BBC2,7 March 1994.

18 *Capital Gay,* 22 May 1992.

19 Ibid.

20 Oscar Watson, 'Black, Queer, and Fierce', in *Over The Rainbow*, winter 1994.

21 Ibid.

22 Cherry Smyth, *Lesbians Talk Queer Notions*, Scarlet Press, London, 1992, p. 21.

23 Ibid.

24 Ibid.

25 *Marketing Week*, 16 October 1992.

4. IDENTITY AND THE LIFESTYLE MARKET

In February 1993 lesbian and gay rights group Outrage! organised a Queer Valentine's Carnival in London's west end 'to celebrate the growing number of shops, restaurants and bars in and around Soho which cater exclusively for lesbians and gay men'.[1] Since then, Soho Pink Weekends have been regular occasions. The events have grown into full-scale carnivals, with gay businesses using the events to promote themselves. Corporate advertising banners, borne by company employees, are carried along the streets in a grotesque parody of a political demonstration. Extolling the potential power of the pink pound to buy influence and legal reform, organisers pull thousands of gay and lesbian people into the shopping area. These defiant tourists crowd the streets, downing cappuccinos, cream cakes and designer beers, manoeuvring packed shopping bags and cheering on a programme of raunchy entertainment. The message is clear: 'We're here, we're queer, get used to it, get out of our faces, we're not going away, we've got talent and a bloody big community. Most of all we've got money. So there.'

Events like this, whether they take place in the gay villages of Manchester, London, San Francisco or New York, express the logical outcome of identity politics. If sexual orientation is the primary factor uniting people who want gay rights, then lesbians and gays can be seen as a discrete social group and potential market sector. Never mind differences in class, wealth and social position. Rich gay business people who own magazines and nightclubs are put in the same category as gay men who work in the printshops or the bars. Property-owning entrepreneurs are classified in the same social grouping as single lesbian mothers on benefits.

Political organisation by lesbians and gay men as a discrete or separate group in society is based in the 1990s on a sense of collective consumer power. This consumer power is perceived as the basis of citizenship: 'we pay our taxes, we should get our rights'. Meanwhile, the establishment of gay markets is applauded as a means of achieving collective, cross-class gay confidence, of proving the significance of the pink economy, of providing a focus for lesbians and gays to recognise common references. These references have to be consumable and are popularly located in fashion, interior design, publishing, restaurants and bars. Through these reference-points is constructed a loose consensus on what constitutes a gay lifestyle and, consequently, what contributes to gay identity. Gay lifestyle is visible as a specialised form of middle-class lifestyle and therefore second nature to some, completely unattainable and meaningless to many.

This chapter argues against the notion that 'buying gay' or attempting to wield power through bolstering the pink economy is a progressive political activity. It shows how the politics of identity are based on misleading and divisive ideas which weaken the fight against gay oppression. Identity, politicised and commodified, is not a basis for unified action; instead it is an insidious and complex framework of competing positions. It creates a false premise upon which to make hopeless and unfounded alliances across class. These alliances do not ensure that the powers of the few ensure the betterment of the many. On the contrary: the gay bourgeoisie (entrepreneurs, intellectuals and media celebrities), which dominates the movement today, sets a political agenda which suits *its* interests alone. This does nothing to increase the power of working-class lesbians and gays to kick back at the bosses and bigots where it really hurts: in the bosses' pockets. Instead it reduces the exciting prospect of sexual liberation for all to a dreary set of proposed legal reforms and isolated single-issue campaigns. It is obviously important to support any move aimed at alleviating oppression. However, there are many reasons why lifestyle and identity politics can never bring about real freedom for all lesbian, gay and bisexual people.

Identity Tags

The politics of identity are about bypassing the roots of oppression and concentrating on the symptoms. Obviously identities exist; they are products of our place within capitalist society. Identities define our place within the global conditions that oppress us: our nationality, sexuality, the social meaning of our gender, our physical dis/abilities, our experience of family relationships. In capitalist society where people's needs are subordinated to the tyranny of profit, identities provide a focal point for making some sense of who we are, what has happened to us and what we would like to do about that. They are a survival mechanism, accommodated within capitalism as a sweetener for individuals who are denied any other control over their lives. They appear to lend a sense of individuality in a world where most people are treated as factory-, office- or gun-fodder. But forming a political agenda on the basis of identity is to mistake identity as an end in itself.

Identity politics celebrate and sanctify our oppression—rooting our individuality in a system of exploitation and compulsion rather than a context where we are free to fulfil our individual potentials. They divide up what we know to be a multiplicity of identities (gay, black, woman, African) into single, monolithic concepts which compete with one another for ascendancy. They say that if you are not specifically oppressed on the basis of identity then you must surely be oppressing. Identity politics separate oppression from exploitation, thus divorcing cause from effect. They assert that only those who personally experience a type of oppression (homophobia, sexism, racism) can lead or even be involved in the fight against

131

discrimination and prejudice. Identity politics revere lifestyle, saying that it is *how you live* that constitutes political action. They concede the commodification of identity and encourage the fetishisation of identities in the marketplace. They compete for visibility and influence. They concentrate on one symptom of oppression—abusive language, say—and promote a futile system of language reform as a way of changing society. The leaders of identity politics fail to recognise class society as the root cause of stigma and blame and enter 'working class' as an optional item halfway down the shopping list, or hierarchy, of oppressions. In identity politics it is what and how you *consume* that defines you, not what and how you *produce*. This ideological distortion, as was seen in Chapter 1, is the basis on which the family is retained as a social norm. Conservatives always try to see people as individuals defined by the methods in which they consume rather than by their role in the creation of wealth.

The Margin Fetish

Gay journalist Colin Richardson describes the cultural marginalisation of homosexuality as an opportunity for radical consumption. He celebrates the building of a corporate 'gay sensibility' as a way of looking at, being in and consuming mainstream culture:

> *We are used to seeing things differently. We grew up in a heterosexual culture which banishes positive images of homosexuality. So we read between the lines, take our own meanings from books and films we are allowed to access and call it camp. Our first images of sex are heterosexual images, but we can still enjoy them. I remember when I first saw simulated sex on TV, putting myself in the place of the woman, the man on top of me. Lesbian and gay porn frees our imagination from such trickery. When I watch a gay video I can imagine myself as any or all of the participants, or just sit back and enjoy being a voyeur.*[2]

Identity politics, fetishising this position of marginalised consumer, essentially seek to *accommodate* gay people within an unjust class society. They do not offer any solution for revolutionary action or change—suggesting that it is within individual lifestyle and personal decisions that political action is wrought. Cause and effect are thus interchanged, with the result that the politics of identity are shot through with themes of guilt, binary oppositions, endless self- examination. Being gay or lesbian means sharing a common victimhood, collectively suffering the oppressive behaviour of virtually all heterosexuals. According to the politics of identity, all women and men in heterosexual relationships are universally privileged as heterosexuality is promoted as the norm. Homosexual relationships are universally oppressed. The idea that it is heterosexuality itself which mainly causes gay oppression, rather than the system which calls it normal, is a misapprehension shared by protagonists across the gay identity politics spectrum.

Sheila Jeffreys is a radical lesbian feminist writer who believes, against evidence to the contrary, that *all* women, whatever their class or position within society, share a common interest in over-throwing what she calls 'male supremacy'. However exploited men are, however poor or abused, Jeffreys believes that they maintain power over women and will always, given the chance, oppress women and treat them as sex objects. She claims that not even lesbians and gay men have any interests in common and defines *all men* as a ruling class. Fantastically, she calls on all women to give up the power imbalances of heterosexuality and embrace homosexuality, or, as she puts it, the eroticisation of 'equality and mutuality':

> *It is not to be expected that men, gay or straight, will voluntarily choose to relinquish the pleasure and privilege they derive from the eroticised subordination of women. Though some are capable of political integrity and of working against their own interests as a class, we cannot expect this to take place on any mass scale.*

As women and as lesbians our only hope lies in other women.[3]

Jeffreys's scenario is profoundly depressing on many levels. Firstly, she denies that there could be any common interest between women and men in improving relationships between them. Secondly, it appears men are, on the whole, so aggressive and abusive they are incapable of any real change. She also ignores the oppressive and exploitative roles played by ruling class and rich women. Finally, she places all hopes for change on women having some kind of inner transformation of their feelings—a metaphysical counterweight to the thought crime of hetero-sex:

> *The 'thought' of women's sexual subordination delivers powerful reinforcement to men's feelings of dominance and superiority. The liberation of women is unimaginable in this situation ... if we cannot imagine our liberation then we cannot achieve it. Male sexuality must be reconstructed ...*[4]

It is inconceivable that any kind of oppression can be got rid of simply by wishing or 'imagining' it away, or by putting forward some kind of model for 'equal' (good, homosexual) sex as opposed to 'oppressive' (bad, heterosexual) sex. Jeffreys's arguments are dangerously close to those of the moralists on the right of the Conservative Party who, quite unrealistically, demand that everyone should aspire to 'normal' family values. Her point is that everyone should aspire to the 'good' sex to which only lesbians (because of their supposed common, cross-class experience of oppression) can point the way. This proscriptive message is thankfully held in disdain by those who position themselves on the left-wing of identity politics.

Many sections of the black, women's and other identity-based movements reply to prejudice and bigotry by creating defensive myths which aim to counteract stereotypes. These responses, however, often end up by reworking the stereotypes and creating new ones. Parts of the women's movement, for instance, have often responded to sexism and misogyny by resorting to right-wing biological determinism. They declare that women are naturally more caring and less aggressive than men. Quite apart from the fact that this can be disproved by any number of the women who do not fit this romanticised model, such a tactic leads nowhere because it suggests that women and men will always be unequal. Similarly, suggesting that gay people are leading a messianic sexual revolution through simply being gay does nothing to address the real reasons for gay oppression. Neither does it explain how gay people who are not even out, let alone participating in the heady, sex-positive, cruisy, commercial scene benefit from this stereotypical lifestyle.

Autonomy Versus Unity

Peter Tatchell, self-styled 'queer emancipation' leader in the UK, is a forceful proponent of lesbian and gay identity politics as the only way forward to equality:

> *What unites lesbians and gay men are our common sexual experiences and our suffering discrimination as a result of prejudice against our sexuality. A wealthy white gay man is in much the same boat if he loses his job because he is gay as a poor, black lesbian who loses her job for the same reasons.*[5]

Tatchell tries to arrive at a state of unity by denying the divisions of class. He ignores the fact that wealthy gay people do not experience oppression in the same way as the rest of us. They can afford to cushion themselves against the sharp ends of oppression. They travel by taxi and avoid being out late at night in the streets, vulnerable to attack. They do not feel the squeeze of insecurity and poverty because they have property and insurance schemes. They do not endure constant fear of ill-health because they can buy private care. They do not feel the grind of daily toil and long working hours because they pay childminders, cleaners and secretaries. Tatchell implicitly defies working-class lesbians and gay men who have no choice but to fight on the basis of class. Whilst setting the ground for inevitable fragmentation he appears to support a united front and leaves the way open to accuse others of divisiveness. His thinking claims to rescue a strategy for 'advancement' from revolutionary black leader Malcolm X. Tatchell advocates the creation of lesbian and gay institutions and a 'community' power-base from which to push for changes in the law and in society. Like other reformists, he writes as though gay liberation can come about without fundamental political and economic upheavals. He also defines mainstream society as 'heterosexual' rather than bourgeois and implies that we can change society simply by enlightenment or persuading the ruling class to change its mind.

> By developing the lesbian and gay community as a focus of counter-culture and counter-power, we are helping to subvert and undermine the ideas and institutions that sustain heterosexual supremacist. In effect, we are withdrawing our allegiance from the dominant culture and denying it moral legitimacy.[6]

By doing this he stamps 'heterosexual' on the institutions and power-structures whose primary function is to control workers. He implies that heterosexual people as a whole have no interest in the eradication of homophobia and that oppressions can be fought on separate fronts with optional co-ordination on special occasions.

> Self-reliance does not mean that we retreat into our own separatist ghetto, give up the campaign for equal rights, or

reject working with others suffering discrimination. On the contrary. It simply means that we make lesbian and gay self-help and community empowerment our priority. From a position of strength, we will be better able to make effective alliances with others fighting discrimination and to bargain with straight society for meaningful legislative changes.[7]

'Prioritising' lesbian and gay rights has turned the lesbian and gay movement in on itself, over and over again. There are continual retreats back into single issues and woolly separatism. This has led to a complete divorce from the revolutionary ideas of lesbian and gay liberation. It has distracted activists from the root causes of gay oppression. It has thrown all the energies of lesbian and gay anger into the marketplace. Tatchell's proposal to 'bargain' for civil rights is a clear outcome of the disaster of seeking 'self-reliance and autonomy'. Factions and figureheads cannot look to a mass movement to demand equality and justice. They really are, as Tatchell knows, not self-reliant at all but heavily dependent upon the manoeuvrings and negotiations between the rich and powerful.

By separating, even for a moment, the fight against homophobia from the fights against sexism and racism, activists weaken the struggle. Our most important task is to show how oppressions affect everyone because they divide us. Racism, sexism and homophobia all come from the same system. Women and black people want and need a movement which links all our concerns. Statistically speaking, the majority of homosexuals in the world are female, non-white and working class or poor. We have to fight collectively against the common enemy.

The fear that there will be no gay movement left if lesbians and gays don't concentrate on the single issues that affect them does indeed echo Malcolm X's early ideas. Malcolm claimed at the beginning of his political life that all whites are racist. He later changed his mind, though, and asserted that black and white workers had a mutual interest in working together to fight oppression and overcome prejudices. He recognised that the roots of oppression were embedded in the common experience of exploitation, across racial differences. His later writings and speeches, when he was breaking with the separatist Nation of Islam, resonate with his growing conviction that the racism of the white working class is a divisive set of ideas that can be challenged and changed—rather than an inherent characteristic born of self-interest:

> *We are living in an era of revolution, and the revolt of the American Negro is part of the rebellion against the oppression and colonialism which has characterised this era... It is incorrect to classify the revolt of the Negro as simply a racial conflict of black against white, or as purely an American problem. Rather, we are today seeing a global struggle of the oppressed against the oppressor, the exploited against the exploiters.*[8]

It was not an imaginary 'white society' that was the source of racism, but a society controlled by a privileged minority consolidating its power by the systematic exploitation of workers: black and white. In the same way there is really no such thing as an oppressive 'straight society' benefiting from gay oppression. The only people who materially benefit from gay oppression are the bosses, property owners and the business classes. For them, racist, homophobic and sexist ideas which confuse, distract and divide workers are useful, ensuring that there is no united opposition to their systems of exploitation. Control of the media is an essential component of a strategy of oppression whereby divisive ideas are continually paraded through our consciousness. It is in this sense that ideology reinforces economic structures, honing, shifting and manipulating their effectiveness.

Many activists and supporters on the left of the gay movement today not only acknowledge but insist that unity with other oppressed groups is essential if any progress it to be made in bringing about equality for gay people. Leaders within the movement pay lip-service to the principle of unity whilst all the time dragging people back to the futile ideas of autonomy. Peter Tatchell believes that heterosexuals, whilst benefiting from gay oppression, also often suffer as a result of homophobia. However, he does not begin to explain that homophobia short-changes straights because it stops them from uniting with gay workers against a common oppressor. His idea is that homophobia prevents heterosexuals from experiencing the liberating erotic and emotional potentials of homosexuality:

> *No-one should have to suffer guilt, ostracism or discrimination because of who they love. Most heterosexuals seem incapable of understanding what it is like to be told that your feelings are immoral, sinful, abnormal and unnatural... Homophobia also forces many heterosexuals to police their own image and mannerisms, out of a fear of being labelled homosexual... The result is that heterosexual women are pushed into a feminine passivity which limits their independence and freedom... Ultra machismo in heterosexual men is not unrelated to social problems such as rape and domestic violence as well as football hooliganism, racist attacks, vandalism and queerbashing.[9]*

Tatchell rightly points to the complex consequences of homophobia and their fatal implication in other forms of oppression like sexism. Homophobia is a powerful weapon preventing people of all sexualities from realising their potentials, socially as well as sexually. But he fails to make the essential connection between the personal responses of ordinary people trying to form satisfying and rewarding relationships and a society beset with prejudices, fantasies and divisions. Demonisation of sexual relationships on the ground of morality, religion, biology, psychiatry and the law is experienced by many sections of society and not just lesbians and gay men. Multi-racial, inter-generational and inter-denominational relationships are all stigmatised to differing degrees. People with disabilities, prisoners, the mentally ill, women of all sections of society, children and many others are constantly told that their feelings and desires are illegitimate.

Lesbians and gay men occupy a pivotal and explosive position within the whole system of sexual regulation, but their experiences are the tip of the iceberg. Homophobia is part of a huge economic, political, social and ideological system of mass oppression. Even if it could be eradicated without changing this system, many other forms of sexual oppression would remain. Tatchell avoids this by ignoring the fact that lesbians and gay men, even those who are out and active, are often limited and constrained by ideals of femininity and masculinity. Lesbians are no less likely than heterosexual women to take passive roles at home and work and have difficulty in asserting their views and wishes. Gay men are by no means immune to the pressures of machismo which enforce codes of behaviour supposedly signifying mental strength, sexual prowess, physical supremacy. Yes, homophobia does indeed affect everyone, but not on the simplistic level implied by idealist radical reformers.

Peter Tatchell's 'solution' is to create an alternative society, a dimension of citizens who share common lifestyles, aspirations and interests based on their sexual identities:

> ... the quality of life for most lesbians and gay men has dramatically improved over the last two decades. This has been largely the result of our own self-help initiatives. We have created a safe and supportive lesbian and gay community; with switchboards and social centres, bars and discos, employment and legal advice organisations, publishers and book shops, housing and immigration rights groups, counselling and befriending services, newspapers and magazines... Effective use has never been made of the

economic power of the pink pound or the electoral power
of the pink vote... We've therefore got to start changing
ourselves and our community, as well as changing society.[10]

This 'self-helping community' would exist to nurture homosexual identity. It would be founded on and strengthened by the power of its own capitalists and bourgeoisie. Tatchell's vision is underpinned by the mistaken belief that only by separate self-organisation will gay people overthrow their oppression. Like Jeffreys's, his is also a counsel of despair because it is founded on the belief that only lesbian and gay people can wage a fight against gay oppression. This can only lead to fragmentation and weakness.

Separatism, whether seen as a political principle of purity or simply a means to an end, is destructive because it alienates and overlooks the mass of potential allies and supporters who have a material and immediate interest in fighting all the forms of oppression which proceed from exploitation and divisiveness. Divisiveness, fragmentation, separation: all these are weaknesses which prevent any force for liberation from gaining strength in numbers. Sharon Smith, in her powerful analysis of identity politics, 'Mistaken Identity', points to the most imperative example of why unity in action is of the utmost importance and why autonomy and all other forms of separatism are deeply dangerous:

> *For people newly active on the left, this way of organising*
> *may seem like common sense: it should go without saying*
> *that those who are oppressed should fight against their*
> *own oppression... For this same reason it follows that each*
> *oppressed group should have its own distinct and separate*
> *movement. Such movements therefore tend to be organised*
> *on the basis of 'autonomy' or independence—from each*
> *other and from the socialist movement. They tend also to be*
> *organised independent of any class basis.*

But this logic is flawed. It would be disastrous for example if the fight against fascism in Europe today were limited to members of those racial groups who are immediately targeted by fascists. The advance of the fascist movement is not only a threat to 'foreign born' workers but to all workers. To most effectively counter the recent rise of fascism in Europe, all those who oppose the far right, whatever race they happen to be, should be encouraged to join the anti-fascist movement. Any fight against oppression, if it is to succeed, must be based upon building the strongest possible movement.[11] *[my emphasis]*

Smith also refers to Lenin's criticism of Jewish separatist organisation in 1903. His warning represents an important lesson for lesbians and gays in the 1990s. Some Jewish workers called for a separate revolutionary organisation, saying that gentile workers were too anti-semitic to unite. Lenin pointed out that autonomous organisation compartmentalises and fragments. He described the Jewish Bund as having 'stepped onto the inclined plane of nationalism' which must inevitably lead to isolation of different groups and weakness in the overall struggle:

One who has adopted the standpoint of nationalism naturally arrives at the desire to erect a Chinese Wall around his nationality, his national working class movement; he is unembarrassed by the fact that it would mean building separate walls in each city, in each little town and village, unembarrassed even by the fact that by his tactics of division and dismemberment he is reducing to nil the great call for the rallying and unity of the proletarians of all nations, all races and all languages.[12]

We can add to that rallying cry: 'and all sexualities'. This call for unity was not one of a movement which ignored oppression.

The Bolshevik revolutionaries were committed to eradicating the many divisions of nationality and racism which existed at that time in Russia, as they do across the world today. Time and history proved that Lenin had been right to argue against autonomous organisation:

> *In 1917 the same Russian workers who the Bund had argued in 1903 were too backward to champion the rights of Jewish workers elected Trotsky, a Jew, as chairman of the Petrograd soviet, Kamenev, a Jew, as chairman of the Moscow soviet, and Sverdlov, a Jew, as chairman of the Soviet Republic.[13]*

The Pink Economy: 'I Shop Therefore I Am!'

Peter Tatchell's arguments expose the nub of the dilemma facing sexual liberationists today. How is it that we have come so far and yet achieved so little? Yes, we have clubs, pubs, discos, magazines and publishing houses. How come lesbian and gay people are still being sacked, deported, separated from their children, imprisoned and murdered for their homosexuality? There are out gay MPs, business people, writers, artists and broadcasters. How then is it that politicians and the media are still continuing to bankroll heterosexuality as the norm? Many more people are out than ever before in recorded history. How can it be that the vast majority of lesbians and gays cannot even begin to explore their sexuality, let alone come out? The power of the gay media has created a dominant agenda for reform and resistance. How is it that gay activists perennially disagree about how to change things? Many journalists and activists welcome the visible signs of a burgeoning pink economy as an indication that the stigma of homosexuality is lessening. How is it then that all forms of gay oppression remain intact?

The 1990s corporate gay markets reflect a combination of evolved monetarism (the emphasis on *making money* rather than *producing things*) and the inheritance of rainbow coalition identity politics originating from the 1960s and gaining mainstream credibility in the 1980s. The prominent gay lobby seeks to gain power and influence by building strong economic and cultural visibility and its appealing rhetoric is culled straight from identity politics movement-speak. Don't Panic, a US-based merchandise company specialising in products for the gay market, launched itself as 'Exclusive Designer for London Pride 94' with a glossy full-colour catalogue picturing T-shirts, jewellery, mugs, hats, tattoos and duvet covers featuring slogans such as 'I can't even think straight!' and 'It's OK to be gay'. These products, the catalogue claims, promote Equality, Pride and Justice. MetroXtra, a London gay listings colour tabloid, announces its profile as 'Proud and Professional' in a shiny brochure entitled 'HOW TO SUCK UP TO OUR READERS'. Its 'not politically correct' approach 'reflects the move towards a positive, enthusiastic and more open approach to our lives ... we're all about just having a good time'. The Lesbian and Gay Pride Festival 1994 took as its theme '25 Years Out and Proud—Equality and Freedom Now!' and, handled by gay public relations agency Detonator, 'adopted an increasingly commercial fund-raising strategy' and 'signed a lucrative concession deal with Charrington pubs'. Clearly, there is no discrepancy or conflict between the politics of identity and the forces of the market. The idea that market forces might be a part of the 'straight problem' is conveniently ignored in the pursuit of lesbian and gay chic.

Ex-socialist Derek Cohen (reminiscing about writing for the British *Gay Left* journal in the 1970s) says:

> *Ironically, capitalism rather than socialism has most furthered gay liberation ... does it really matter whether 100,000 lesbian and gay men fill a park in South London to shop for T-shirts and sex-toys rather than to parade and*

protest? ... They have Ideal Homes, we have Ideal Homos. They go dancing in Hell, we go to Heaven. And we all cruise the aisles at Sainsbury's... We made demands of the capitalist state and it delivered some of what we wanted. That's what capitalism is good at, delivering the goods. And it seems it can easily deliver gay liberation as Gucci loafers.[14]

Following *that* logic we may as well demand the reinstatement of the poll tax. Gay liberation hasn't been delivered, or we would have seen an end to gay sackings, gay murders and homophobic headlines. Cynics, like Derek Cohen who is indignant that gay liberation and international socialism didn't come about whilst he was on the editorial board of *Gay Left*, have capitulated to the archetypal Tory notion that you can have your liberty, your vote and your influence so long as you can afford to pay for it.

Cohen is a serious victim of the splintering, subdivisions and guilt- trips of identity politics. He is one of many gay activists who write and act as though they have grown out of effete socialism and into the sophisticated marketplace of modern gay identity where barriers only come up when you can't pay for your ticket.

The idea of a significant pink economy is related to the apparently high disposable incomes of unmarried gay men. Double male incomes and no dependants mean high spending power and potentially substantial consumer influence. Market researcher Overlooked Opinions Ltd put the US national annual gay market value at $514 billion and the average household income for gay men at $51,325, compared with the national average of $36,520.[15] A UK survey of 1,788 lesbians and gays in 1994 estimated that on average lesbians and gays were better educated, with 27 per cent having degrees as opposed to 9 per cent in the general population. Lesbians were said to earn £3000 more on average than heterosexual women.[16] These surveys and figures are slanted because of the nature of the gay movement and the effects of a homophobic class society. It is easier for

145

middle-class lesbians and gays to come out. Market researchers do not have access to working-class gays who can't come out or who do not come into contact with the commercial gay scene. These distortions lead inevitably to ideas that lesbian and gay people have special 'sensibilities' and tastes. They work against the unity the movement needs. But they work very well for the business people who are desperately seeking new markets.

Gay public relations executive Stephen Coote points out that 'Manufacturers and the media should take note and understand the commercial potential of Britain's biggest minority.' Lifestyle journalist Frances Williams asks: 'How can lesbians begin to exercise their economic muscle and claim a share of the burgeoning gay market and announce the lesbian pound?' She answers her own question with the now-conventional corporate ideological synthesis: gay liberation will come through consumer power:

Ultimately the market will depend on the increasing visibility, confidence and opportunities that lesbians can achieve for themselves in society at large. But then, as the old inspiring adage goes, 'lesbians are everywhere', so the market must be somewhere, ripe to be tapped.[17]

The politics of identity evidently offer a self-selecting, self-defining market for entrepreneurs wishing to cash in. Ultimately gay identity is a consumer category that does its own market analysis, offering up the results to the business class with an order note attached. The purveyors of 1990s gay identity politics, whether knowingly or unknowingly, are participating in the sale of liberation, accessory by accessory, instalment by instalment. Defining gay sensibility, gay taste, gay lifestyles are all about identifying a market and lining it up for a killing. Becoming a recognised market sector, even if we can afford to be included, will not bring about the sexual liberation we all deserve. Gay oppression will remain intact. Fundamentally, the 'freedoms' offered by the market will be under constant pressure from the capitalist mechanisms of morality and social control. Homosexuality for any but the select and visible few will never be incorporated into corporate Europe or America.

The Posturings Of Post-Marxism: Where Identity Politics Come From

How have we arrived at this stage where we, as a movement, have become so confused and divided over the route to gay liberation? An important factor in the fragmentation of the left into identity politics and groupings around personal characteristics has been the growing influence of the theories of post-modernism and post-Marxism across political, social and cultural fields.

Post-modernism is discussed further in chapter 7, however, both of these inter-linked schools of thought are based on the ideas that the old certainties of class and a society divided by wealth and class interests are over. The idea that the world is largely divided into exploiters and exploited is simplistic and out-dated. Workers experience modern capitalism as individuals, not collectively. They therefore identify not with a large working class, but severally, across alternative groupings, according to their particular individual identifications (national, racial, gender, sexual etc.). Hence the collapse of class struggle into various 'movements' (environmental, gay, women's, disabled etc.)

Furthermore, because ordinary people are so divided and so fragmented by the present system, they will never again organise on the basis of class to improve their conditions or to take control of the means of production. The academics and intellectuals who articulate these new conditions are therefore crucial to any form of resistance because it is their ideas (of identity, of groupings) which make sense of the apparent lack of cohesion. Any revolution, revolt or reform will therefore be led by intellectuals rather than workers.

Post-Marxist academics and intellectuals fill a lot of published space with theoretical writing intended to be read by other academics. Their writings tend to be highly obscure and full of impenetrable jargon. Their treatment of sex, whilst often providing in-depth explorations of the highly complex ideological function of 'sexuality' in capitalist culture, does little to offer any kind of tangible theoretical basis for ordinary people working in the world to tackle sexual oppression at the roots. For instance cultural theorist Dugald Williamson is willing to approach the much neglected subject of bisexuality and its position within contemporary ideas about individuality and gender. This issue could be of interest to all women and men wishing to create a society where everyone has the right and the opportunity to explore their full sexual and creative potentials. Williamson, though, submerges the implications of talking and writing about bisexuality in a morass of abstraction with no connection to the material world:

> *In some current writing, a notion of bisexuality has been invested with a new (or greatly altered) potential, where it can give sexual content to a residually Romantic notion that true subjectivity is to be found in the incompletion of the self, the active tension between thought and feeling, mental consciousness and pulsasional experience, and indeed, between the masculine closure of representation and the feminine possibility of excess. In this case, it becomes possible to speak in the same breath of a plethora of unrealised differences for the subject positioned in the signifying process, and an oscillation between sexual polarities, not bisexuality in any fixated form, but a continual, androgynous deferral of identity, the intermediate space of desire: these two terms coming together to create a sense of the radical possibilities of the subject's realisation in history.*[18]

Academic theories are generated to provoke further theoretical response, not to inspire revolutionary action amongst ordinary people. However, we need to be clear that ideas are not the property of an intelligentsia or academic elite. Issues of sexuality, representation and liberation belong to everyone and they relate to all of us on a theoretical level as well as a practical and everyday basis.

Post-Marxists deny that the root of oppression lies in class society. Oppression itself, instead of being objectively identifiable through systematic discrimination, media misrepresentation and popular prejudice, is seen as something only definable by the people who experience it. They see the state itself as essentially neutral and not inextricably bound up with the interests and methods of capital. They deny, for instance, that the welfare benefits system is a means of class control. The state, according to post-Marxism, is up for grabs to anyone who can get the power to influence it. This concurs with the current Tory philosophy of free market choice. Under this system public services are privatised. This involves 'contracting out' health care, education and advice provision to independent 'providers' who are forced to monitor their clientele as 'units' or sources of income which collectively attract the providers' cash. Thus, for example, services for people with sickle-cell anaemia are put in competition for funds with services for people with HIV. Refugee students needing English language support are put in competition with women students needing creche provision under the 'special needs' budgets. In reality, the free-for-all is a free-for-no-one. The choice on offer is obliterated by a total absence of opportunity. In the same way, by offering all things to all people, post-Marxism ends up by articulating almost nothing which relates to the everyday experiences of ordinary people. In this sense it would be more accurately described as 'anti-Marxism'.

Post-Marxists explain that more fragmented, individualised identities are really the basis upon which people are galvanised into radical or reformist action, because they do not see class divisions as universal and applicable to everyone. Thus movements based on identity politics can compete with one another and with institutions to influence the 'neutral' state. Sharon Smith points out yet another feature of post-Marxism which helps to explain the divisions and squabbles within the gay identity politics movement:

> ... according to Laclau and Mouffe [post-Marxist theorists], oppression is not only completely subjective, but it can also result from any relationship in which one group of people are subject to the authority of another or others. This method borrows heavily from the blind anti-authoritarianism of anarchism—which opposes any form of authority, regardless of who is wielding it and for what purposes. But there is a difference between the authority of those who are democratically elected and of those whose authority is imposed from above. Similarly, the authority of a picket captain in a strike is of an entirely different nature from the authority of a police officer, based upon each one's objective interests—based upon class position. But taken out of the context of class society, all forms of authority are equal and should be equally opposed... The forms of struggle which flow from post-Marxist theory consist of separate, autonomous struggles against specific relations of 'subordination'.[19]

By this logic we can begin to see how identity politics so frequently collapse into bitter schisms and antagonisms. If oppression 'can also result from any relationship' then political differences and various tactics can be ascribed to oppressive behaviour. Women declare they can't fight alongside 'oppressive men'; black people won't unite with 'oppressive whites'; lesbians and gays (if they get as far as working together) won't align with supportive heterosexuals—seeing them instead as 'oppressive straights'.

Signposts to Utopia:
Radical Pluralism and Multicultural Democracy

The proponents of post-Marxist identity politics describe their ideas as a radical step forward, leaving behind the old-fashioned Marxist ideas of class analysis and class struggle. Their rhetoric, however, reveals a deeply reactionary despair that socialism is no longer possible or even desirable. Cloaked in language which suggests optimism based on fresh, diverse and vibrant new energies, their vision suggests an illusory 'pluralistic' society where all kinds of different groups compete on a friendly basis for ascendancy within the neutral state:

> ... the central questions confronting the left aren't located within the left itself but in the broader, deeper currents of social protest and struggle among non-socialist, democratic constituencies—in the activities of trade unionists, gays and lesbians, feminists, environmentalists, people of colour, and the poor... This means advancing a politics of radical, multicultural democracy, not socialism.[20]

So, not only are identity politics entirely compatible with the forces of market capitalism, we now see that they are entirely incompatible with socialism. Unsurprisingly these ideas of pluralism find support in intellectual coteries which once supported the now defunct Soviet Stalinist regime, believing it to be a progressive socialist society, and who now find themselves floundering without a substantial political programme. Rosalind Brunt gives a good account of the appeal of identity politics to those who want to stay on the left but who don't want the embarrassment of admitting that they might have been wrong. She cheerfully paints a horrifying picture of a political programme with no basic philosophy or analysis. Brunt also denies the disastrous splits, accusations and fragmentations resulting from the worst excesses of 1980s identity politics and

151

buys wholesale into the idea that politics should be expressions of people's personal feelings:

A politics of identity... is indeed a very welcoming kind of politics because everyone can have a go at defining it in their own terms ... [It] has been current for some time as a contextual shorthand for movements organising around sexuality, gender and ethnicity and working to translate 'the personal is the political' into everyday practice. Learning the lessons of these movements, we can begin applying notions of identity, and identities, to a political agenda for all. A politics whose starting point is about recognising the degree to which political activity and effort involves a continuous process of making and remaking ourselves—and our selves in relation to others—must rightfully be available for anyone to make up as they go along.[21]

Celebrating fragmentation to this extent goes hand in hand with the consumer lifestyle politics of the gay bourgeoisie. Identity politics are claimed as the potential liberator of everyone, as though everyone in society has the same interests. Quite clearly this is not the case. Class interests are, by their very nature, oppositional and cannot be reconciled through an attractive-sounding programme for breaking down sexual boundaries. The post-Marxist proponents of identity politics see a multiplicity of identities being marketed to consumers through the sounds and images of advertising. They claim that 'old certainties' are 'gone' and that people have become caught up in the plethora of options and identities on offer through consumerism. They cannot be 'made class-conscious'—the argument goes—their imaginations and their aspirations are too fragmented. The left intelligentsia, then, must respond to this psychic splintering with a programme of political ideas that will appeal to these fragmented consciousnesses. There's no point, they say, in reiterating 'the old certainties' because people will just not understand them. They ignore the fact that society is galvanised by a continual struggle between those who produce the wealth and those who own the wealth.

Underpinning this position is the conviction that working people need the intelligentsia to construct palatable theories which will enlighten and liberate them. Ex-Communist Party member and post- Marxist Frank Mort waxes salesmanlike:

'Depoliticisation' registers much more than a pessimism about the political process. It speaks of a growing disengagement of 'life' where people choose to put their energies and invest their hopes, from 'politics'. For more and more people it is outside work, outside the formal political structures, in the world of holidays, home interiors and superstores, that they have a sense of power and freedom to express themselves, to define their sense of self, to mould the good life... So, to put it polemically, should we just sit back and let the marketeers get on with it?... Responding to consumption means recasting our thinking... Most of the new politics have been saying much the same thing, yet rarely have they put consumer culture centre stage... Privatised car culture, with its collective red nose days and stickers for lead-free petrol; shopping as the quintessential expression of consumer choice now carries social anxieties over eco-politics and food pollution. These are the localised points where consuming meshes with social demands and aspirations in new ways.[22]

Substitute 'freedom towel' or 'rainbow jewellery' for the red noses and we're back to the glossy 'liberation through lifestyle' politics of the pink marketeers and their cynical theorists in Gucci loafers. Mort, Brunt and those on the 'democratic left' want to compete with the advertising milieu for the dreams and imaginings of ordinary folk, inserting the politics of social change into the multiple messages of commercial communications, like a free gift in a packet of breakfast cereal. Like Don't Panic!

merchandising, with its Pride Tumblers, Freedom Wristwatches and Removable Gay Tattoos, the theories of identity politics are packaged to fulfil our Utopian dreams of pleasure and contentment.

Imagined Utopia, not revolution, is in fact the object of the pluralistic politics of identity. Socialist gay historian Jeffrey Weeks confronts the limitations of identity politics and criticises gay essentialists who see their sexual identity as an end in itself and the sole defining factor about themselves as people. But he then attempts to put forward a theory of sexual liberation which is similar to the theories of post-Marxists in that it aims to appeal to academics and cultural critics and uses language which suggests that class antagonisms are a thing of the past. He suggests that:

> *Identity may, in the end, be no more than a game, a ploy to enjoy particular types of relationships and pleasures. But without it, it seems, the possibilities of sexual choice are not increased but diminished. The recognition of sexual identities, in all their ambivalence, seems to be the precondition for the realisation of sexual diversity.*[23]

For Weeks, the politics of identity provide a way of making prohibited sexual practices visible. In a society where moralism and homophobia are rampant, they offer a limited opportunity for people to recognise that human sexuality is multidimensional and unpredictable, completely uncontained by the representations and regulations which are produced to control it. But Weeks makes the mistake of asserting that it is possible for people like himself—sexual theorists and academics—to develop an abstract framework for universal sexual liberation, which will filter down, presumably, to ordinary people through the cultural transformations engendered by such inspiring critical illuminations. He outlines his theoretical project thus at the beginning of the book:

I want to canvass...what I shall call the 'radical pluralist' position. Like the liberal position at its best, it speaks out for individual needs. Like the libertarian approach it embraces the legitimacy of many hitherto execrated and denied sexual practices. Unlike the absolutist approaches, whether the old absolutism of religious dogmatism or the new, born of political certainties, it speaks out for the acceptance of diversity... an approach which is sensitive to what I believe to be the really fundamental issues around sexuality today: the social nature of identity, the criteria for sexual choice, the meaning of pleasure and consent, and the relations between sexuality and power.[24]

Weeks, like the post-Marxists, sees social relationships as largely unrelated to class, entrenched instead in multifarious, complex structures of 'domination and subordination'. Like most gays and lesbians he is uncomfortable with the flashy commercialisation of 'gay lifestyles'. But he believes that the ruling class, the common enemy against which workers of whatever sexuality, gender or race can unite, has been laid to rest with the supposed death of Marxism. Consequently he sees any notion of class as more or less irrelevant in the creeping progress towards 'radical pluralism'.

In his theory oppression originates 'in the multiple forms of domination and subordination that flaw our society and which the New Right seeks to reinforce'.[25]

Oppression should be got rid of 'in a project of the thorough democratisation of society...democratising the processes of economic decision-making, opening up the different communities to popular involvement, and realising a sexual democracy'. This democratisation can be achieved by:

... an education of 'desire' in its widest sense, an imaginative encouragement to feel and relate differently in a better future...the vision of a freer, unalienated sexual world

155

powerfully survives as an antidote and alternative to the meretriciousness, restrictions and oppressions of the present ... All we need is the political commitment, imagination and vision.[26]

The fundamental flaw in Weeks's proposal is the critical gap he leaves unfilled between his legitimate aspirations and his interesting and insightful criticisms of the sites and discourses (such as sexology, psychiatry, radical feminism, gay essentialism) which fixate on questions of sexuality now. By not pinpointing the roots of oppression in the systematic exploitation of workers in capitalism, he resorts to a woolly explanation of oppression and an even less concrete programme of action for achieving his aims. Ultimately Weeks points the way to a dream because, tragically, he offers us no real clue as to how to achieve this truly democratised and sexually liberated society.

Unite! Don't Follow These Leaders!

Proponents and supporters of identity politics were very active in the 1980s in city-based movements to reform public and social services. Their aims were to pressurise local governments and city councils—from the inside or from the fringes—to accommodate diverse lifestyles in their policies and practices. Whilst the demands for equality had clearly emerged from the sense of confidence which had been built by the class struggles of the 1970s, the pattern of 'interest groups' and 'movements', all trying to push for their particular projects of advancement, owed its origins to the diverse radical struggles of the 1960s. During this period modern ideas of feminism, black liberation and gay liberation were formed and they went on to become the basis of identity politics in the 1980s, through a process of pluralistic accountability based on the politics of identity. The 'top down' consultative democracy that grew up in this brief era of reform holds many attractions for lesbian and gay 'opinion formers' today. But for many others, this outcome heralded the virtual collapse of any kind of popular belief in working from inside to change the system. Many socialists are still wondering nearly ten years later where gay liberation will come from.

The danger is that the lesbian and gay leaderships in Europe and the US will step even deeper into the pitfalls and minefields of identity politics, embracing wholesale the cynical business solutions of buying our way out to freedom. Most lesbians and gays know that a new brand of sexual politics is desperately needed, one that will make sense of the failures and splits of reformist organisations, one that will be able to explain why lesbians and gays cannot unite across chasmic class differences, one that will offer a way forward for black and white gays to unite and fight a common enemy. But while a comprehensive class analysis of gay oppression remains sidelined this development is inhibited. It is not in the interests of the bourgeoisie and their supporters (business people, managers, media cliques) to admit the truth about where sexual liberation for all will come from. It is only the working class which has a material and unifying interest in bringing about a society where sexual oppression is no longer needed. Identity politics offer none of the crucial theoretical and practical links between gay oppression and the exploitation which workers experience every day of their working lives. They foster the illusory hope that the state is indeed neutral and that by increasing pressure we can gain more influence over it. They encourage those of us who are not in influential positions to hand over the task of gay liberation to a select few who set themselves up as our representatives. Yes, we have to recognise and confront the awesome developments in the modern world which have alienated millions of people from any sense of control over their own lives. But at the same time we have to be aware that the 'old' divisions, the ones which divide people through society and create basic antagonisms, are still very much alive and still the primary influence upon our lives.

The proliferation of identities in modern capitalism is about the commercialisation of 'alternative lifestyles'. It is not about sanctioning diversity or undermining the structures and systems which create oppression. Whilst the institution of the family may appear to decline, its ideological function as a regulating ideal remains intact. At best, identity politics offers a route for oppressed individuals to understand the symptoms of their oppression—on the way to understanding its causes. At worst, the politics of identity provide a vehicle for the middle classes to make money and nurse their own careers, enabling the capitalist state to continue repression whilst appearing to bow to organised pressure. Identity politics only offers solutions to certain individuals through selective 'empowerment'. It has nothing to offer the mass of people for whom sexual liberation will be attainable only when the battle against class oppression has been fought. This battle can only be won by a movement which unites all workers across boundaries of race, gender and sexuality.

Notes

1   *Capital Gay*, 5 February 1993.
2   Colin Richardson, 'Porn Again' in *High Risk Lives*, eds Tara Kaufmann and Paul Lincoln, Prism, Bridport, 1991.
3   Sheila Jeffreys, *Anticlimax*, Women's Press, London, 1990, p. 313.
4   Ibid.
5   *Gay Times*, August 1993.
6   Peter Tatchell, 'Self Reliance: The X-Factor in Queer Polities', Gay Times, April 1993.
7   George Breitman, ed. *Malcolm X Speaks*, New York, 1990, p. 217.
8   Ibid.

9   Peter Tatchell, 'Realising Your Potential', *Pink Paper*, 18 February 1994.

10   Ibid.

11   Sharon Smith, 'Mistaken Identity', *International Socialism* 62, March 1994, p. 4.

12   VI Lenin, 'The Latest Word in Bundist Nationalism' quoted by Sharon Smith, 'Mistaken Identity', p. 44.

13   Ibid., p.45

14   Derek Cohen, 'Full Marx', *Rouge* 15,1994.

15   US figures from *Pink Economic Facts, Detonator Briefing for Gay Lifestyles Exhibition 93.*

16   UK figures broadcast on *Out*, Channel Four, 9 August 1994, reported in Pink Paper, 12 August 1994.

17   Frances Williams, 'Dykes Mean Business', Gay Lifestyles 1994 *Gay to Z Business Directory.*

18   Dugald Williamson, 'Language and Sexual Difference', *Screen*, vol. 8 no. 1, winter 1987.

19   Sharon Smith, 'Mistaken Identity', p. 30.

20   Stanley Aronowitz, *The Politics of Identity: Class Culture, Social Movements*, New York, 1992, pp. 269-70, quoted in Sharon Smith, 'Mistaken Identity'.

21   Rosalind Brunt, "The Politics of Identity', *New Times,* eds Hall and Jacques, Lawrence and Wishart, London, 1989, p. 151.

22   Frank Mort, 'The Politics of Consumption', *New Times*, pp. 170-1.

23   Jeffrey Weeks, *Sexuality and its Discontents*, Routledge and Kegan Paul, London, 1985, p. 210.

24   Ibid., p. 56

25   Ibid., p. 257.

26   Ibid., p. 260.

5. HOSTILE BROTHERS

Anybody who is running a business which happens to be in a gay market, if they have their head screwed on, knows that that business has got to work. Most people who are running businesses are so preoccupied with trying to make the business work that the community is totally secondary. If the business doesn't work, people are not employed and gay issues and things don't really matter because the business doesn't exist.[1]

—Gordon Lewis, businessman

The capitalists, like hostile brothers, divide among themselves the loot of other people's labour...[2]

—Karl Marx

The dominance of identity and lifestyle politics in the lesbian and gay movement today leaves many in a quandary. Millions of lesbians, gays and bisexuals experience oppression and discrimination as just part of a whole range of obstacles and difficulties at home, school, college, in the workplace and the streets. Yet they have little opportunity to link these experiences because the ideas put forward by gay community leaders leave no room for applying the politics of class. Many people express deep uncertainty about the role of entrepreneurialism in lesbian and gay rights organisation. They know that capitalism is at the root of oppression. But they cannot let go of the fallacy that all lesbian and gay people are in the same boat. They sense the betrayal by figureheads and people of 'influence'. However, because they fear real revolutionary change may be impossible, they settle for the limited goals of law reform and look to media coverage to change people's attitudes. Cutting loose from the reactionary ties of lifestyle and identity politics is the only way of breaking out of this quandary. For this to happen it is necessary to understand gay entrepreneurialism for what it is: its motivations and its priorities. The gay business class is not a stepping stone but a big wall between us and the liberation we are fighting for.

This chapter is about confronting the real divisions in the lesbian and gay communities. It shows that differing class interests will always underpin social relationships whilst exploring how—especially in relation to the gay community—market changes and the fluidity of class definitions affect our sense of alignment. It will examine the development of the pink economy, the gay market and gay business protagonists' motivations. Class, wealth and private property lie at the root of gay oppression. Only by recognising this can gay liberationists understand fully the limitations and weaknesses of the gay movement in the UK and the US. Then the hopes, disappointments, misplaced trusts, fragmentation and frequent sense of betrayal which characterise contemporary gay politics will fall into place. In order to begin to set this political confusion in context, it is necessary to look at the burgeoning gay business class, the rising prominence of gay markets and the political meaning attached to pink economic 'muscle' by gay business people themselves.

Organising as a Business Class

The notion of pink economics is not new. Ever since class society began there have been places where people who love their own sex can gather to meet, relax and interact sexually. The explosion, since the 1960s, of historical writings which explore same-sex relationships of the past testify to such gatherings and communities in all parts of the world since ancient times.[3] The very existence of private property, the family and class society ensure that there is ghettoisation and therefore opportunities for money to be made. The enterprising entrepreneur recognises a market and begins to tap it by ostensibly offering its deprived members what they want and need. This is the beginning of the idea that business people catering for 'oppressed minorities' are somehow perpetrating a neo-charitable social good, investing in a stigmatised community living on the margins of mainstream society.

The gay market is big business. Self-defined, gay-run businesses tend to concentrate on the market sectors which are particularly associated with the gay social scene: clubs, bars, merchandising, sportswear, publishing, entertainment, specialist retailing (books, greetings cards, gifts, magazines, sex toys). A newer breed of gay professionals are offering legal, financial and property services to the gay community, their selling point a promise of 'understanding', 'sensitivity', 'supportiveness', 'confidentiality' and 'friendliness'. Fashionable areas in city centres, such as London's Soho, are seeing the growth of a new kind of gay venue: continental-style cafes and bars with windows and doors onto the street and tables and customers spilling out onto the pavement. Unlike the traditional British gay pub or club, with shutters, bouncers and side-doors, the new venues reflect a growing sense of consumer confidence and construct a visible social presence for bourgeois gay sophistication. Whilst they are competitive, gay business people, like all business people recognise the need to organise amongst themselves for mutual benefit. In this way they can avoid treading on one another's toes as well as share opportunities for expansion and inter-trading. Mike McCann of the gay lifestyle chain of shops Clone Zone explains how the UK Gay Business Association (GBA) was founded in 1984. He expresses his belief that the gay 'business community' is an important subsection of the gay population as a whole, offering more of that population the opportunity to buy all the different attributes of a gay lifestyle:

We did it, if anything, because of unfair competition. I remember when I first started I didn't know very much about the gay community. We wanted to buy from people and all of a sudden people were being difficult. I had been in conventional business for twenty years, handling budgets of six million pounds and all of a sudden someone's frightened I'm going to take away their business because I'm selling a few vests. Amazement. It occurred to me that people were being very small-minded and believing that the market was small. I realised that there was a tremendous number of gay people and much more business to be had. There were about seven or eight of us at the time who wanted to talk: Clone Zone, Expectations, the Market Tavern [pub/club in South London], Man Around [travel company], and a couple more. We put a constitution together and it's grown wonderfully [130 members by 1994].⁴ Attitudes have changed. There's more cooperation and we help each other now. There's lots of ways in which the business community can help each other. It also helps the punters because you've got the Gay Business Association to fall back on if you've not been treated correctly or the product isn't good.⁵

Whilst the gay market is primarily identified as white and male, given the traditionally higher earning power of that group, the increased openness surrounding gay identity in the commercial lifestyle world has brought an increased interest in the fashion-value of lesbians. Once stereotyped as women too ugly to attract men, chic lesbians are now elevated to cult status in the fashion stakes. Their collective image is one of super-sophistication and cultural innovation. The role of individual lesbians in the new commercial environments is not as proprietors or publishers but as managers, marketing executives and commissioning editors. It is an asset for a thrusting gay company to feature a well-dressed lesbian in its executive line-up.

The classic gay lifestyle, as defined by the media, is in fact a distilled replica of a traditional middle-class lifestyle and is a concrete indication of the dominance of middle-class cliques within the gay movement. The editors, journalists and designers who create the glossy images are identified as representatives of lesbians and gays *per se*. Of course their interests in opera, designer clothing and Scandinavian furniture are inaccessible to the vast majority of lesbians and gays. The powerful myth that all gay people are united by a common interest has obscured the fact that gay taste, gay sensibility and gay lifestyles are in fact merely middle-class taste, sensibilities and lifestyles. The preoccupations of working-class lesbians and gays — police harassment, job losses, wage cuts, benefit cuts, homelessness, domestic violence—are excluded from the editorials of lifestyle magazines, except as copy documenting the activities of middle-class led reformist and campaigning organisations.

A burgeoning sub-industry in public relations and business consultancy provides a cushioning interface between established mainstream companies, who wish to target the lucrative gay market, and gay business people themselves. Marketing and business consultants, by offering their services to gay and straight companies alike, reveal the essential material similarities between all business people—whatever their sexual orientation. The consultancy selling point is clearly expressed by Brian McLaughlin of Conference and Marketing Associates Ltd (CMA):

We believe that the time is now ripe for major companies to take a serious look at marketing to the gay consumer, especially as there is now such a broad choice of media to use. However, despite being a trend-setting group, the market is sensitive to ill-considered campaigns, and is especially looking for activities which will put some investment back into the gay community. We hope to give an insight into these areas.[6]

The CMA-organised Gay Lifestyles event—an annual exhibition featuring presentations, shops, entertainment, fashion shows, discos with top gay DJs, bands, seminars and restaurants at the London Olympia centre—offers an opportunity for marketing executives to get a feel for the potentials of the gay market. The event is delivered as a one-off social extravaganza to the punters, and a unique opportunity to enter the bottomless pit of gay spending to the businesses. The hard sell is combined with a 'community feel'. Voluntary organisations, especially those involved in HIV and AIDS work are also assigned a role at Gay Lifestyles alongside campaigning and political organisations like the gay rights lobbying group Stonewall and the Tory Campaign for Homosexual Equality. Lifestyles 93 also saw the confident first presence of the Metropolitan Police, touting for recruits. Altogether, the sense is one of a 'good cause', and non-gay-specific companies are treated as guests on probation, courting their intended clientele. The 'news' is that gay life is no longer covert, ashamed and carried on in the back rooms of pubs. Fashionable, up-to-date marketing executives know that to be gay-friendly is to be on the cutting edge of contemporary commerce, bringing the gay lifestyle out into its rightful place at the forefront of fashion and interior design, home furnishings, music and entertainment, arts and literature. National newspapers and the marketing trade press run a steady stream of features heralding the coming age of liberated gayness, a world where modish homosexual women and men openly lead the way in all aspects of style and good taste.

Kim Watson, Managing Director of the *Pink Paper*, a UK national free newspaper, interprets the motivations of 'straight' companies targeting the gay markets as an attempt to recoup recession losses:

I think there are a lot of products out there which, whether they like it or not, are very dependent on money from the gay community. Levi is a classic example, so is Virgin.

166

They partly recognise that they are hitting the gay market with their sales and a gay video section has recently been set up within the Virgin Megastore. But there is still this part of the threshold that they have to cross over. A lot of them don't seem to be actively pitching to that marketplace because they're worried about their existing clients in the mainstream. It's very challenging. We had a degree of success with Absolut Vodka and I think that has to do with the fact that they had an international policy to advertise in the gay press. What we have in [the UK] is still a lot of traditional values. People whisper about going in the gay press in the most subtle way possible but there is a recognition now that it is a viable marketplace. That's a post-recessionary trading tactic. Economically it could go either way. For instance Bass Charrington [major brewery and owner of a major share of the London gay pubs] do advertise their gay-run pubs in the gay press occasionally but they could turn round and open up all their London pubs as champagne bars for yuppies. It's all quite fragile. I think it's going to take a couple of years before we see the kind of advertising that we see in the States like the magazines OUT *and the* Advocate *which carry Gordon's Gin and Marlboro cigarettes. [In 1993* OUT *attracted 400 per cent more national advertising than it had in 1992.[7]] It's unfortunate, there are one or two clothing companies like Levi and Gap but the majority of those mainstream people in the gay press in the States are alcohol and tobacco. I think that low end of the market will be the first to jump in with the gay press...[8]*

Despite a certain level of cynicism and recognition of te barrier of 'traditional values', Kim Watson sees any advertising development as having a direct impact on the positive development of the 'gay community' through the channels of the gay press:

Economically it ensures the future of the publishing houses. It can only strengthen the publishing houses and in turn it will strengthen the gay businesses and the gay community. Until there is a time when the gay press is more accepted through the news trade and until such time that gay publishing houses are structured to be in a position to put out papers through the newsagents, a lot have to rely on their own distribution services and advertising revenue to support them.[9]

Experience with working on the edge of the gay market has forced Kim Watson to face the reality of anti-gay prejudice in commerce and its relationship to the brutal reality of a 'free' market economy. She looks to a form of coordination or organisation as the catalyst for making the pink economy really work:

There's one thing that's overlooked in this 'I have a dream' mentality which is that there are ludicrous price wars in the rest of the consumer press at the moment. By consumer press I mean Cosmopolitan, GQ, car magazines and so on. To expect to come into that marketplace and get an asking price for a full colour page is incredibly optimistic. I think in many respects there's a lot of myth attached to the pink pound and the gay consumer...there are a lot of people who come onto the scene in terms of gay businesses who really do believe it's going to be a much bigger, brighter thing, this booming industry, changing people's lives. Until it's actually turned into constructive action it just won't happen.[10]

The Fine Line between Commerce and Politics

Ivan Massow of Ivan Massow Associates, a company of independent gay financial advisers, firmly believes that commercial development is essential in the process of making gay people more accepted and respected in society. He identifies a necessarily close relationship between law reformers and business people:

We have to recognise that phobias, fears and misconceptions about homosexuality can only be straightened out not by confrontation but by actually getting people to like us. And so my form of politics is by being absolutely wonderful and always doing everything right and making people want our service regardless of whether they are straight or gay, creating a whole sort of culture where homosexuality can be admired. It goes hand in hand with one side forcing our rights and the other side saying 'look, we're fucking brilliant anyway'.[11]

Mike McCann, gay retailer, explains what he sees as the benefits to gay people of the success of gay businesses in London's Soho:

Soho is now like a gay ghetto in a way. Things have mushroomed, there are more bars, other shops, hairdressers, the restaurants are becoming very continental with seating on the street. It's exciting because there's always been the element of almost being underground for the lesbian and gay community but now it's not like that at all. The atmosphere is terrific. If you go into Soho there's lots of people milling around and the cafes are full of sophisticated people.[12]

The theory is taken a step further by Gary Henshaw, gay business consultant and co-owner of the Kudos cafe-bar at Charing Cross in London. He sees his own commercial success as a natural development from the gains of the gay movement in the 1970s and 1980s, and looks to a future career in politics as a consequence of his own commercial success:

169

I think there's a very fine line between commercialism and politics. I am motivated by money and power. There is a certain amount of power and prestige in being recognised as a businessman on the gay scene and I do enjoy that. I happen to be a capitalist to the extreme, I grew up watching Dynasty *and I believe that dream that you must struggle forward, you keep expanding and getting bigger until some day I would like to build an empire. Power is very much connected with wealth. The more powerful gay people there are the better off we'll be. Ten or 15 years from now you're going to have an awful lot of very powerful influential gay people around and I think they will use their backbone at that stage to really shake things up. I recently met with two people and we've all come from the political to the commercial and we all three agree that in the future we see ourselves back in the political field again because I think that once you get out and once you get wealthy it's almost the next step.[13]*

On the other hand, most gay business people are wary of appearing to support or identify with any particular set of political beliefs. They know that party politics are a potential minefield for prominent personalities who want to maintain prestige within a cross-class gay 'community'. Their statements, however guarded, express considerable discomfort about the apparent conflict between gay rights and business values, despite any beliefs they may have in the power of the pink economy. Gordon Lewis appears confused about his political allegiances as a businessman and his interests as a gay man:

Edwina Currie [Conservative MP and instigator of the parliamentary debate on the age of consent for gay men in February 1994] has thoughts and views of trying to help the gay community that are very, very good. We all vote for a party because we believe in that view, but when you get a situation like gay politics and you get one particular MP, Chris Smith, who happens to be a Labour politician and he doesn't stand with the conservatives, it puts you in a very unusual position. You start thinking 'Can he actually make any impact on that issue?' It doesn't matter what my political connections are. It doesn't come into the equation. I don't see myself as a political animal. If I was, I would be leading the campaign.[14]

Mike McCann is quite explicit about his perception of a political dilemma around gay rights:

I don't think gay rights needs to be political. It's been made that way but if people support the idea of an equal age of consent they don't have to agree on other political matters. I am not political in that respect. From a financial point of view I would probably vote Tory but I have found the Tory campaigns against gay people in the last elections so offensive I just haven't voted at all. From a social point of view I think you'll get a better deal with the socialists.[15]

Ivan Massow understands the importance to a business person of maintaining an open position on almost everything. However, his conviction that the customer must always be right forces his hand, in spite of his determination to be independent:

I have my economic views and my social views and my homosexual views and all of them are completely appropriate to whatever I feel the climate is at the time. I quite resent the way Gay Pride tends to offer homosexuality to the Labour Party. For lot of people who are my clients those politics aren't necessarily appropriate to them.[16]

171

Jobs for the Gays?

Most gay businesses catering directly for the gay market and with a high level of client contact tend to employ gay people to work for them. The provision, by employers, of jobs for workers, is regarded in modern capitalism as a great service to society. Gay employers credit themselves with even more beneficence. Mike McCann is quite definite about his contribution to the gay economy as an employer:

> *The most obvious thing that gay businesses do is to provide people with jobs. Lots of pubs and clubs, if they didn't exist, then there would be fewer people with jobs. Not only that but the jobs we provide enable people to be out. Clone Zone hasn't made me terrific amounts of money or anything like that. What it has done is to give me a different level of confidence. It's allowed me to come out but it's also allowed me to think I help the community. We've got 30 employees, that's 30 people who would not have a job in the gay community if Clone Zone wasn't there.[17]*

Ivan Massow also prides himself on his employment style in the traditionally stuffy insurance industry:

> *There's no commission, it's all on salary. I tend to wear a suit but most of the boys, they all have to be smart, but they wear jeans and things. It's just not a typical insurance environment. I think we have a better relationship with our clients than I have ever experienced in any other company. We're a lot ruder to them! We just have a lot more fun. And we get a nice rate of referrals. It so happens that everyone is young and quite good-looking but that's more to do with the age-group mentality I wanted to employ.[18]*

Gary Henshaw goes one step further yet again by claiming that working within an all-gay environment is tantamount to liberation for the workers. He describes the good fortune of those in his employ:

> *I think it's a good environment. A lot of young people go and work in a gay business basically to liberate themselves, they've grown up with problems being gay, suddenly they come out and they work in a gay bar or a gay club and they find people accept them and they have a great time. Then they can go back into the straight environment with total confidence in themselves.*[19]

On being asked if he actually paid his workers any more than a 'straight' employer would, Henshaw replied with an authoritative and emphatic 'No!'.

The Enemies Within: Them or Us?

The idea that lesbian and gay people can be 'helped' to liberation by the prowess of a successful gay business class or community is a curious one. Whether they are gay, straight, black, white, male or female, bosses, employers, business people and their managers have interests which are *diametrically opposed* to those of the people who work for them. John Rees explains how this is endemic to capitalist society:

> *To survive, each boss has to avoid being beaten by his competitors. So every capitalist tries to get his workers to work longer and harder in return for less than his competitors can. Competition forces each individual capitalist to attack the jobs, wages and conditions of workers. Because this pattern is repeated in every firm it results in a struggle between the whole class of capitalists and the class of workers.*[20]

Such a conflict of interests is not brought about by the individual greed or ruthlessness of particular capitalists. Indeed, the gay business people interviewed for this book were, on the whole, charming and amiable people. Many business people are not personally particularly greedy and dislike the idea of cutting workers' wages or making people redundant. The system they benefit from forces them to do it. To maintain competitiveness, to ensure that they make a profit, they find themselves in a position where they have no option but to displace their losses onto their workers. Thus, however nice or kindhearted a businessperson is, ultimately, they will be forced to take a position of conflict against their workers. Similarly, there is no boss who can afford to put the interests of his or her workers before the pursuit of profit in competition. That competitiveness and drive for profit is the nature of business and the principal motivation in the movement of capital around the world, in whatever industry, sector or market. Some bosses are certainly more humane than others. They may wish to ensure that their employees have decent working conditions and a reasonable level of pay. But since workers are paid only a fraction of the real value of their work (the rest kept aside for profit and reinvestment to stay competitive) they are inevitably exploited. There is no worker in the world today who is not exploited to a greater or lesser degree. Employers may be 'good' or 'bad' but in terms of class, the bosses will always be opposed to the rest of us.

This is clearly illustrated in the awareness of the gay business cliques of the need to organise *as a class*. Claims by individual gay business people that they are not particularly political, or that they try to stay out of politics, are a smokescreen. They mask the necessity of acting politically (either in the workplaces through their employment and business practices or by bringing pressure to bear upon the state) to protect their essential interests. Workers who organise, who unite and campaign to fight cuts and protest against job losses are often accused of being too political. The fact is that politics is about wealth, property and power. The business people who have a stake in the accumulation of wealth hang onto that stake by means of a political system which favours their interests over the interests of the people who work for them and create their wealth for them.

The aims and objectives of the Gay Business Association provide an example of the ways in which the business class shares common interests and is committed to protecting the interests of employers and honing the reputation of the market.

Sexuality and identity may make gay business people socially aware on a very limited level but they share material interests with other bosses and business people, not ordinary lesbian and gay workers. At the same time, they recognise that ordinary lesbian and gay workers make up the majority of the market they wish to target. It is crucial that they do not alienate this vast group of potential customers. They do this by taking a public stand against bigotry. But their contribution to the fight against homophobia is strangely constrained. Because they oppose homophobia but do not wish to acknowledge or discuss where it comes from or its function within capitalism, they put forward a pessimistic view that there will always be anti-gay feeling in society. The idea that society could change sufficiently to make homophobia irrelevant and a thing of the past is not only unthinkable but undesirable because in such a society workers would not be divided and therefore could not be exploited. They therefore use the tired argument that socialism is dead and that those who are seeking a fairer society are wasting their time. Gary Henshaw prophesies that poverty and suffering are inevitable:

> *If they want to have a government that will look after them, fantastic, but life's not like that. If we had that situation... there wouldn't be homeless people and all that. Maybe that will come in the next hundred years. We've gone through communism, we've gone through a form of socialism.*[21]

175

Ivan Massow offers his version of a materialist future:

I feel that things like communism fail because everyone is a capitalist. Under a socialist framework, nothing would survive to support it. It would destroy the things that give us something to complain about! It would destroy the businesses. At the moment we can afford to push money around because there's an infrastructure of greedy people above us that are working away to make profits for themselves but are indirectly employing us and providing us with money and taxes. I would hate to take away the incentive to make money. I think we'll always have an eager infrastructure and that's what I believe as a businessman. I make a nice profit and I can use my influence for charity. I can do so many things now I'm Ivan Massow.[22]

These arguments assume that the rich and powerful have an unshakeable grip on the use of wealth and resources. But the working class has enormous and overwhelming potential power—and it's this power that we need to harness in our fight for liberation. The major difference between the working class and the ruling class is the question of competition and division. What benefits one section of the working class (free health care, gay rights, women's equality, cheap transport, higher wages) materially benefits the whole working class. When the working class unites, the potential for greater unity increases and the power to halt the system grows. However, the ruling class, whilst sharing common interests with one another in maintaining class control and class divisions, are in effect in constant competition with one another. Under pressure and during crises, they fall apart, they quarrel and fight over territory, markets, capital and produce.

For bosses, one way of 'keeping in' with workers is to promise jobs. The level of homophobia in society means that the vast majority of lesbians and gays cannot be open about their sexuality at work. For many people who do work in, say, a gay bar or a gay bookshop, it can be a relief to be out. But there is no haven in capitalism, no place where we can hide from the injustices and divisions that hinder us from realising who our real enemies are. Whilst a lesbian or a gay man might not encounter anti-gay prejudice inside a gay company, the company—be it a pub, shop or office,—cannot protect them from homophobia on the street, on a housing estate or from their family or neighbours. Moreover, being employed in a gay business does not ensure protection against racism, sexism or discrimination on the basis of disability. Ivan Massow's description of his easy-going office is a good example of discrimination against older people and women; he states openly that he will only employ young people, mainly 'boys'. Bar-owners of whatever sexuality will always testify to the importance of employing 'attractive' bar staff—be they male or female. Like straight bars which use women bar staff as bait for male customers, gay bars will employ 'cute' men for precisely the same reason.

Waged labour is no gift, no boon. It is simply a means of exploitation to a profitable end. If you are a worker it doesn't matter whether you are a teacher, a graphic designer, a nurse or a shop assistant, you share the same material interests as all other workers, whatever their race, sexuality, gender or nationality—wherever they are in the world. There are employers who wish to present themselves as 'good employers', bosses who 'care' about the welfare and working conditions of their workers and who describe their employment practice as a contribution to society. The danger for us is when this belief is transferred over to workers. Workers' consciousness and organisation is damaged when workers believe that their interests lie in the principle of capital and that their lives are improved by the use of capital in purchasing and creating objects. We are often told that the job market will be improved by 'investment'. We are told that business is good because 'profits are up'. In reality production and profits are achieved by labour and the control of wages.

There is no example of employment under capitalism where any worker can hide from exploitation. A gay business may allow a few gay people to be out at work, a black company may offer rare opportunities for career development, a women's business might represent a chance to make it into higher management. None of this in any way alleviates the acute symptoms across the whole of our society of racism, women's oppression and homophobia. Far from it, these initiatives use the mechanisms of the very system that causes oppression and prejudice in the first place. Whilst employers may deny and even genuinely oppose certain forms of discrimination, they all, without exception, benefit from the perpetuation of divisions, bigotry and prejudice. They benefit from prejudice as materially as they benefit from tax cuts for the rich, the abolition of health and safety standards or any other attack on workers' lives we might care to mention. They benefit because prejudice enables certain sections of the population to be *paid less*.

Homophobia, like racism and sexism, is full of ideas which are useful weapons against working people. These ideas provide convenient explanations for the misfortunes that befall us. When unemployment rises, we are told that it is because there are too many immigrants and black people taking away jobs from white people. When there is a chronic housing shortage we are told that this is because refugees from other countries have gone to the front of the queue. When local services are cut we read articles in the newspaper saying that the money has been spent on 'loony' schemes like a gay helpline for victims of queerbashing or a lesbian and gay advice project. The reality of course is that the ruling class is using every means at its disposal, economic and ideological, material and political, to deflect the blame for its heinous actions against the working class and slap it on any vulnerable group who happens to be to hand. Homophobia works in the same way. It cannot be separated from other false, divisive ideas which make workers suspicious of one another. It is endemic to a culture where people compete with one another for employment and promotion and blame one another, instead of the real culprits, for job losses and housing crises.

Mistaken Identity

Frustration with the commercialisation of gay politics is constantly echoed on the pages of the gay press in letters complaining about being ripped off and private profit being put before the interests of the gay community. However, the lack of class consciousness in the gay media means that such expressions of discontent tend to focus on the questions and problems of identity rather than material interest. There are two main critical responses to gay entrepreneurialism. The first is that gay commerce is good and progressive, provided that it is *purely* gay. Proponents of this view are convinced that by buying gay one actually supports the gay community. They insist that heterosexuals are the guilty perpetrators of oppression and that 'straight business' is simply exploiting a vulnerable group. A letter to *Capital Gay* newspaper in January 1994 took two gay journalists to task for accepting the job of creating a new glossy gay lifestyle/culture magazine with multinational 'adult' publishers Northern & Shell:

> *I refer to Paul Burston and Pas Paschali and their employment by heterosexual publishers. It seems to me that one is a gay journalist, writer, actor, poet, painter, or whatever, only if one is working in and for the gay community. Either one is part of the solution or part of the problem. What shocks is that these two prominent figures have no understanding of our oppression.*[23]

This viewpoint is not informed by any sense that the gay 'community', such as it is, is in fact riven by acute and stark class divisions. It is content to assume that what is in the interest of one gay person must also be in the interest of another. There is an alternative to this viewpoint which points out that all business, whether 'gay' or 'straight', is carried out in the pursuit of profit. Spy, *Capital Gay*'s anonymous critic of the gay scene, makes the following observations about the new breed of cafe/bar in London's Soho and offers an astute comment on the ideological significance of gay enterprise:

> *There are two schools of thought about the creation of this new type of venue. The Businessman's view is one of pound signs... Shops, hairdressers, cafes, cab firms, even peep shows have arisen as a result of the receding economy and the success of these venues which can only benefit the gay community. Then there is the Cynic's view, unfortunately the one to which I ascribe... This pathetic belief in some new-found solidarity is not based on homo-identity, but rather on a number of people's obvious intent to create their own wealth. A gay ghetto masquerading as a safe haven for fags whilst milking the pink pound (natch) from their designer pockets.*[24]

The article ends on a promising note:

> *I certainly don't believe the scene is a classless society. Walk into half these places in the wrong clothes or with the wrong face and you know you are not welcome. If anything, the burgeoning gay village is only serving to drive a wedge into our so-called community. My opinion, for all it's worth, is that it won't be long before something gives.*[25]

Spy is right. The emergence of a new kind of gay business mentality which not only underpays its workers but charges its clientele exorbitant prices for designer consumables, is serving to highlight the social differences and divisions between the many hundreds of thousands of people who identify as lesbian or gay. At a time when people are losing their jobs, homes and civil liberties, the idea that a seriously oppressed minority can be helped along by a few rich gay people getting even richer is something of an insult.

So who *does* believe the pink pound will buy us our equality?

Notes

1   Gordon Lewis, interviewed by the author, 1993.
2   Karl Marx, *Theories of Surplus Value*, vol. 2, Moscow, 1963-72, p. 434; quoted in Alex Callinicos, *The Revolutionary Ideas of Karl Marx*, Bookmarks, London, 1987, p. 125.
3   See, for instance, Patrick Higgins, ed. *A Queer Reader*, Fourth Estate, London, 1993.
4   *Capital Gay*, 6 May 1994.
5   Mike McCann, interviewed by the author, 1993.
6   Lifestyles 93 Press Release from Detonator Ltd, 18 November 1993.
7   *Pink Paper*, 3 September 1993
8   Kim Watson, interviewed the by author, 1993.
9   Ibid.
10 Ibid.
11 Ivan Massow, interviewed by the author, 1993.
12 Mike McCann, interviewed by the author, 1993.
13 Gary Henshaw, interviewed by the author, 1993.
14 Gordon Lewis, interviewed by the author, 1993.
15 Mike McCann, interviewed by the author, 1993.
16 Ivan Massow, interviewed by the author, 1993.
17 Mike McCann, interviewed by the author, 1993.
18 Ivan Massow, interviewed by the author, 1993.
19 Gary Henshaw, interviewed by the author, 1993.
20 John Rees, *The ABC of Socialism*, Bookmarks, London, 1994.

21 Gary Henshaw, interviewed by the author, 1993.
22 Ivan Massow, interviewed by the author, 1993.
23 Letter to *Capital Gay*, 21 January 1994.
24 'Cruising with Spy', *Capital Gay*, 4 February 1994.
25 Ibid.

6. Reform

Good will costs money. Make it financially advantageous
to someone to participate and they will. It's just the way
things work.
> —Ivan Massow, independent gay financial adviser

You've got the lifestyle ... now get a life!
> —Advertisement for Stonewall,
> UK national lesbian and gay lobbying organisation.

Being involved in lesbian and gay politics today means
participating in a reform movement. This movement looks
to bring about equality for gay people without addressing or
acknowledging the causes of gay oppression. As a social force it
concentrates all its activity on bringing pressure to bear on the
state. This activity is based upon the belief that agencies and
institutions which discriminate against lesbians and gays can be
reformed in order to make them operate more 'fairly'.

This political strategy is part of reformist tradition at the
centre of which is the idea that fundamental social change
will eventually be brought about by changing the law, slowly
and gradually. Reformism adheres to a conservative version of
history. This version puts the actions, pronouncements and
achievements of prominent individuals at the centre of social
development. In lesbian and gay reformism, the principles
of lobbying, small direct action protests, business influence
and political negotiation are anchored in the activities of
unaccountable leaders and personalities. These self-appointed
representatives and co-opted figureheads are identified as the
centre of political and social meaning around which historical
events are shaped. Like school history lessons which focus on
the antics of kings, queens, generals and bishops, this version of

change doesn't take into account the movements of people who, drawn by events into mass action, change the course of history and pressure the system into fundamental transformations. Gay visibility today seems to be about the extent to which prominent gay individuals have been permitted to enter the mainstream corporate, media and political sectors. The achievements of the gay movement are measured by the number of gay MPs, journalists, businesspeople and respectable lobbyists there are working with the media to promote single issues and reform proposals. The multilayered, complex lives of lesbian and gay workers who face many forms of oppression and exploitation as well as anti-gay discrimination, are not reflected in the stated objectives of the professionally-led gay leadership. The objectives centre on a handful of proposed law reforms which, whilst important, go nowhere near offering any kind of solution to the brutal and pervasive reality of gay oppression in people's lives.

The Impossible Dream

In 1993 a campaign was started which aimed to force the UK government to equalise the age of consent for gay men.

Prior to 1967 sex between men was illegal in the UK and liable to result in criminal prosecution and frequently imprisonment. The 1967 Sexual Offences Act partially decriminalised male homosexuality by legalising sex in private between two consenting men over 21 (the age of consent for both women and men for heterosexual sex is 16). On top of this discrimination, gay men were far more likely to be prosecuted for breaking the law on the age of consent than heterosexual people. In 1991 nearly 1500 men had been arrested for having consensual sex with men under 21 years of age. Of these over 1000 were convicted and some of them received prison sentences. Men arrested on under-age gay sex charges were five times more likely to be prosecuted than men who had sex with girls under 16.[1]

The Sexual Offences Act claimed to protect young men from the unwanted seductions of older men. In effect what the law does is to criminalise those young men for having consensual relationships. It does not stop young men from having sex. Neither does it provide any protection from abuse or sexual attack. A discriminatory law on the gay male age of consent means that health educators are not free to provide the kinds of safer sex information that young gay men need to protect themselves and their partners from HIV infection and other sexually transmitted diseases. Neither are young gay men themselves lawfully allowed to seek such information. In the light of these issues, Stonewall launched a campaign to get the law changed. The object was to equalise the age of consent for gay men, bringing it down from 21 to 16.

The reformist gay movement extends across many apparently disparate groups. In Britain and America lobbying organisations attempt to bring together gay people of many political persuasions and from diverse walks of life in order to broaden and popularise questions of legal and social reform. In the US, the National Gay and Lesbian Task Force, the Human Rights Campaign Fund and gay military personnel joined forces in coordinating the million-strong 1993 March on Washington with direct-action cells the Lesbian Avengers and Queer Nation. In Britain, Tory, Liberal Democrat and Labour MPs (notably Edwina Currie and Chris Smith) and Stonewall worked together with action-pack Outrage! to campaign for equalisation of the age of consent for gay men. On the face of it this makes sense. Strength comes in numbers and the more we get out on the streets the better. However, both the coalitions described above have been subject to fierce and angry disagreement between activists on the right and left of the campaigns. It has become clear that while business people, legal lobbyists and street activists can *inform* one another, they cannot *unite* because they have opposing interests. Lesbians and gays, whilst coming from a multitude of political, cultural and social positions, are still divided by the antagonisms of a society ruthlessly riven by class and its determinants: wealth, control of production and private property. This means that a political movement which aims to unite lesbians and gay men across these barriers will run into problems.

All political movements which aim to fight the oppression of a minority seek to build unity on the basis of identity. Their leaders have swallowed the right-wing and liberal media propaganda that there is no longer any such thing as a working class. When they come to organise, against specific laws or in support of a proposed piece of legislation, they do so by focusing their attention on a single issue which they believe will unite all parts of an oppressed group. The problem comes because members of that oppressed group experience their oppression in different ways. Gay lawyers may find they cannot advance quickly enough in the profession because of prejudice at the Bar. Gay business people may find they can't get backing from a bank because the gay market is not being taken seriously. But a lesbian who is facing redundancy on top of racial harassment whilst about to lose her kids in a custody case is being attacked from all sides. In a movement based on identity and focused on single issues, whose experience, whose interests are likely to be in ascendance? The most influential and powerful, of course: the professional, the lawyer and the business person. In other words, the people who support the idea that gay issues can be divorced from other kinds of oppression and who need to separate gay oppression from the threatening agenda of class struggle.

The effect of this 'movementism' is that the symptoms of oppression are separated from the cause. All the issues which do not appear to relate directly to the single issue of identity-oppression are stripped away. Simplifying the issues, reducing them to a question of basic decency and common sense not only prevents any kind of debate about the root material causes of gay oppression. It also provides a basis upon which groups in society who have clearly opposing interests can be seen to be united. Angela Mason, Executive Director of Stonewall, describes what she sees as the positive signs of lesbian and gay advancement:

> *This year lesbians and gay men have achieved a new degree of visibility. 120,000 people came together to celebrate this year's Pride festival. Armistead Maupin's* Tales of the City *is a major TV series. The* Evening Standard *told us it's cool to be a lesbian. Major companies like Kingfisher (owner of Woolworth, B&Q, Comet and Superdrug) and British Telecom are among the growing number of employers with company policy on sexual orientation. Lesbian and gay police officers can be increasingly open about their sexuality.*[2]

Note Mason's choice of achievements: a TV show, lifestyle journalism, the policies of massive companies, developments in the police force. This new-found media visibility is headed by a sincere contingent of middle-class lesbians and gays who find it much easier to come out. They are not forced to live at home with parents, wait around at night for public transport or live in poor housing with little privacy. They are able to afford to be part of the growing pink economy. Going to pubs and clubs, and dressing in fashionable clothing: these things make it easier to be out, to live a 'gay life'. Angela Mason, like many reformists and gay leaders, talks as though living that life is the way to beat oppression. But whilst that life remains inaccessible to the vast majority of gay people, it remains little more than lifestyle politics: the use of the personal, the consumable, as the political.

In a round-table discussion Angela Mason reinforced her view that gay politics are primarily about personal experiences. She reiterated her belief that the ability to be out is evenly distributed across society:

The key political moment for all lesbians and gay men is coming out, being able to articulate your feelings publicly and without shame. The whole reason we are in the position...to advance further with law reform, is because, it is far more possible now to be out. It is the translation of hundreds of thousands of individual lesbian and gay lives coming out, able to take up the potential for political action in all walks of life, which will lead to major change in public policy.[3]

Proponents of this kind of 'lifestyle politics' debate and organise as though all lesbians and gays experience oppression in more or less the same way. Thus the career enhancement of a journalist, the opening of a new gay bar or the coming out of a gay policeman are interpreted as somehow benefiting all lesbians and gays. On this basis the lesbian and gay reform organisations are able to get all kinds of apparently dissimilar people and groups to work together. Equality is reduced to a media-friendly single issue which will rally all sections of the lesbian and gay middle-classes and persuade them to give their influence, their money and their abilities to the cause. This also provides an easily-identifiable focus to attract people in the public eye who are not gay but who wish to lend their name and support to a clearly expressed goal. Conservatives, gay and straight can then be attracted to a campaign which has stripped away all possible inconvenient political 'side issues'.

The Tory Input

What effect does twisting the gay rights agenda so as to attract the support of conservatives have on the politics of sexual liberation? An answer to this question can be found in the story of one Tory MP's involvement in a famous gay rights campaign.

The Stonewall-led age of consent campaign provided the first opportunity for campaigning gay Tories to enter the main body of UK gay rights political activism. This was made possible not because gay Tories had in any way dropped their right-wing views, but because activists had allowed the issues to be so far removed from any radical agenda of equality that it finally became acceptable to those on the political right.

Edwina Currie MP, former Junior Tory Minister, re-entered the political arena in 1994 by fronting the Equality Now! campaign to get the age of consent for gay men reduced from 21 to 16 (there is no age of consent for lesbian sex). As the MP tabling the relevant amendment, she soon established herself as the key figure within the campaign. For many gay activists the fact that it was eventually a Tory MP who paved the way for potential law reform on one of the central aspects of anti-gay discrimination, was somewhat confusing.

Currie has long argued for all barriers in the pursuit of wealth by the ruling class to be abolished. She is well known for expressing views which even members of her own party find embarrassing. As Junior Minister for Health her answer to poverty and hunger was to urge people on low incomes and benefit to not go shopping on an empty stomach. Her advice to old people unable to afford domestic fuel and worried about hypothermia was to wear a woolly hat in bed. She blamed the ill-health of the poor in the north of England, not on damp and substandard housing or the inability to afford good quality food, but on an uneducated insistence on eating fish and chips to excess. As an 'ambassador' for the British ruling class in Europe she has argued for the removal of minimum wage levels and the abolition of large chunks of health and safety regulation in order to allow British companies to become more 'competitive'. In short, she has never shied away from unpopularity and controversy in her zeal for authoritative and unyielding penny pinching. She voted for Section 28 of the 1988 Local Government Act preventing the use of public funds in the 'promotion of homosexuality'—a piece of legislation which preceded the wholesale defunding of local lesbian and gay service organisations. During the parliamentary debate on the age of consent she stated that she was *not* a supporter of gay rights.

Currie's brand of 'courage', therefore, made her a prime candidate for proposing a potentially controversial piece of legislation. Stonewall welcomed her with open arms, making no demands that she support any other aspect of lesbian and gay equality. Edwina Currie is not the only Tory to get involved in gay politics. The revamped Tory Campaign for Homosexual Equality (TORCHE) boasts leading lights Paul Barnes and David Starkey, both committed to TORCHE's aims to 'persuade the Conservative Party to support full legal equality', 'to provide a platform for all Conservatives...who wish to ensure that the views of gay people are properly represented throughout the Party' and *'to put the Conservative case within the gay community'* (my emphasis). Aware of the strong tradition of gay rights organisation on the political left, gay conservatives base their arguments around deeply conservative notions of privacy and choice. David Starkey, for instance, denies any correlation between economic policy and the promotion of morality— despite the Tory Party's long-standing insistence on family values as being essential to the economy:

> *... the notion that because I fuck in one way I should vote in one way I find preposterous. In my view, your views on economic management are quite separate from whether or not you have a happy family life. Your politics are one thing and your private life is another.[4]*

Paul Barnes reiterates the commonly-held misapprehension (so useful to reactionaries) that the majority of people are naturally non-political and basically, irrevocably conservative:

> *If the lesbian and gay movement is only seen to be putting forward what is a left-wing agenda in left-wing language,*

190

it's not going to appeal to the likes of me, or my mother, or most people down the road.[5]

Torchebearer, the newsletter of TORCHE, provides some insight into the political interests of organised gay Tories. The Party Conference edition in 1993 recorded the inception of TORCHE as the dawn of a new age of concern about gay equality in the Conservative Party. It noted that the proposed campaign on the age of consent offered a new opportunity for Tories to become more involved in gay political organisation. In fact, Stonewall's pleas to gay people across the country to give momentum to the campaign by writing letters to and lobbying MPs locally, is laid out in this edition of *Torchebearer* as the foundation-stone of gay political organisation.

Under the heading 'The Love that Picks up the Tab' a *Torchebearer* contributor spells out a belief in liberation through the pink pound.

> *The still developing Soho is a wonder to behold—not because there are so many gay businesses but because these are so visible and yet so totally integrated... You can flaunt it if you want but a pin-striped suit is just as welcome...in post-recession London pink money talks. Gay men and women have stepped out of the ghetto and into the High Street. Economic recognition will lead to political recognition; we are strong and becoming stronger.*[6]

After becoming chair of TORCHE in March 1994 Paul Barnes explains his experience of gay oppression and his particular approach to gay identity. A million miles from the everyday hazards which face the millions of lesbian and gay people (out and not out) in Britain, Barnes's airy pronouncements reveal a cynical and individualistic approach to personal and political advancement:

191

'I realise I am fortunate to be a director of a company where [being gay] has never been an issue...'. In a few year's time he plans to sell out of his political consultancy and 'settle into gentlemanly pursuits with my millions... I don't think people should do the same things all their lives and I certainly don't want to be doing at 53 what I'm doing at 33'. He also says he now has no interest in being an MP. 'You have to commit yourself to all sort of vacuous associations...and at the end of the day you could get chucked out at the next election... One of the best ways to get into Government is to get a peerage. You can't be sacked'.[7]

Invaluable career advice for us all!

Pink Pounds, Pride, Parades And Politics

Many gay leaders, including those on the left of the movement, have embraced the emergence of a gay business class and looked to this clique for political support. Why?

The increasing efforts of gay rights campaigners to gain footholds in mainstream politics has meant that great importance is placed on professional leadership and influential representation. Gay business people see their role not only as increasing credibility for a marginalised minority by enhancing its economic muscle, but also as rationalisers of gay protest, 'modernisers' of liberationism, shifting the politics of gay liberation to the right and eliminating any trace of class consciousness within the organised gay community.

Business people are an important part of the lesbian and gay reformist process. They provide a respectable image to the establishment. They give funds to the campaign so that it can continue its work. Their input is rewarded with a political framework which can benefit them. Profile, visibility, publicity and the breaking down of market barriers—all these things help them to make their profits more successfully as Gary Henshaw explains:

> *I think the commercial gay scene has a lot of political clout but unfortunately at the moment it's not organised enough to be used like that. I think the day will come when it will be used like that. People are getting wealthy from it and that's the difference and people see there's a reward there. It's getting much more serious. From what I know of the people involved, if you want to call them the gay capitalists, all of them have got definite political interests... If you have a gay bar you need people to come in there... The more* people who come out onto the gay scene the better for everyone.[8][my emphasis]

The annual UK Pride event has now developed from a protest march into a full-scale festival showcase and opportunity for bars and businesses. Through Pride, employers, breweries and business people have become important motivating aspects of gay political activity. Many lesbians and gays have expressed deep concern about what they perceive as an essential 'depoliticisation'. Has the effort to attract more people compromised the political significance of the gathering itself? *Or have the politics merely shifted towards the interests of the business cliques which increasingly control it?*

Mike McCann, member of the Pride Organising Committee, on the occasion of his re-election to the Chair of the Gay Business Association in April 1994, announced 'the increasing self-confidence of the gay business community in general'. He went on: 'The GBA is proud to have been involved in the success of Gay Lifestyles: and the more commercial approach taken by Gay Pride.'[9]

McCann reveals the ambivalence of the Pride membership's feelings about the increased commercialisation of what had once been a purely political event:

I went to an open forum about Pride not long ago. Pride took a bit of a pasting. There were groups saying 'this was necessary and that was necessary and you should be providing these services' and I said I agreed but that all of these things cost money. The chair called me down to the front and introduced me as from the GBA and as I was walking down people were actually hissing... People seem to forget: Pride can't happen without funds. I remember walking off to the most stoniest of silences![10]

Gordon Lewis, owner of the Village bars in London, argues that Pride is nowhere near commercial enough, that the attempt to retain the 'community' feel is totally misguided. In his view it should be completely shaken up:

Here's a situation where they're trying to create the awareness and the profile and all the splendid ideas and so forth and yet they've never made a bloody profit. This is where you need to become aggressive but when you've got people sitting on those committees and they don't want to make an entrance charge they'll never make a profit... I actually wonder whether putting on an event like that in the park is relevant in the current '90s. Maybe they ought to be looking at Olympia or Earl's Court where they can run it as a commercial venture... All I do know is that it's an amateur night out and it'll always be that way. They ran it as a business and they went bust and the only way they got started up again was companies like mine giving them money for their new campaign. The intentions are great but at the end of the day it's Mickey Mouse operations.[11]

For the bars and breweries which form the centre of the gay social scene, Pride is a battleground where the prize is big money. Ivan Massow is highly motivated by a desire to professionalise it:

Even without party politics I think Pride is almost too political. I saw a presentation that Australia did for the Olympic Committee and in it there was a massive picture of the Gay Mardi Gras. That's one of the things they are proud of as a nation. I thought imagine if England [sic] put in our presentation a picture of Gay Pride as something to be proud of. That's probably politically more powerful than stonking through with banners and hating people.[12]

Like all good capitalists gay business people have a substantial contempt for the kind of protest which erupts out of anger and defiance because they themselves have no sense of the material effects of oppression. For most lesbian and gay people, though, Pride remains the single most powerful opportunity to express the determination of lesbian and gay people to fight for their rights. It is therefore a controversial space of crucial political importance.

The Age of Consent: Riot or Regulation?

During the parliamentary debate over the gay male age of consent, 6000 demonstrators patiently kept a candle-lit vigil in the freezing cold February night outside the House of Commons. When the news came that MPs had voted not for 16 (equality) but for 18, the protesters broke ranks in a riot of outrage and fury. While Stonewall stewards appealed for calm and lesbian and gay 'leaders' inside the House bemoaned the lack of decorum outside, working-class gay people fought the police and barraged the doors of democracy in a powerful spontaneous show of defiance. Divisions immediately rose to the surface:

Shouting 'Shame!' and 'Bastards!' and with many people openly weeping, the crowd surged forward through police

195

crash barriers and began banging on the door of Parliament's St Stephen's entrance. As Stonewall stewards struggled to push protesters back, an angry demonstrator shouted at campaign leader Sir Ian McKellan: 'Send your knighthood back, Ian!'. Inside, police hurriedly barred all exits to the Palace of Westminster. In the Commons car park, Tory members including Currie and fellow Tory campaigner Jerry Hayes were among nervous MPs prevented from leaving by an angry crowd rattling the gates. 'I am damn well walking out through the front gate', bristled one anti-gay MP, only to turn back in the face of protesters shouting 'Lynch the bastards!'.[13]

Later, Angela Mason, director of Stonewall, declared that she 'regretted the violence' whilst a representative of the Stonewall Group announced that the 18 vote had been a success, that Stonewall had done 'a bloody good job' and asked, incredibly: 'Why use a different system when you've got one that works?'[14]

Further reports revealed that the vote had been lost because an unexpected 36 Labour MPs had opposed equalisation, including the shadow health minister David Blunkett (who was responsible for the party's policy on HIV prevention). Peter Tatchell of Outrage! promised a spate of civil disobedience: 'We will never again trust Parliament. We put our faith in MPs and they have let us down ... they voted to treat us like criminals so we are going to act like criminals'.[15]

During the period that followed there was a sense of disorientation as people asked themselves and each other: 'Who are our friends? Who are our enemies? Did our leaders sell us out? Whose side are they on?' A *Capital Gay* correspondent took Stonewall to task for trying to distance itself from the scenes of furious protest after the 18 vote saying:

The response of that wonderful crowd was entirely appropriate—anything less would have been shameful.

As things turned out that show of anger, that tremendous outpouring of contempt was the only thing worth celebrating on Monday night.[16]

The betrayal by Labour MPs, coupled with widespread publicity surrounding Edwina Currie's active support of the Equality Now campaign caused many lesbians and gay men to question the long-held tradition that gay liberation should necessarily be associated with the left. Those who had been drawn into the rhetoric of the single issue had taken on board the implications of the single-issue package: that gays were a class in themselves, that all gay people were in the same boat, that only lesbians and gays could effectively fight discrimination. They were floundering. The options left to them appeared two-fold. They could abandon the idea that gay liberation can be part of a more widespread fight against oppression and exploitation, denounce the uprising that occurred outside the House of Commons and place all their hopes on a personality-led parliamentary campaign to win the votes of MPs. Alternatively, they could ditch all faith in the parliamentary process and cast around for new, more direct and radical ways to fight for gay liberation, for real and powerful alliances *that would not let them down*. Inevitably, the splits became chasms and the community debate over how to achieve civil rights for lesbians and gays was once more split down the middle.

The gay leadership itself was also caught in a dilemma. How do you get more people to be involved in fighting oppression whilst at the same time retaining credibility with a community furious at ceaseless harassment, discrimination and homophobia? Trapped in the constraints of identity politics and locked in the grip of a reformist lobby which depends on the support of people of influence, gay activists shift from one strategy to another. They are constantly searching for a political programme which will weather the apparent contradictions of gay oppression and gay resistance, that will allow for meaningful alliances whilst at the same time not bending to compromise.

197

The Dangers of the Single Issue: Gay Rights at Work

In 1993 a bitter debate over the meaning of Pride dominated the pages of the gay press. Peter Tatchell of Outrage! demanded in the *Pink Paper* that the Pride Trust turn the festival into a full-scale civil rights march:

> *With good planning we ought to be able to mobilise a hundred thousand people. Another idea that could help increase participation and media coverage is a specific theme ... A simple and concrete human rights demand that all can agree on such as 'Equal Rights at Work'.*[17]

The Pride Trust, geared as it is to private money from 'gay' and 'straight' businesses, understood that adopting an anti-employer theme (as an 'Equal Rights at Work' demand would have been) would inevitably alienate powerful and influential support:

> *Pride means many different things to different people. Even within the Pride Trust, directors have differing personal responses to the meaning of Pride... To impose such a theme on the Parade such as equal rights at work would be divisive and set a very dangerous precedent.*[18]

Tatchell had touched on a sore point. Workers' rights are not popular with employers, be they gay or straight. The destiny of lesbian and gay workers is irrevocably bound up in a much wider tradition of struggle for decent treatment, justice and equality. Employers throughout the history of capitalism have opposed all attempts to regulate employment practices. Measures such as health and safety regulations, the Sex Discrimination Act (1975), Race Relations Act (1970), the Equal Pay Act (1976), sickness pay and minimum wage levels necessarily impose restrictions on employers which cost them money and put pressure on their profits. Such measures are tiny attempts to protect workers against the full force of the most brutal aspects of exploitation. Most of them are ignored, avoided or side-stepped by employers. We are now seeing an escalating campaign by western governments to erode and destroy these minuscule protections. There is a sharp shift across Europe and the US towards deregulation and 'flexible' working practices. In other words, workers' rights are being broken down. This general trend is presented as a move towards the 'freedom' of the marketplace. Many New Realists, commentators, employers and politicians who support this trend, or see it as inevitable, explain the increase in low-paid employment in the US in the 1990s as a direct result of the fact that, unlike Europe, the American economy is not 'burdened' by social legislation which requires employers to fork out redundancy payments, maternity benefits, sick pay and holiday pay.

Equal rights for lesbians and gays at work, even in principle only, would entail, at the very least, the introduction of a fully-fledged piece of legislation in defence of those workers' rights. Employers will not welcome this, whatever their sexuality. Those who claim some sympathy with the gay rights lobby, who want to appear progressive, will prefer to introduce equal opportunities policies (EOPs) which are legally unenforceable. On that basis it was no act of liberation but a canny move when Kingfisher plc funded Stonewall's survey into private sector employment policy of lesbians and gay men with a view to extending private companies EOPs. In one inexpensive swoop it defused Stonewall's campaign on equality at work and put itself on the map as a 'good' employer.

Of course any move which improves workers' rights is to be welcomed. But it is essential to understand the severe limitations of some concessions and the motivations behind them. To do this, I shall take the examples of two specific major UK employers, British Rail (BR) and the British Broadcasting Corporation (BBC). The issues raised are relevant to all workers in Europe and the US who experience job insecurity and wage cuts.

In April 1994 BR, a nationalised company, incorporated sexual orientation into its equal opportunities policy. Why? The campaigns for equality at work for lesbians and gay men had been at their height during the 1980s. Surely, if BR had been keen to improve, that would have been the time to have pushed the policy through. But the demands of employees at the time were ignored. The actual adoption of the policy in 1994 appeared to be coming from the management: 'Clearly on examining the equal opportunity policy and its implementation, we observed the omission of sexual orientation and corrected this in our strengthened policy,' says Gareth Hadley, a BR spokesperson.[19]

The policy offered welcome redress for all employees affected by harassment, whether sexist, racist or homophobic. But on closer examination, the process of BR's EOP development, as with many other companies adopting such policies in post-recessionary Britain, appears to be closely connected with the anti-worker measures of 'modernisation'. To understand this it is crucial that we look at the wider context of worker's rights in Britain over the past few years. In the case of British Rail, it is easy to understand that BR management have faced a massive task to win workers and the public over to the idea of privatisation. Privatisation meant the breaking up of the rail network into regions and selling them off to private operators to be run for profit. It was necessary to convince people that privatisation was not only inevitable but also an improvement. BR workers knew that both of these claims were untrue and had proved themselves, as a workforce, to be committed to taking industrial action in an effort to stop the process of sell-off and its disastrous consequences for their employment.

With the steady expansion of privatisation and the consequent reduction of workers' rights, attacks on pay and conditions, redundancies and the abolition of vital health and safety regulations, it may appear somewhat inconsistent that big, powerful companies, especially those preparing for privatisation, should adopt such pro-worker positions, especially on an 'unpopular' topic like gay rights. However, this is not necessarily so. The adoption of such policies offers a sop to workers about to be plunged into the nightmare of market forces. EOPs, which are subject to interpretation and unenforceable by law, offer an easy and cheap way of looking like a decent employer. With no extra outlay, BR can boast of its staff benefits, effectively throwing a bone to the workforce to keep it quiet whilst plans are cooked up for massive staff cuts. In this context BR management's claims sound at best hollow and at worst downright hypocritical:

> *Everyone has the right to be treated with respect and I think the message we are sending out by launching revised policies with significant amounts of support and information is that all our employees are valued and harassment has no place in British Rail.*[20]

In May 1993, two years before the date set for rail privatisation, rail workers, through two paralysing one-day strikes, forced BR management to promise to make no compulsory redundancies in the run up to privatisation. There were no promises about redundancy *after* privatisation however, no halt to the attacks on rail workers' pensions and conditions and no U-turn on the creeping new practice of employing staff on short-term contracts rather than giving them proper jobs. The announcement of the EOP can be seen as potentially divisive, implying to straight BR workers that whilst management are decimating their jobs, they are bending over backwards to give concessions to lesbians and gays. They calculate that this may pay off for them when the real fight takes place as privatisation draws nearer and workers are forced to choose whether to stick together or fall apart. The effect is to create mistrust, to separate the issue of lesbian and gay rights from other worker's rights and to place all responsibility for anti-gay harassment and prejudice on their fellow workers rather than on management itself.

The example of the BBC takes the issue of gay rights in the workplace further into a moral political context which touches on questions of nationhood, the ownership of public wealth, the family and the market. Since introducing television into Britain, the BBC had funded its productions through a licence fee payable by all households with a television. Following the 1989 Broadcasting Act, deregulation of the television industry meant that the hitherto 'public service' company was obliged to begin the reshape under a model of private enterprise. Inevitably this meant cutting costs, especially staff costs: pay and conditions were under savage attack; workers at all levels below senior management faced real wage cuts and basic benefits like sick pay were to be 'rationalised' and reduced. Staff also began to report endless examples of ridiculous red tape. In May 1994 members of the National Union of Journalists and of the broadcasting union BECTU forced their leaders to call a series of one-day stoppages. The BBC was facing massive and formidable opposition to its plans and workers were determined to stick together and fight for their common interests.

Suddenly, just two days before the first day of action was due to take place, it was reported that the BBC had decided to extend its marriage benefits to lesbian and gay couples who had undergone a formal ceremonial commitment. Such couples would receive the standard £75 voucher 'wedding present' and a week's paid "honeymoon leave'. Iain Davidson, a lighting director, had requested marriage leave following a 'confirmation of love' ceremony with his partner Scot Love. Davidson's request was initially refused but granted some five months later. (This decision followed a long campaign by workers involved in the BBC's Lesbian and Gay Group.) Tories greeted the news with disgust and outrage. They argued that the BBC licence fee should not be used for the purpose of sanctioning homosexual relationships.

The BBC responded to tabloid and Tory hysteria by withdrawing the voucher scheme from all employees, whatever their sexuality, on the first day of industrial action. The 'honeymoon leave' scheme was left in place pending a review. Scot Love explained how the BBC's move had effectively proved to be an attack on all BBC workers and showed his anger that the principle of lesbian and gay equality had been used to undermine workers' rights:

We thought our victory would mean other gay couples being treated just the same as anyone else. That was the best wedding present the BBC could have given us... [But] the BBC had folded under criticism. It has given equal rights with one hand and taken away everyone's rights with the other.[21]

The episode was clearly reported to time with the strike. For politicians and business people in favour of and about to benefit from the BBC commercialisation plans, the idea of a 'gay wedding present' offered a golden opportunity. It enabled them to appeal to homophobic ideas and promote market forces by arguing that governors at the BBC were not capable of spending public licence money responsibly. Since very few people had been aware that wedding presents were a tradition within the corporation, the episode also cast public doubt over the striking workers' case. If attacks on conditions meant removing extravagant gestures like wedding gifts then perhaps it would be a good thing to cut back on other staff benefits. TV critic John Naughton, writing in support of the strike in the *Daily Mirror*, fell into the trap of blaming the 'gay wedding present' concession on John Birt's 'political correctness' and thereby implied that such equality measures were part and parcel of the rationalisation programme!

This latest wheeze by the equal opportunities unit to bring homosexual employees into line with heterosexuals is the latest example of how out-of-touch John Birt's management style has become. But most staff will regard it as further proof of management lunacy... As they struggle to cope with Birt's hair-raising system of internal markets known as Producer Choice, the staff are bound to conclude senior management is more preoccupied with slogans that sorting out the corporation's continuing problems.[22]

The stories of British Rail and the BBC reveal themes which touch on many people's experiences. Token reforms and empty gestures are familiar to all who campaign for equality and justice. Understanding the basic conflict of interest between employers and employees means that we can begin to comprehend the reluctance of Pride organisers to identify the annual march and celebrations with the struggle for workers' rights.

Repositioning Pride

The *Pink Paper* responded to the Pride Trust's ambivalence over gay rights at work with a rare and powerful editorial which captured the mood of frustrated lesbians and gays who had always associated gay rights with political courage and resistance:

We want the most public route, past the most important institutions and monuments. We want to make our public statements about equality, age of consent, HIV and AIDS, and work rights... Gay Pride has got to be more than a car boot sale with bars ... As Martin Luther King put it, civil rights have always been won by 'an explosion from below'. Pride is the time we explode onto the streets, calling the ruling class to account.[23]

Film director Derek Jarman also added his voice to the call for a radical resuscitation of Pride:

Does the Pride Committee live in cloud-cuckoo land? To say that an equal rights policy is divisive is so foolish it leaves me gasping... Last month one gay man came to support Bart's Hospital's attempt to save its HIV unit. So where were the 40,000? Drunk in Old Compton Street. Do we really want to be just selfish hedonists? Who cares if 40,000 people have a good time for an afternoon? I don't... We really should look at our history.[24]

So, many people view with concern and foreboding the progress of the business class as it moves in on Pride. Casting round for answers and solutions they blame the Pride organisers and label their efforts a betrayal. Some even pit one capitalist against another by arguing for the interests of one bar over another in the carve-up of marquee space at the carnival. But the Pride organisers only really reflect the direction of the gay movement in society as a whole. Market forces and business practices are being inserted into all kinds of aspects of our lives which we have been brought up to expect as a public service. Cuts in education and health, privatisation of utilities and services, cutbacks on public spending—all of these things affect everyone, lesbians and gays included. How can we resist the privatisation of our liberation?

Transforming Radical Reform into Revolutionary Action

Contrary to what we hear from the New Realists, who claim that the working class is dead and that all people want are holidays abroad, video games and cable television, it is clear that the anger at injustice and oppression is very much alive and kicking. If anything oppressed people are more determined than ever to get out and get even. Direct action organisations like Outrage!, the Lesbian Avengers and ACT UP, aim to represent that anger and channel it into civil disobedience. They organise street actions aimed at forcing confrontations with homophobia. The style of the organisation is to target institutions and 'zap' them with one-off actions which expose discrimination, homophobia and hypocrisy. Many of the most effective actions have been designed to draw attention to ruling-class bigotry such as anti-gay sex education in schools, cuts in invalidity benefit for people with HIV and laws which criminalise public displays of affection between people of the same sex.

All of these actions provide an important focus for fighting homophobia. However, the lack of clear position on class and the avoidance of addressing the all important questions about where homophobia comes from means that Outrage! itself is failing to seize fully the potential for mass action. Moreover, the failure to understand class conflict between gay people leads Outrage! (and its US counterpart Queer Nation) into a series of disparate actions which lack consistency and continuity. For instance, it was Outrage! which organised the Queer Valentine's carnival in London's Old Compton Street in 1993. Derek Jarman, in his capacity as archbishop of the radical drag group the Sisters of Perpetual Indulgence, 'blessed' Soho gay businesses. This was followed by a demand by the group for the Gay Business Association to set up a permanent lesbian venue in Soho on the basis that it was sure to be 'financially viable'.[25] This kind of intervention frequently confuses and alienates potential supporters with its alternating support for gay business and complaints at the lack of radical politics on the gay scene.

Logically and laudably, Outrage! claims to follow the lead of the black civil rights activists who coordinated civil disobedience in the US in the 1960s against state-sanctioned segregation. Organised mainly through the churches, the anti-segregation campaign involved groups of activists openly defying racist laws as part of a widespread mass campaign involving black—and white—workers who understood the importance of smashing racism. The best organised and most effective activities involved thousands of people, like the Montgomery bus boycott, where people, *en masse*, refused to use segregated buses. All of these activities were underpinned by a series of mass national demonstrations where the sheer power of numbers served to intimidate the racists and also provided a basis from which angry people could build up the confidence to fight bigotry and racism in their neighbourhoods and workplaces. Quite rightly, those angry at the commercialisation of Pride understand that if a national mass demonstration becomes nothing more than a huge drunken party and spending orgy, it cannot provide any sort of basis for ordinary lesbians and gays to fight the real, everyday hazards of harassment, poverty, discrimination and violence. A safe space to party only lasts as long as the party. Once that's over, reality starts up again.

A real fightback can no longer ignore the wider struggle of workers against the tyranny of capital. We need to face the fact that we live in a society which claims to be democratic, even 'classless', but which is ruled by a class which is totally unaccountable.

The attempts of Stonewall to distance itself from the House of Commons riot were not simply the result of squeamishness on the part of the campaigners. They were the inevitable squeaks of dismay of an organisation which uses the strength of mass anger to build a campaign but then jumps back when that anger erupts into a burgeoning consciousness of class divisions. The tradition of protest, of mass demonstrations, of confronting the strong arm of the law, is a massively powerful weapon in the hands of people who are clear about who their enemies are. It is also deeply disturbing and threatening to reformists who prefer to tread carefully, making deals rather than demands.

Labour's Shame

In Britain, it is generally hoped that a Labour Government would be rather better than a Conservative one, in the same way that many Americans believed Clinton would bring better times than Reagan or Bush had. But is Labour really a vehicle for change?

There have certainly always been sincere socialists in the Labour Party, working within the system to try to curb the worst excesses of brutality carried out by the state against the poor. However, they have been able to do little other than act as a minority pressure group within the party. Often they are simply too weak to oppose the main right-wing dominated body of the party or they capitulate to the leadership. Out gay MP Chris Smith, for instance, a founder of Stonewall, has moved consistently rightwards in his progress up the party ladder. Socialists' numbers were severely depleted in the 1980s when Neil Kinnock became party leader and carried out a number of purges!

The only consistent thing about Labour has been its gradual shedding of socialist principles as it became more and more electorally unsuccessful throughout the 1980s. The Labour Party does not sell out all the time simply because it attracts hypocritical and power-hungry careerists. On the contrary there are many examples of politicians who have started out by trying to make Labour more socialist but ended up by either caving in or becoming isolated. Many of those who do compromise their beliefs, argue that this is necessary to win votes with an electorate which is racist, sexist and homophobic. The problem is that Labour never attempts to challenge these ideas for fear of losing support. It therefore ends up reinforcing such ideas.

There is a notorious example of this from the 1980s, at a time when the left's hope of standing up to the Tories through control of the town halls—municipal socialism—was fading away. The councils had failed to mount an effective fight against Tory cuts. Now their equal opportunities policies were vilified by the tabloids and then the Labour leadership.

Many lesbian and gay Labour supporters were dismayed by a letter written by a high-ranking party official in 1987.

Labour had just lost the Greenwich by-election to the centre-right Alliance candidate. Neil Kinnock's press secretary, Patricia Hewitt, wrote to a London MP: 'The lesbian and gay issue is costing us dear among the pensioners.'

Her letter was leaked to a right-wing tabloid, the *Sun*, which then used it to attack lesbian and gay rights. Many gay activists were rightly outraged. They saw Hewitt's comments as homophobic and a betrayal. But, as Noel Halifax explains, Hewitt remained quite loyal to her political interests. Her comments were not in the least bit inconsistent with the inexorable logic of parliamentary politics:

> *The Labour right, who had long wanted to ditch any support for gays, jumped on the bandwagon immediately. Hewitt was no right-wing bigot. As secretary of the National Council for Civil Liberties in the 1970s she had pushed it into taking a principled stance on discrimination against gay people. She was simply expressing particularly clearly the logic of electoral politics from which the Labour Party cannot escape: gay rights is not a vote-winner and should therefore be dropped.*
>
> *The vast majority of the Labour left made no protest over the Hewitt letter. Instead they joined in the rout. But ...concessions made to the bigots only increase their appetites. Labour's refusal to fight, given the increasingly right wing climate, made more attacks from the right inevitable. And as the attacks have become increasingly fierce, so the Labour Party has retreated further and further.*[26]

This disappointment which followed this incident has been felt by people over and over again in many countries. Reeling from draconian cuts and attacks from right-wing governments, centre-left parties are voted in on promises of reform and reinvestment. Bill Clinton promised a free health care system for all, full gay rights, abortion on demand, more public housing and an end to the grinding poverty experienced by millions of Americans. He has delivered virtually none of his promised reforms because the banks, businesses and unelected civil servants who run the economy haven't let him. The same process happens in Europe when centre-left parties like Labour are finally voted in. Labour will inevitably sell out. John Rees explains why:

> *The Labour Party is founded upon the belief that capitalism is here to stay. It was built by the trade union leaders and it shares their view that there may be an improvement here, a reform there, but there can be no thought of workers themselves taking control of society. The market is here to stay. So when the system can afford a little change, Labour may be willing to implement it. But when the system can't afford to give more, Labour acts for the system, not for the workers. Labour is a 'capitalist workers' party'—a party supported by and voted for by workers but which has no greater ambition than to run capitalism according to the system's own rules. Inevitably this means it ends up implementing anti-union laws, regressive taxes like the poll tax, and making cuts in hospitals and schools.[27]*

Lesbian and gay reformists have a close relationship with Labour and other centre-left parties in other countries, because they do not really believe that the root causes of homophobia can be got rid of. They merely seek to make the existing system a bit fairer. Labour tries to tinker with capitalism, making adjustments at the top of society, striking deals with judges, business people, civil servants, the political opposition— whoever. The protagonists at Stonewall think that change is best effected by manoeuvrings at the top of society. They hope that the deals struck will eventually filter down and gradually transform the 'ethos' of society as a whole without too much real upheaval.

This hope is false. It has no grounds in history and no prospect of becoming reality. Reformist proposals, when they are issued as isolated demands, can come to nothing more than limited concessions and grossly disappointing compromises. Time and time again lesbians and gays have been betrayed, let down and sold out by leaders and politicians. Reforms are needed. But they are needed as part and parcel of more fundamental change.

Notes

1 Figures drawn from 1993 Stonewall briefings on the age of consent.
2 *The Case for Change*, produced by the Stonewall Lobby Group Ltd, 1993.
3 *Gay Times*, August 1993.
4 Ibid.
5 Ibid.
6 *Torchebearer*, (Party Conference edition), Tory Campaign for Homosexual Equality, 1993.
7 Paul Barnes, *Pink Paper,* 13 May 1994.
8 Gary Henshaw, interviewed by the author, 1993.
9 *Capital Gay*, 6 May 1994.
10 Mike McCann interviewed by the author, 1993.
11 Gordon Lewis, interviewed by the author, 1993.
12 Ivan Massow, interviewed by the author, 1993.
13 *Capital Gay*, 25 February 1994.
14 Ibid.
15 Ibid.
16 *Capital Gay*, 4 March 1994.
17 *Pink Paper*, 9 May 1993.
18 Kim de Testre, chair of the Pride Trust, *Pink Paper*, 23 May 1993.
19 *Pink Paper*, 20 May 1994.

20 *Capital Gay*, 29 April 1994.
21 *Daily Mail*, 24 May 1994.
22 *Daily Mirror*, 24 May 1994.
23 *Pink Paper*, 6 June 1993.
24 *Pink Paper*, 30 May 1993.
25 *Pink Paper*, 16 May 1993.
26 Noel Halifax, *Gay Liberation and the Struggle for Socialism*, Bookmarks, London, 1988, p. 35.
27 John Rees, *The ABC of Socialism*, Bookmarks, London, 1994, p. 29.

7. POLICE:
THE STRONG ARM OF THE STATE

There... needs to be a forum for constructive criticism.
There's no use in just telling the police they're wrong—
someone, somewhere, has to help them get it right.
— Gay policeman Tony Murphy[1]

On Cable Street, East London in 1936, the police, much
as they tried, could not clear the 100,000 anti-fascists
from the path of Mosley's British Union of Fascists. In
Lewisham, South East London, in 1977 the anti-fascists
took on first the police and then the National Front,
smashing the Nazis off the street. Needless to say our
'freedom-loving' media condemned with ferocity the
'violent tactics' of the anti-fascists. Yet who but the
Tories and the fascists themselves would criticise the
Cable Street and Lewisham mobilisations today?
— Mark Brown[2]

One of the most significant and perilous projects of the gay
reformist lobby in the 1990s has been to enter into consultation
and liaison with the police. Perhaps this more than any other
'gay rights' issue betrays the polarised interests within the gay
community as a whole. Certainly, the frustrations and setbacks
which have accompanied all talks and deals between police
representatives and gay spokespeople have led to bitter splits
over whether 'we' should talk to the police at all.

Activists have tended to fall into one of two main camps.
On the one hand there are those who value and emphasise the
progress and improvements in relations between the police
and gay people. On the other hand there are many who argue
that lesbians and gays, as citizens, deserve an appropriate

policing service, that the police are no nearer offering anything approaching such a service and that all police consultation with the gay community is merely a PR stunt.

Both reactions—I will call them respectively 'loyalist' and 'cynical'—are understandable. Lesbian and gay people have for over 150 years suffered acute police harassment, the brutal and vindictive enforcement of homophobic laws and a widespread contempt for their rights as victims of violence and intimidation. Any improvement in police attitudes towards gay people has to be welcomed. However, many of the agreements struck between police and gay groups have been blatantly disregarded. Progress in making even tiny changes has been painfully slow. It is hard to believe that the handful of efforts by police chiefs to initiate changes are any more than devices to stop the gay community from declaring all-out war on the police. However, both the loyalist and the cynical points of view neglect to examine the central position of policing in the maintenance of an oppressive state. Because of these omissions, activists from both camps fail to engage with the mood of ordinary lesbians and gays, most of them not out, who experience hostile policing as one of many hazards in their everyday lives.

The Role of the Police in Lesbian and Gay Oppression

Homophobia, like racism and sexism, runs through the whole of society. It affects individual people's psychology but it also shapes and conditions institutions. Its perpetuation is part and parcel of capitalism's need to keep workers divided from one another through prejudice, mistrust and an artificial sense of competitiveness. Homophobic ideas also serve to uphold the ideal of the family and the imposition of 'family values' on workers, forcing them to accept the oppression of waged labour. The police play a vital role in the whole process of maintaining class control. Along with the other powerful institutions of the state—the armed forces, the judiciary, the prisons and top civil servants—they protect the interests of the ruling class, by inhibiting social protest, protecting private property, breaking strikes and facilitating scab labour and by singling out particularly vulnerable groups like black people, gays, the homeless and prostitutes for harassment and intimidation. In this way they forcibly divide sections of the working class from one another. Punitive and aggressive policing of these groups is class control in action. It is an intrinsic part of the police's core role.

Spurred on by anti-gay laws and the need to chalk up arrest quotas, the police have traditionally treated gay men as one of a number of easy targets. Police operations take many forms. Raids on known gay venues, stakeouts at 'cottages' (public toilets) and surveillance of outdoor cruising areas are common. Victimless crimes perpetrated by men who may simply be in search of companionship or sexual fulfilment are treated as serious crimes and great effort is put into ensuring that many arrests lead to conviction. Cottaging has been routinely policed through entrapment. Lesbians and gay men have been arrested for kissing or holding hands in the street, on the grounds that their behaviour is 'insulting' or 'likely to cause offence'. In the spring of 1994 four men were arrested and strip-searched in a park in Wimbledon, south London. The police were looking for condoms which could be used as evidence that the men might be about to commit a sexual offence. Not long afterwards another man was arrested outside a gay club in Manchester and held for several hours for 'stealing state property'. All he had done was to carry his boyfriend's unemployment card in his pocket.[3]

It is well known that police rarely treat sympathetically and seriously anti-gay crimes, even violent ones. There were 129 known gay murders in Britain between January 1986 and February 1994. Thirty one of those remain unsolved at the time of writing.[4] In addition, the police have been known to use information to bring charges (usually of gross indecency or underage sex) against people who report and bear witness to anti-gay crime. There have been many instances where lesbians and gays have called on the police to defend them from attack, and then found themselves being arrested on public order or indecency charges. At the Pride 94 celebration, there were at least 11 serious cases of homophobic violence; 'most of the victims complained bitterly about slow or non-existent police responses on the day'.[5] At the same event police vigilantly inspected a safer-sex stall run by Gay Men Fighting Aids and took the time to remove posters, cards and other health promotional materials because they depicted gay sexuality. This incident reveals the whole police force's priority in relation to the lesbian and gay community: to maintain an atmosphere of terror and fear amongst people who have or want to have homosexual sex.

Given this record, it is not surprising that the police command little respect or trust amongst gay people. As with racist attacks and violence against women, the number of homophobic attacks which actually take place far outnumber those that are reported. Victims are far too wary of the way they might be treated by the police, and afraid that if they complain this might lead to trouble for themselves or their loved ones. Many people who suffer homophobic attacks are not out and are afraid that if they report an incident they will be forced to 'go public'. Thus homophobia in the police and in wider society combines and interacts as part of the same oppressive system.

The Metropolitan Police, under pressure from gay community activists and leaders, initiated a scheme in selected London boroughs in 1992 to monitor anti-gay violence. In two years only 65 attacks had been reported. The police tried to use this as an excuse to abandon all monitoring of anti-gay crime. By contrast, when *Capital Gay* appealed in the summer of 1993 (following a spate of gay serial killings) for people to ring or write anonymously with details of violent incidents it received 60 replies within *three weeks*.

Liaison Initiatives and Where they Came From

The police force was formed and organised to protect the interests of capital. This became particularly evident during Margaret Thatcher's government in 1980s Britain. This was a time when workers faced great repression from a government determined to destroy workers' organisations and crush protest. The police were given a key task in this battle: their presence was needed to physically prevent and break up demonstrations and pickets. The Police and Criminal Evidence Act 1984 was passed during the year-long miners' strike. This Act gave the police the power to arrest and detain people they suspected were on their way to join demonstrations and picket-lines. The Public Order Act of the same year outlawed mass picketing and forbade secondary picketing and secondary action (the methods used by workers to support one another's struggles). At the same time Thatcher promised almost unlimited resources to the police. Thousands of officers were recruited. Methods of 'crowd control' were extended. Riot police were equipped with new military-style shields and helmets. There were threats to regularise on mainland Britain the riot control methods in customary use on the streets of Northern Ireland.

The police had new confidence and a sense of almost unlimited power. But with this increased brutality came widespread unpopularity. The people who took part in the mass campaigns which fought and defeated the Poll Tax, if they hadn't before, saw first-hand the violence and barbarism of the police. By the 1990s the police had lost credibility with huge sections of the population. The police force as a whole recognised that it faced a huge task in trying to rebuild its credibility and reputation. It therefore set about a 'soft' programme of community relations. This was the point where liaison with the lesbian and gay community really took off.

The police have always had consultation and deals with

gay business people. Though they are gay and run events and services for the lesbian and gay community, like clubs, pubs and shops, gay business people are property owners and employers. Their interests include being on good terms with the enforcers of law and order. The police have always been willing to negotiate deals over licences, and gay club-owners have often drawn on their links with the police to handle prostitutes, drug-dealers and anyone else who threatens the smooth running of their business. The gay business class are the touchstone of lesbian and gay police liaison. They provide the police with a 'way in' to talk to gay community leaders. Mike McCann of the Gay Business Association describes the origins of the first official consultative process between the gay community and the police. His account clearly indicates the aim of the business class to minimise commercial disruption by the police:

> *The Gay Business Association [GBA] was the instigator of dialogue with the police. Way back in 1986 there was a problem with a police raid on the Vauxhall Tavern [in south London]. The GBA decided this was really not on. We got together lots of groups and decided that we should go to the police and contest the action. At the same time that this was happening there was a murder [of a gay man] in Kennington Park and police found that they were being hindered by the community. People were giving them false leads because they were angry. So the police came to the GBA and said 'would we be prepared to go to the press and ask the community to at least if they didn't want to cooperate, not to hinder the investigation?'. So we said that we would be prepared to do so if we could start some dialogue about some future action.*

This offer from the GBA resulted in the very first liaison between the police and the leadership of the gay community in London. Mike McCann again:

A chap called Ian Buchan who is a very sensible practical sort of person, an inspector at the time and now a chief superintendent, agreed to set up meetings at Scotland Yard. Capital Gay were involved, the Pink Paper at various times, the Friend organisation, and we started doing human awareness courses, going to Hendon [to the police training centre], talking to new recruits. We didn't get paid to do it and it was all fairly low key. We were not getting desperately far and the Outrage! decided the whole thing should be stepped up and kicked into the political arena. From that, the London Lesbian and Gay Policing Initiative (LLGPI) was set up, with the GBA involved.[6]

The direct action group Outrage! was founded in May 1990, following the murder in Hanwell, west London, of Michael Booth. He had been kicked to death in an outdoor cruising area. By creating more high-profile publicity, Outrage! managed to capture the attention of the national press and provoke a wider debate about the methods used by the police in reaction to gay people and venues. The crucial issue of resources was placed firmly on the agenda. Why were the police spending time and money hanging around in public toilets and parks, when the real crime problem in the gay community was the violence being perpetrated against gay people themselves? Why did the police not recognise anti-gay violence as an offence and why were they not monitoring such crimes so that effective protection could be offered? By the end of that year the Metropolitan Police had agreed to have talks with LLGPI. In keeping with its policy not to have dialogue with police monitoring groups, however, it refused to permit the Gay London Police Monitoring Group (GALOP), to enter the talks.

This consultative initiative set off a catalogue of events which meant that gay community relations became one of the highest—profile policing developments in the early 1990s.

In 1991 a London-based scheme to monitor anti-gay violence was set up in four divisions of the Metropolitan Police. This was later spread to nine divisions and the policy decision was circulated as information to all forces in England and Wales. Police plans to abandon this scheme after two years were met with dismay by LLGPI, so in April 1994 Chief Inspector Roger Kember announced that computer monitoring of homophobic violence was to be introduced across the whole Metropolitan force: a new computer code HO (signifying Homophobic Offence) would enable cases to be cross-referenced. This new scheme also provided for police officers to be trained to recognise and understand homophobic violence. However, no indication was given of how long the scheme would last and what would be done with the information collected from monitoring.

Meanwhile, sexual orientation was incorporated into the Metropolitan Police's equal opportunities policy. Gay awareness sessions were included in police recruitment training. Then, guidelines were issued on the policing of public sex which ordered that cottage entrapment operations should be abandoned in favour of the use of uniformed officers and warnings published in the gay press. Gay community leaders responded by helping with a major police investigation. The Pride Committee distributed police leaflets at Pride 93 asking for people to cooperate in the hunt for gay serial killer Colin Ireland. The first gay pub police-watch, to prevent homophobic violence, was set up at Vauxhall Cross in south London.

The talks broadened. GALOP dropped the word 'monitoring' from its name and was allowed to join in the liaison process. The organisation became a referral point for the police when they needed specialist help in dealing with cases—which was often. A public debate started about police homophobia and the need to break down prejudice. The Lesbian and Gay Police Association was formed and a handful of police officers went public in the gay and national press, as well as in the professional police press.

The social/pressure group SM Gays ran an educational workshop for police and others on issues of consent in sadomasochistic sex. (This followed the imprisonment of men for having consensual SM sex in the notorious Spanner case and a police raid on a private party in Hoylandswaine, Yorkshire, where SM equipment was seized.) Lesbian and gay police liaison groups were set up in several other British cities, including Manchester and Birmingham.

The Metropolitan Police Charter, published in September 1993, stated that it would not discriminate against members of the public on the basis of their sexual orientation. Police officers began to be appointed as liaison officers with the lesbian and gay communities in several areas of London and other cities. Gay policeman Tony Murphy was given £8,100 by the Home Office to research the policing needs of lesbians and gay men in the UK. Manchester-based safer-sex project MESMAC and Manchester Metropolitan University teamed up with the Greater Manchester Police to conduct a survey into homophobic attacks in the city. In the much-touted shift away from heavy policing tactics, male prostitutes in London's Earl's Court were handed preventive letters warning them that soliciting and importuning in public places is illegal. Gay people began to achieve redress for the intimidation and harassment they had experienced. Phil Burke, a gay man in Liverpool, won a case against police for homophobic harassment. Alan Strong, a London gay man, won more than £12,000 from the Metropolitan Police in an out-of-court settlement after suing the police for unlawful arrest, false imprisonment, malicious prosecution and assault. He had been wrongfully arrested on a cottaging charge, held for four hours, beaten in his cell and denied a police doctor.[7]

However, the results of liaison were not all successful. Things began to go wrong right from the start. It was clear that entrapment operations were still going on. Raids were still being carried out. The promised warnings in the gay press about forthcoming police operations in particular areas were at best inconsistent and at worst non-existent. Gay police constable Lee Hunt was sacked for tipping off gay men about cottage surveillance. Police officers were pleading ignorance when questioned about the new anti-discrimination guidelines in court. People began to be reminded that equal opportunities policies are not always very effective.

The mixed results of police-gay community relations began to create splits amongst the groups who had been taking part in the consultative process. Outrage! and UK lesbian organisation Sappho withdrew from LLGPI late in 1993 saying that the whole process wasn't delivering and that police treatment of gay people had not substantially improved. This led Mike McCann of the GBA and Tony Murphy of the Lesbian and Gay Police Association to make public appeals for the community to retain faith in the liaison process. But by this time cynicism within the gay community boiled over into downright anger.

Divisions in the Ranks and on All Sides

The story of the raid on the Mineshaft club in Manchester indicates the severe limits of police reform. It also illustrates the interest the gay business elite retains in pursuing close liaison with the police.

In January 1994 *Police Review* proudly reported on a pioneering scheme in Manchester's 'gay village', a result of two years of liaison between the police and gay community representatives. PC Butterworth, a man 'chosen for his level-headed, no-nonsense approach and his calm easy-going manner', had been given the job of patrolling the gay village. His beat included the many gay clubs, pubs and shops in the area and his role was to reassure the gay community that their policing needs were being met. By appointing Inspector Tom Cross as lesbian and gay liaison officer for the Greater Manchester Police, the force intended to dispel its reputation as the most homophobic in the country. This reputation had been well-deserved under the aegis of ex-Chief Constable James Anderton, who had described the victims of AIDS as 'people swirling about in a human cesspit of their own making'.[8] After Anderton's retirement, a series of guidelines for policing the gay community had been drawn up. These included a procedure for acting on complaints of sexual activity in pubs and clubs. Instead of coming in on a raid, police officers were now supposed to contact liaison groups and licensees, giving them a chance to stop illegal activity and avoid police involvement.

Nevertheless, on 23 April 1994, only three months after Police Review boasted of PC Butterworth's gay village beat, police, some in uniform and others in plain clothes, swooped unexpectedly on a gay Manchester club called the Mineshaft and arrested 13 men, most of whom were clad only in their underwear. Without allowing them to dress, the police handcuffed the men and dragged them out into the freezing night. Those arrested reported that they suffered painful lacerations and open sores from the handcuffing. One man sustained lasting nerve damage. They were kept handcuffed most of the time they were kept at the police station, despite being guarded by police officers. They were not allowed to retrieve their clothes, nor were they offered any form of covering, being forced to stand around almost naked in reception and administration areas. Unsurprisingly, they endured barracking from other people who had been arrested, while police officers joined the laughing. One of the men later wrote:

> I am still in shock, I can't sleep and I have the shakes. My experience has totally changed my attitude to the police force. I will never again help any police officer, no matter how serious the situation.[9]

The Mineshaft raid revealed deep divisions within the police force. Community liaison officer Tom Cross, clearly furious at the complete disregard of the new guidelines, described the fact that the men were denied their clothes 'out of order' and called the whole incident 'a major setback'.[10] Community groups organised a demonstration against the raid. Under the banner 'Stop Wasting Time, Fight Real Crime' protesters questioned the value of the liaison initiatives. During this demonstration policemen laughed and exchanged homophobic remarks. When demonstrators began pointing at these officers and shouting 'Shame', the officers got in a car and began to drive very slowly away from the area. An eyewitness commented that this behaviour was 'deliberately provocative... It was quite clearly an attempt to provoke the crowd.'[11]

Policing Protest

Oppressed groups in society fight for their rights through social protest. When it comes to issues like the age of consent, civil rights or resisting fascism, one of the most powerful tools of protest is public demonstration: the gathering of a mass of people in the streets to show anger, defiance and determination to fight. The official role of the police, in a society where dissent is supposedly permissible, is to keep public protest 'peaceful'. In reality, the police try to disrupt protests and make them as ineffectual as possible.

The organisers of the Pride march in 1994, despite their efforts to de-politicise the event and turn it from a protest demonstration into a 'parade' still found that the police were unwilling to permit a high-profile route. Organisers and activists were furious:

Steve Cook of Outrage!, who is helping to plan the Pride march, described police plans as 'totally unacceptable'. 'The Met [Metropolitan Police] do not seem to comprehend how vital a high-profile route is for this occasion. This year is internationally recognised as a landmark in the life and history of our community, with the 25th anniversary of the Stonewall riots.'[12]

This statement is true but misses the point. Stonewall is a bleak anniversary for the police. During the 1960s the Stonewall was a gay bar in Greenwich Village—a gay area of New York. It had been routinely raided by police, to whom it had paid regular backhanders, for years. Like most of the bars it was Mafia controlled. On 27 June 1969 eight policemen raided the bar and, as usual, began to load the customers into police vans. At the station they would be questioned, searched, held pending identification and charged with anything from underage sex to dressing in drag. But on this particular night a crowd began to gather as the raid was being carried out. No longer willing to tolerate the interminable harassment, people saw what was going on and, *en masse,* decided to fight back. The crowd moved in on the police pushing them back into the bar and imprisoning them there. The customers in the police vans were then released and everyone gathered round the bar. The police inside the bar called the station for help and the 'Tactical Police Force' swiftly arrived, ready to break up the demonstration. The crowd rioted and fought the police for three nights in a row, forcing the police eventually to withdraw. Similar smaller incidents took place throughout summer 1969 and in August the militant Gay liberation Front was formed. So Stonewall and its outcome was about confronting the state, fighting it *and winning.* Gay activists can draw inspiration from this event not by merely incorporating it into a diary of social events for a commercialised gay community, but by openly reiterating the Stonewall story as a lesson in defiance, courage and victory. The riots were not planned, or routed or timetabled. No publicity was sent out, no sponsors were secured: there were no stalls or marquees or floats or maps. Ordinary people—gays, workers— organised themselves to fight and win. This event is as relevant in the 1990s as it was in the 1960s. Despite a flowering of the pink economy, despite an explosion of gay culture and despite puny attempts by the police to improve their record on gay issues, attacks on gay people and raids on gay venues are still common.

The dangers are not going to go away. World economic recession, the inevitable crisis of modern capitalism, has seen an escalation of ultra-right organisation. Nazi leaders, preying on the despair, anger and hopelessness of people desperately looking for someone to blame for their sufferings, have fostered an upsurge of racist violence on the streets. In Britain, the fascist British National Party (BNP) set up its headquarters in Welling, south-east London. This heralded a 300 per cent rise in local racist attacks and the murder of three young black people.

Gay people are also the targets of Nazi violence. A lesbian living in Tower Hamlets reported that hours after BNP member Derek Beackon won a council seat in 1993 groups of thugs were walking round yelling 'Queers out of the area'.[13] A teenage student was beaten up by six white men shouting homophobic abuse in October 1993, claiming that Beackon stood by and watched the attack.[14] In April 1994 a gay pub in Derby was graffitied with the words 'Queers Out' as well as swastikas and the letters 'BNP'. The following evening, despite the presence of a police officer stationed outside, two men were seen running away after a gallon of petrol was poured into the cellar of the pub.[15] Over a year after the arrest and conviction of Colin Ireland as the killer of five gay men in London, members of the BNP splinter group Combat 18 claimed they encouraged the killings and labelled Ireland 'the Fairy Liquidator'.

Similar threats and incidents are also being experienced in the US where a rise in racist nationalism and Christian fundamentalism is fostering an increase in anti-gay and racist violence. A group called the Christian Coalition has been coordinating campaigns in several cities and states to repeal anti-discrimination laws and equality policies. Using newspaper and television advertisements to boost their anti-gay crusade, the organisers argue that homosexuality corrupts 'moral values'. There has been a corresponding rise in violent homophobic attacks and gay sackings in the wake of their campaign.[16]

Conservatives and bigots have clearly gained confidence from the public statements of homophobic activists. In September 1993 conservative groups in Oregon called for the release of serial murderer Jeffrey Dahmer because 'all he did was kill homosexuals'.[17]

No Justice, No Peace ... and No Consultations!

The police have no interest in fighting racist or homophobic crime. They do have an interest in undermining, disrupting and breaking up all attempts by working people to fight together against oppression and exploitation. In every situation where people are prepared to stand up for their rights, the police do their best to stifle protest. At the same time they are committed to protecting the interests of the rich and powerful. If necessary, the police will not hesitate even to protect fascists whose activities effectively divert the spotlight of blame onto black people, immigrants, gays, lesbians and disabled people.

Recognising the real role of the police in society enables us, whatever our race or sexuality, to identify the common enemy we face and to recognise our own power to fight back collectively. It also frees us from the confusion brought about by the splits and frustrations of community police liaison. Any improvements in their treatment of gay people are to be welcomed. But these improvements are severely limited. On the countless occasions the police have broken their own rules, or ignored their own guidelines, they have got away with it.

Being lesbian or gay will not exonerate a police officer from institutionalised homophobia. The state requires that the police are police officers first and individuals second. A gay police officer is primarily a member of the police force. If they want to keep their jobs, then their private sensibilities must be set aside. As gay police officer 'Dave' explains:

If one of the bosses decided that a particular facility was unacceptable then steps would be taken to bring it into line. And it would not be my place to question that. If it came to the crunch then that I was involved in some kind of operation then I would do the job.[18]

If gay community leaders want to liaise with the police, their intentions will probably be sincere. At worst they may be seeking detente with local police forces in an effort to ensure trouble-free commercial enterprise. But the police will never be reformed to the point where they no longer harass gay people. Their homophobia is rooted in their intrinsic opposition to equality. Reformists and business people may shift farther and farther into negotiations with the state and its agents, but the state and its agents will never leave go of the principal means of social control and class oppression: force, ideology and profit.

Notes

1   Letter to the *Pink Paper*, 27 August 1993.
2   'The Coming Storm', *Rouge*, 15, 1994.
3   *Capital Gay*, 13 May 1994.
4   *Gay Times*, April 1994.
5   *Capital Gay*, 24 June 1994.
6   Mike McCann, interviewed by the author, 1993.
7   *Pink Paper*, 5 November 1993.
8   *Guardian*, 12 December 1986.
9   *Pink Paper*, 6 May 1994.
10   Pink Paper, 13 May 1994.
11   Ibid.
12   *Pink Paper*, 25 March 1994.
13   *Pink Paper*, 24 September 1993.
14   *Pink Paper*, 8 October 1993.

15 *Pink Paper*, 22 April 1994.

16 *Pink Paper*, 19 November 1993.

17 *Pink Paper*, 13 September 1993.

18 Duncan Campbell, 'The Bent Copper: Confessions of a Gay Policeman', *Observer Magazine*, 5 September 1993.

8. CULTURAL ACTIVISM

... art *does* have the power to save lives, and it is this very power that must be recognised, fostered and supported in every way possible. But if we are to do this, we will have to abandon the idealist conception of art. We don't need a cultural renaissance; we need cultural practices actively participating in the struggle against AIDS. We don't need to transcend the epidemic; we need to end it... Cultural activism is only now beginning; also just beginning is the recognition and support of this work by art-world institutions.[1]

—Douglas Crimp

The intelligence of millions of creators provides something infinitely superior to the most gifted individual insights.

—V.I. Lenin

By their very nature, art and culture are produced by human beings out of their social conditions. Individuals are creative in order to express something about their relationships with aspects of the world, or to examine their own responses. In this sense, culture is deeply implicated in class conflict. Across the world, liberation, reform and revolutionary movements have been accompanied by astonishing periods of cultural production. Historical moments of great social upheaval have always been accompanied by explosions of artistic activity and the evolution of new forms and genres. This is also true of periods of catastrophe such as wars, epidemics and disasters, when communities fight to resist obliteration and seek out the causes and perpetrators of their suffering. But culture is frequently also used self-consciously as a weapon of resistance, a deliberate act of subversion. Forms of culture have been implicated in politics since the very beginnings of class society. When integrated with organisation for political and social change, culture can be an irresistible touchstone of communication.

The nightmare of AIDS has inspired in the West a powerful cultural reaction which heralds a dramatic fusion of political resistance with furious creative expression. As gay writer Douglas Crimp explains (above), such creative acts of resistance are politically significant because they represent both a challenge to, and a contribution to, established cultural traditions. Culture on its own, however, cannot bring about change and social justice. It is a serious political mistake to look to culture to transform society and to substitute cultural activity for political activism. This mistake has been made frequently in the name of gay rights and AIDS activism. It is one of the key developments resulting from an explosion of commerce and the prevalence of identity politics surrounding 'homosexuality' in the 1990s. From its intensely militant political beginnings in the 1970s, the gay movement has gradually transformed into a primarily cultural or counter-cultural force. It operates within the structures of capitalism (the art market, the corporate world, the established political system) on a reformist programme to achieve a measure of equality. The present-day gay leadership does not seek a material transformation of society as a whole in order to eradicate the causes of oppression.

The transition of gay activism from the streets to the marketplace and the corridors of power has led to the development of a whole new school of culture which styles itself as 'cultural activism'. Cultural activism is based on the idea that by making challenging art we can thereby challenge and change the world. It reflects the tendency in the wider movement to embrace the dangerous strategies of reformism and attempts to bypass the material causes of gay oppression by creating a culture of resistance. Its rhetoric claims to be revolutionary. But tragically, whilst often powerful and poignant, cultural activist art displays an idealism which counters its own revolutionary aspirations.

Cultural Activism and the Creation Of Aesthetics

The prominence of cultural activism in gay political structures is connected to the predominance, in those structures, of notions of identity. The gay community is understood to be a 'counter-culture', with its own cultural references and codes. Participation in this counter-culture is rooted in a political agenda which derives from individual sexual identity. Commonality between all lesbian and gay people means sharing that sense of identity. The rejection of class interest as a basis upon which to organise has led to the proliferation of identity in an attempt to create a focal political point. Moreover, cultural activism shifts the location of crucial political activity from collectivised places where working people have power (the workplace, the estate, colleges and schools) to galleries, theatres, studios. The power of the imagination is harnessed, not as a touchpaper of collectivised action but as a substitute for it. Thus gay counter-culture, instead of engaging with class struggle, is preoccupied with cutting a path into the convention of the art market. The issues and difficulties faced by gay cultural activists are therefore centred on aesthetics, problems of representation, notions of identity and the creation of diverse cultural space. These preoccupations have come to replace more political questions about unity and resistance.

Aesthetics operate similarly to morality, promising a set of codes by which 'real art' or valued art is defined and judged, whilst other products of creativity are excluded. Certain kinds of cultural production are marginalised. The bourgeois aesthetic is necessarily 'western'. African, Aboriginal and Indian art are seen as 'ethnic' and outside recognised forms. Work which is produced without the influence of bourgeois training is seen as 'naive'. Art which breaks the bourgeois boundaries of erotic 'taste' is dismissed, even censored, as 'pornographic'. Work which exposes the secrets of the state is made illegal.

Bourgeois standards can also change and shift as they appropriate different forms and genres. What they appropriate is usually derived from innovative counter-cultures. This mirrors the fluctuations of morality. Thirty years ago unmarried heterosexual couples were often regarded as 'living in sin'. It is now considered entirely acceptable not to get married. What is acceptable in the art market follows similar patterns. For instance, the photographs of artist Delia Grace, with their graphic depictions of lesbian sexuality, were once vilified as sadomasochistic and obscene. They now represent the standard for a growing culture of lesbian photographic erotica. The counter-culture becomes absorbed into mainstream culture and newer aesthetics are developed in opposition and resistance. The process is one of patterned chaos; 'acceptability' is a movable feast and there is never any one fixed boundary. But there is a kind of logic to the way the boundaries shift—and this logic reflects contemporary concerns about democracy, community and nationality.

The Stonewall riots and the subsequent flowering of a gay liberation movement precipitated a new wave of artists who seized the opportunity of 'coming out' to create a new iconography of 'gayness'. Emerging from the shame, guilt and secrecy of the past, the new art images celebrated gay desire and asserted a small but powerful male homosexual presence on the art scene and within the art market. This new subject was fashionable, shocking and exhilaratingly erotic. The work of Andy Warhol and David Hockney, the precursors of today's cultural activists, took on a full social significance. The birth of the gay movement projected such art into the centre of the art world. It could no longer be aesthetically marginalised or dismissed. In the 1990s it is no longer shocking to see overtly homoerotic paintings, to visit plays with lesbian and gay characters in them, to read stories, novels and poems written by openly lesbian and gay people. 'Out' gay art has been, and continues to be, accepted into the mainstream. What is considered 'good' art and what is considered suitable subject matter for art within the mainstream tradition, can now include homosexuality and homosexual 'issues'.

The prevalence of identity politics in gay, black and feminist cultural activism means that mainstream culture is often framed, respectively, as 'straight' culture, 'white' culture, or 'male' culture. Mainstream culture, however, whilst often influenced by heterosexist, racist and sexist ideas and motifs, is primarily bourgeois culture, sanctioned by the establishment as a fit representative of society's development. This development is connected to the representation of a nation's mood. It does capitalism no good to hang on the walls of the national galleries work which expresses the experiences, moods and creative responses of women, men and children at the bottom of society whose everyday life is a pattern of poverty, struggle and oppression. What does the nation good is a canon, or body of approved work, which can suitably and safely express a particular version of a nation's artistic expression and will include a healthy smattering of artwork which chooses to intervene, to protest, to criticise. How much is permitted is very much to do with the confidence of the classes in conflict and the ideological ascendancy of progressive or reactionary ideas. Artists and styles go in and out of fashion. Radical forms are one year sought after, the next 'debunked'.

British art can therefore encompass the obsequious flourishes of Gainsborough and the pastoral idylls of Constable at the same time as admitting access to the iconoclasm of Bacon and Freud. More internationally, the very gayness of artists like David Hockney, Arthur Tress and Robert Mapplethorpe has become part of their acceptability because their images, like those of Bacon and Freud, can be captured by the 'art world' (which is really an 'art market') and incorporated into an established canon. They can also be reproduced and packaged commercially as an illustrative blueprint for gay culture—the visible gay presence within a nation's cultural statement. The photograph-like figurative paintings of British lesbian artist Sadie Lee have achieved unprecedented exposure. Her 'Erect', a double portrait of two rigidly upright women side by side on armless chairs, at once embracing and hold themselves apart, was used by the National Portrait Gallery in London to promote the British Petroleum Awards show. It was therefore to be seen on hoardings and underground walls all over the city. Lee herself is acutely aware of the contradictions of becoming 'known':

What I want to do is to bring lesbian art into the mainstream... When I started out I tried to present alternative role models, but now the goal posts have been moved and everything I've been trying to do is being done. What was a struggle is almost a cliche.[2]

Ultimately this kind of appropriation (the very lifeblood of the art world) can seize on challenging work and reinvent its qualities by calling them 'painterly' rather than 'political', 'expressive' rather than 'angry'. This is precisely what happened to Turner, once a cultural radical and political dissident who, in the early nineteenth century, revolutionised painting with his rebellious romanticism in the face of emergent industrialisation. Today Turner is an embodiment of conventional British art. His work is now seen as a projection of bourgeois cultural values. His protest has been submerged in and defused by the needs of corporate capitalism with its constant need for good public relations and its technique of subordinating the facts of history to the interests of the nation-state.

The Myth of the Artist

Central to the traditions of bourgeois art is the question of 'the role of the artist'. The established art world often sees the artist as working outside society, as a kind of soothsayer or commentator, not really involved in the action. Being separate, the artist can then be said to have a unique view of the world, a detached and objective position. This idea gives rise to idealist notions of art being separate from society and of culture being separate from social change.

Artists are also understood to be uniquely gifted. Only a very few are permitted art education beyond their early teenage years, if at all. Art education for working-class children is usually either non- existent or a 'soft option' for those considered to be academically weak. Consequently only a tiny minority, a privileged elite, are allowed to take on the hallowed role of 'artist' and work in the 'art world'. Their insight is forced upon us, as a crucial and perceptive commentary upon the world in which we live, as though our everyday experiences are not enough to tell us how things really are. The values of bourgeois art tell us that ordinary people see the world from a very mundane point of view and artists understand it on higher and deeper levels. To declare art to be politically neutral and transcending the seedy workings of the political sphere is to deny the close and dynamic relationship between ongoing class conflict and cultural production.

Counter-cultural movements, springing as they do from liberation or reform strategies, have challenged many of these bourgeois notions. Black art, women's art and gay art have asserted that art and society are irrevocably intertwined and that artists work *from* the position they occupy in the world, not outside of it.

British gay academic Alan Sinfield convenes an MA course entitled 'Sexual Dissidence and Cultural Change', with deliberate emphasis on locating sexuality within a cultural rather than a material framework. Sinfield enjoys the fragmentation of the lesbian and gay movement and see the divisions as being primarily related to a diversification of identities:

Sinfield talks with a sense of pride about the fractures that have emerged in the lesbian and gay community since the early, optimistic days of liberation. 'I think community is the wrong word. What we actually want is people arguing … that's what a lesbian and gay subculture should be about.[3]

He supports the idea that lesbian and gay counter-culture is a substantial basis upon which to build a movement for equality. Essentially an idealist, Sinfield thinks that sexualities studies will give rise to significant social change. He believes that the articles he writes and the ideas he formulates are in the vanguard of lesbian and gay liberation strategies. He understands that the appropriation of lesbian and gay counter-culture by mainstream cultural institutions should not be a primary political goal. However, he mistakenly retreats back into the inevitable isolation of gay cultural activism. He believes culture will change the world and knows that this won't happen if we go mainstream. The only response must therefore be to stay in the counter-culture. That way, he avoids discussing thorny political topics like economics and unity and can advocate a comfortable career structure for academic enquiry:

… It's subculture that he is happy to work within. 'It's a mistake for subordinated groups to feel they've made it when they've really made it into the mainstream… The goal is actually to have lesbian and gay intellectuals in a social role within the movement, salaried to sit around reading and talk about books, not jump through the academic hoops'.[4]

The double-bind in which left-wing or radical artists and academics find themselves illustrates one of the many contradictions within capitalism. The enforced ideological position of art, on the edges of society (or beneath the surface), means that it often leads artists and audiences to question and criticise, even rage at the system. At the same time it operates within a market which displays all of capitalism's hallmarks: competition, the drive for profit, the creation of surplus value and so on. People employed in the arts industry are also subject to the pressures which face all workers: low pay, worsening conditions, cuts in funding and the threat of redundancy. The arts environment is especially subject to the creeping control of business 'sponsorship' and consequent fears of 'frightening away' potential backers with left-wing politics or anything which challenges society's oppressive norms. Radical artists are therefore forced to engage with influences and systems which, through their work, they are attempting to reject or criticise. Caught in this dilemma and grappling with seemingly intransigent institutions leads many radical artists into cynicism. Others collapse even further and embrace the reactionary ideas of post-modernism.

Fetishising Hopelessness: From Modernism to Post-Modernism

Modernism gained currency in the early years of the twentieth century as a way of understanding and defining the cultural changes resulting from developments in capitalism. These changes reflected the establishment of the modern nation-states, the forging of imperialism, the growth of racial and national 'identities' and the development of theories of 'society'. Modernism in practice, through the paintings of Picasso, the novels of Joyce, the drama of Brecht and so on, expressed a sense of fragmentation, of things being fluid, changing fast, of not being fixed. Whilst national boundaries were being moved around according to imperialist interest, the growth of mass industry was continuing to move whole economies from the country to the city. Transport was speeding up with the introduction of motorised transport, aeroplanes and integrated rail networks. Communications were transformed with the aid of more printed newspapers and books, the telegraph and the telephone. Working-class men, then women, gained the right to vote. Work patterns changed. Contraception became accessible to ordinary people. The old order seemed to be falling apart.

Culture reflected and expressed this fluidity. Narratives were no longer 'objective' but subject to the perceptions of the narrator or author. There was a sense that everyone could have their own reality, that there may no longer be any objectivity. The process of making a work of art became the subject of the art work itself. Content, method and meaning were intertwined. Things were no longer whole but broken into parts, made up of fragments, constructed and therefore subject to deconstruction. This was reflected dramatically in the development of montage techniques in film and photography. Cubism emerged as a way of looking at and representing things as a collection of parts, rather than as an organic whole or 'body'. Surrealism reflected the growth in psychoanalysis and the discovery of the unconscious as a driving force behind social experience. Even the individual subject—'I'—was now open to question.

The themes of modernism remain at the heart of the 'post-modern condition' but all vestiges of left-wing or class politics have been eradicated. Post-modernists adhere to fragmentation, fluidity and subjectivity but dismiss any basis for or reason to try to effect social change. They claim a real break from modernism but in fact merely represent a right-wing version of it. Mistakenly, they see the shift during the 1980s in western Europe and America from mass industrial production to services, finance and the elevation of consumerism (the rise of 'design' in everyday commodities) as a signal that we are now in a completely new age which has nothing in common with previous phases of capitalism. People's identities, their methods of communication and their working practices (computer networking from home, flexi-time) now define their place in modern society. Marxism, which explains social development in terms of material and ideological change brought about by class struggle, is dismissed as obsolete and flawed. Post-modernism rejects the idea of any kind of progressive social change. Post-modernist theorists put forward their ideas in a verbal complexity which is largely unintelligible to people who do not have endless hours to devote to the interpretation of single paragraphs. Post-modernism is the embodiment of abstruseness because it has 'given up on' the real world and offers to hopeless cynics an avenue of debate which does not require much reference to the workings of the material world. Post-modernists celebrate the modernist principles of heterogeneity, plurality and fragmentation. They then go further to advocate the instability and loss of political cohesion which such fragmentation brings. They reject scornfully any analysis which could possibly explain the chaos of the modern world. Influenced by post-structuralists like Derrida, Kristeva and Foucault whose anti-realist theories have come to dominate all academic debate about language and sexuality, post-modernists even go as far as to say that there is no such thing as experience or history in the West, that we only learn about events through the media, which offers a subjective representation, a fantasy. According to post-modernism, we are now in a post-capitalist era where class struggle is non-existent. There is no point in trying to change the world because it is so amorphous it will transform itself before you have time to do anything.

Idealism In Action

The significance of post-modernism in relation to gay culture is not that gay artists and writers are post-modernist. Indeed, most radical artists, those working within a gay milieu, reject outright the extreme anti-realist stances of post-modernism. Cultural activism itself powerfully refutes the idea that there is no point in trying to change the world. Cultural activists defiantly engage with social issues and contest the propaganda of the state. But while they may reject the notion that there is no point in trying to change the world, as a whole they accept the idea that there is no longer a working class which has the power to overthrow the roots of homophobia. As a result their work reflects their acceptance of the notion of irrevocable social fragmentation in the modern world. All too often their 'radical' message is that counter-culture, in the form of art, conventional lobbying, identity politics, consumerism and small pockets of stunt-type protest, are the only sites where people can be political.

The activities of lesbian and gay radical direct action groups, with their emphasis on street wit and style, crystallise this need to shock into a fast-growing tradition of demo-cum-performance art. Outrage!, for instance, reacted to a clampdown on naturist sunbathing at Highgate men's pond in north London with a defiant nude protest. Characteristically this protest was ultra media-friendly: the gay press was filled with photographs of naked men sporting 'Outrage!' stickers on their bodies, posing as Greek sculptures amongst the trees and outhouses. It was a type of protest which would necessarily involve a very small number of people who railed against prudishness and 'those who have a phobia about male genitals'.[5]

These kinds of protest, and the groups which organise and carry them out, have little to say to the working class as a whole. The 'New Realism' of post-Marxism has been taken as gospel, almost a principle of protest. Activity is carried out on the basis of identity and from the position of cultural leadership. This has nothing to do with revolutionary organisation. The launch of the Lesbian Avengers in London (taking its objectives from the New York based group of the same name) declared itself dedicated to 'creative activism and the celebration of lesbian identity'. Printed T-shirts were worn and organiser Lynn Sutcliffe declared, paradoxically, 'The two things which are needed now are mystique and secrecy, to keep up the intrigue and get even more women involved.' It's a significant but not enormous step from such 'clique-ism' to the fatuous antics of gangs uniting around a common consumer fad. Under the heading 'Suburban style guerrillas' six 'DIKEAS' are pictured jumping for joy clad in boiler suits with logos and little dyed caps. The copy reads:

> *The IKEA catalogue is their manifesto, they're 17 strong and they're coming to a Swedish furnishing store near you... 'Dykes like IKEA and it's as simple as that,' explain Penny, who lives with fellow DIKEA member Lesley, and who boasts a sumptuous red sofa, an aluminium light shade...a set of coffee cups and a chandelier...*[6]

Obviously the DIKEAS do not pretend to change the world. But, in keeping with the identity politics of post-Marxism, they attempt to create a focus around minority consumer taste upon which to build a credible lesbian visibility. This kind of hopeless consumer politics is the logical conclusion of radical action which demands rights on the basis of consumer-citizenship.

If liberation can be achieved through identity politics and the power of consumerism, then it follows that the radical action cultural leaders will need their own team of marketing and PR consultants. Michelangelo Signorile, founder of the now defunct American radical gay magazine *Outweek*, sees his mission primarily as a PR executive and 'cultural terrorist' for the gay counter-culture. His radical solution to homophobia is to expose famous closet homosexuals through the media, especially the gay media. Operating exclusively from within a middle-class gay commercial enclave, having joined ACT UP because the recruiters were 'cute',[7] Signorile outlines a number of specious arguments to back up his theory that outing is the major contribution anyone can make to breaking down the barriers of homophobia. Signorile's book *Queer in America* argues that outing powerful closet gays will break down the stigma attached to homosexuality. At no point does he address the reality of homophobia for the majority of American lesbians and gays who stay in the closet simply to survive. The subtext is that he wishes to smooth the path for himself and his colleagues to build careers for themselves in culture and politics. His idealist logic contradicts itself but makes clear his interests in reformism and the gay market:

Clinton created an entire wave of things beyond politics just by coming in as a gay-friendly candidate. His election affected Hollywood, the media—it pushed forward a huge cultural change. And culture leads politics. I'm convinced of that. Clinton helped to create an atmosphere for American Express [who used a gay couple in an advertisement] to embrace the gay community.[8]

Individuals like Signorile and groups like Outrage! and the Lesbian Avengers have abandoned mass activity and the importance of finding a basis upon which to challenge the homophobic ideas of the working class. Questions about the causes of oppression are ignored. It is assumed that oppression is so personal and individualised that there is no common ground between gay people and their fellow students, colleagues or neighbours. So distant are they from any kind of analysis which addresses the material conditions of millions of gay people's lives that their solutions veer between pointless, misdirected haranguing and petulant shock-tactics. They miss the point that since the establishment will never bring about gay liberation, there really is very little mileage in addressing themselves exclusively to it. In many cases, the nebulous fluidity of post-modernism (instability, uncertainty, incoherence) is embraced by cultural and radical activists as a preferable option to the rigidity of, say, Tory values. This is understandable, given the overwhelmingly reformist context of virtually all gay political activity in the 1990s. But it is also a very dangerous strategy. Gay liberation is no nearer now than it was in 1968. Homophobic violence, some of it organised, is still part of the everyday life of working-class gay people who cannot buy themselves off the streets and out of the cottages. The way forward is to restore a revolutionary focus to the politics of gay liberation.

What's Wrong with Just Ranting and Raving?

A basic flaw of cultural activism is the failure to examine the material causes of homophobia. A theatre production presented in 1993-4 by the Wild Justice Company in London was a good example of cultural materialism in action—post-modernist influences and all. 'What's Wrong with Angry?' was a fringe success, soon turned into a film—and deservedly so. Set in middle-class Basingstoke it was a moving and furious exploration of the effect of the age of consent laws which criminalise teenage boys for being gay. However, its confusion about the causes of prejudice and the sources of hypocrisy meant that the message of the play was unclear and ultimately pessimistic about the possibilities of change.

The two protagonists are teenage boys at a fee-paying single-sex school who fall in love with one another. Stephen is sixteen and determined to defy taboos and experiment with sex. His surreptitious adventures lead him to cottaging and Cruising in parks and woods. He is sickened by the barrage of heterosexual propaganda and 'peer pressure' around him at school, at home and in the media. He seeks some refuge in literature and camp culture. John, his heart-throb, is a little older, the head boy at school and successful with girls. He has experienced sex with a man at a cruising ground but remains adamant that he is straight—until he falls for Stephen. The play tells the story of how their relationship is beset by the problems of parental prejudice, fear of legal redress and queerbashing by other boys. The pompous hypocrisy of their headmaster echoes that of the Tories, press and television. Stephen wants to defy the world and be true to himself whilst John desperately tries to conform, betraying and embracing Stephen by turns. Throughout the play Stephen's teacher acts as a narrator. He comments on Stephen's experiences as being an echo of his own early life when he came out onto the gay scene and experienced the excitement of a seemingly uninhibited sexual culture in the pubs and clubs of the big city. At work, though, he is firmly in the closet. He wants to support Stephen but is afraid of being professionally compromised. When Stephen is repeatedly queerbashed by his classmates, the teacher tries to get him to save his sexual openness for the commercial gay ghetto, saying 'this is where you belong too, Stephen'. His one attempt to make a stand, when he appeals to the headmaster for action against queerbashing, is a failure and results in Stephen being forcibly outed to his parents.

The play clearly represents a cultural response to gay oppression and openly engages with the issues surrounding the criminalisation of gay teenagers. Like other art works, it uses cultural forms and practices to define a political position and advocate specific reform and change. However, since (as previous chapters have described) the roots of homophobia lie in the structures and institutions of class society under capitalism, statements against gay oppression which do not address this fundamental relationship are weakened. They lack a clear focus on the causes of anti-gay violence and prejudice and sound unconvincing when proposing a solution. 'What's Wrong with Angry?' fell into this trap and its message to the gay community was ultimately one of despair. The play sees heterosexual people as inherently homophobic.

It implies that only gay people are capable of understanding that the family is not a natural way of life but a social construct propped up by the law and the media.

The leaking of identity politics into literature, theatre ad so on is signposted by a culture of despair, a landscape of isolated communities all wrapped up in oppression and having to turn in on themselves in order to survive. Lesbian and gay culture is a prime example, with its 'in-jokes', its satirical honing of what is seen as 'generic gay experience' and its disastrous conviction that only gay people have an interest in fighting homophobia. The best we can hope for, we are told, is to find a nice ghetto to escape to in the evenings.

For most of us this vision is not enough. We need real change, we want to see and imagine and work towards a society where you don't have to spend lots of money or risk arrest simply to find a bit of pleasure and companionship. A society where, whatever your sexuality, you can express it however, wherever and whenever you want to. This is a million miles from the so-called 'sexual freedom' of lesbian and gay discos, saunas and clubs. The pursuit of sex on the commercial gay scene is analogous to the ancient ties of religion. Marx wrote that religion is not simply a set of false beliefs, a collection of delusions peddled by the manipulative to the weak. He argued that religious faith, especially Christian faith, is an expression of people's real needs. Tragically, though, these real needs are distorted by class society. They are transformed in people's psyches, lives and relationships into hope for the impossible. Religion offers people something that is wildly unrealistic: an all-knowing, supernatural, omnipresent, omnipotent Being. Into this fantasy are poured the distorted needs of workers desperately seeking meaning, explanations, understanding and liberation. Christianity claims to offer real comradeship, cooperation, equality, selflessness, collective responsibility, a caring and sharing community. All these things are worthwhile goals to strive for, and important 'traditional values' of the international working class. However they are denied us by class society under capitalism. Instead of comradeship we find ourselves jealous and possessive of one another; instead of cooperating we are forced to compete—for jobs, for promotion, for shelter, for benefits; instead of collective responsibility we are drawn into blaming and scapegoating in the false hope that we can divert suffering and hardship from ourselves and our children.

Our alienation, our oppression, our obsession with identity and our invisibility are not a result of our willingness to submit. They are symptoms of the society we live in. They are the only ways we can survive if we are isolated as individuals. They are also the very means of our enslavement. That is why we have to act against the causes of gay oppression; that is why we have to unite and act on the basis of our class and not our sexual preferences. Gay people are too weak, too divided, too small in number—in short: too oppressed—to act alone. We need more than just to survive. We need to win.

Notes

1 Douglas Crimp, 'AIDS: Cultural Analysis/Cultural Activism', *October*, no. 43, winter 1987, p. 3.
2 *Pink Paper*, 2 September 1994.
3 *Pink Paper*, 19 August 1994.
4 Ibid.
5 Peter Tatchell, quoted in *Capital Gay*, 15 July 1994.
6 *Pink Paper*, 17 June 1994.
7 *Capital Gay*, 17 June 1994.
8 *Pink Paper*, 17 June 1994.

9. BISEXUALITY

At the party I met a very glamorous straight African-American woman called Troy, who walked up to me and said, 'I just lurve English men'... She was hot, she was raunchy and she scared the shit out of me. Why? Because she raised some heterosexual feelings in me that I thought had disappeared years ago. I often see women that I'm attracted to; not sexually, but aesthetically. But Troy was so beautiful that I could have spent the whole night with her. As you can imagine this threw me into a bit of a panic. It took me years to sort out my true sexual identity, and the last thing I need at this point in my life is to do a turnabout. Four days after the party I confided my worries to Michael: 'I don't know why I found Troy so attractive. I haven't felt like that about a woman for years.' Michael laughed; 'Oh Sukie! So she fooled you too!... Troy is no woman. Troy is a man. And, honey ... I don't mean part-man, I mean all-man!' Oh god, the relief, the blessed relief!

—Sukie de la Croix, letter from America[1]

Someday being a bisexual faghag will be 'in'. But first we have to get *our own look*!

—Susanna Ventura as Penny Arcade in
Bitch! Dyke! Faghag! Whore!

Bisexuals experience homophobia. Like the majority of lesbians and gay men they can be sacked, have their children taken away, lose their homes, be parted from lovers, family and friends by immigration laws, be denied benefits like pension schemes, marriage and compassionate leave. They can feel ostracised and compelled to hide their relationships. They can be abused and attacked because of their sexuality. They can be thrown out of families and denied the support and information they need. They can be arrested, criminalised and imprisoned for having consensual sex.

Despite all this, bisexual people often find little welcome within the modern lesbian and gay communities. Publications from the developing bisexual movement in Britain and the United States testify to a palpable hostility against bisexuality within the ranks of the organised lesbian and gay communities. Bisexual people are perceived as 'half-gay, half-heterosexual' and accused of having one foot in the 'enemy' camp. They are feared and excluded as part-time oppressors masquerading as 'real' gay people, hovering permanently on the point of betrayal. As a consequence, and as lesbian and gay identity has grown more and more market-orientated, the politicising of bisexuality has meant the building of a separate bisexual movement based on diverse but shared 'bisexual identity'. Looking for liberation through the politics of identity makes lasting unity an impossibility. A broader fight against the causes of homophobia and bi-phobia is needed. This chapter looks at the ways in which the question of bisexuality offers a key for understanding the meaning of sexual oppression in capitalist society. This analysis will involve a reassessment of the implications of closetry in a homophobic society where many people cannot be open about their homosexual desire, let alone their homosexual relationships. It will examine bisexual lives and bisexual politics alongside commercial lesbian and gay identities. It will ask whether the commercialisation of bisexual identity can be an option for a separate bisexual movement. It will question what is gained from the isolation of 'bisexual issues'. In this context we must be able to confront the fact that in order to be accepted within gay and lesbian circles, many people have kept silent about their own bisexual desires and practices. We can then ask how a lesbian and gay movement, which does not permit the full expression of sexual orientation, can effectively lead the fight against sexual oppression?

The Fear of Bisexualtty

Re-reading Sukie de la Croix's story of mistaken gender identity at the beginning of this chapter is a reminder of how deeply many lesbians and gay men fear bisexuality. To some extent this fear mirrors homophobia.

Homophobes fear homosexuality as a form of social cancer, invisibly undermining the moral fabric of the nation. The bigot's nightmare features homosexuals on the rampage. In this nightmare, perverts are uncontrollably sexual, infiltrating everywhere, seducing and preying upon the young. They lure vulnerable and confused individuals into the addictive vice of unnatural acts.

Similarly, lesbian and gay bi-phobia is also a fear of colonisation. Bisexuals are people who look like 'us' but aren't really 'us'. People who claim membership of 'our community', who may at this moment be standing right next to you, are not the 'real thing'. Capable of the taboo crime of voluntary sexual contact with the other sex, bisexuals pose a threat to the purity of lesbian and gay social kinship. Lesbian and gay bi-phobia is not, however, a complete mirror image of homophobia. It comes from a position of defence rather than morality. It is not about upholding the capitalist state and the interests of 'the nation', but about defending the fragile institutions of gay identity. Lesbians and gays are viciously oppressed. They are forced to defend themselves and do this in a number of ways: protest, organisation and the creation of a gay community. This gay community is centred on commerce and the marketing of gay identity and gay lifestyle. Its purpose is to create a sense of safety, an illusion of a 'nation apart', where people can take refuge from homophobia and oppression. Clubs and pubs and gay-only holidays contrive to create the illusion that gay commercial spaces are havens from prejudiced society. The drive for profit and the relationship between capital (the club owners) and labour (the people who work in them) ensure that this is far from the case. But part of the attraction of such venues is that they are places where, apparently, there is no homophobia. Gay identity politics, the mainstay of commercialised gay culture, incorporate the essential idea that anyone who is not gay or lesbian is automatically homophobic. Even if they are not apparently anti-gay, they have the potential to be. For this reason bisexuals are suspected of not being 'proper' gays or lesbians.

Sukie's story shows how suspicion deepens into fear when the bisexual interloper appears to be actually within the gay body itself. He is sexually attracted to a person he believes to be a woman, a woman who has expressed an open sexual interest in him. He describes his feelings of desire towards her as specifically 'heterosexual'. The implication is that this desire is fundamentally and substantially different from the desire he might feel for a man. Moreover, Sukie's gayness is not simply a sexual preference but a political identity in which he takes refuge. The thought of sexual contact with a woman threatens this identity, makes this refuge seems unsafe, unsealed. Fancying Troy is an unwelcome reminder that there is no such thing as a separate gay world, and, more importantly, that *there is no such thing as a gay psyche or gay biology.*

The entire international commercialised gay culture is founded upon the illusion that there is something that can be experienced as a gay world. Whilst this can accommodate people who have changed from being heterosexual to homosexual, it cannot openly tolerate those whose sexualities change from being exclusively homosexual to becoming open to the possibilities of sex with someone of the other gender. Sukie has identified himself with the gay scene: its body politic is located within his own body. If he is attracted to a woman he panics and fears a 'turnabout'. When Michael reveals that the panic was a nightmare, Sukie can wake up. Order is restored. The end is not nigh. Sukie doesn't even have to worry that he has unwittingly fallen for a male-to-female transsexual or a man who has been castrated. His desire was good, wholesome and purely homosexual.

The Cultural Cleanse

Sukie's story, entertaining and honestly written, is not an isolated incident. Mistrust of bisexuality has become an entrenched and permanent feature of mainstream lesbian and gay journalism and culture. Sue George, in her book *Women and Bisexuality*, describes how bisexual women have often been pilloried as traitors through the construction of 'lesbian identity':

> *Lesbians in particular have said that bisexual women will always retreat into a heterosexual identity when the going gets tough, wanting conventional homes for our children and a man's wage.*[2]

Bisexual activist Kate Fearnley has encountered similar fierce, moral judgements amongst gay community activists:

> *I helped to organised a Lesbian and Gay Socialist Conference, at which I insisted there should be a workshop on bisexuality ... Almost all those present glazed over at the very mention of bisexuality as if it wasn't relevant to them... One gay man I'd known for years refused to believe that I could be bisexual, because, 'they're all political cop-outs!'. Then I moved to London and got involved in the London Lesbian and Gay Centre. Another manifestation of the 'more right on than thou' syndrome struck, and bisexual groups were banned from meeting there...there was no proposal to ban individual bisexuals ('We feel that it's a phase that many people go through on their way to being lesbian or gay' said a management committee member.)*[3]

Anti-bisexual positions within the gay community add up to a fairly rigid sexual political orthodoxy. Some activists and commentators explain this as a form of gay self-protection: the gay community is under such vicious attack that it needs to close ranks, to protect itself from any potential weakness. The corporate gay world therefore needs to find powerful and effective public spokespeople who will defend gay identity. Those who identify as bisexual, rather than lesbian or gay, are simply letting the side down. An interview in *Gay Times* with Right Said Fred lead singer Richard Fairbrass links his popularity to his insistence on being identified as bisexual, rather than gay:

> *Richard called himself bisexual, and knows that the likes of you and me would only doubt this... To his credit though over the last year he's clarified his position: 'There's a lot of misunderstanding about what a bisexual is. The most common is that you've got twice as many people to screw. The other is that you're bisexual all the time and of course you're not. Sometimes you're gay and sometimes you're straight... I'm mostly gay at the moment, but I wouldn't like to think I'd never have another physical relationship with a woman.' It would be quite a coup for us if Fairbrass was simply 'gay', but his popularity is intrinsically tied up with the 'fact' of his bisexuality... It makes him more of a man rather than less of one.*[4]

The implication of this comment is clear: the interviewer believes that Richard Fairbrass is indeed 'simply gay' but won't come out and is peddling a lie that he is bisexual so that he will sell more records and have a more virile public image. What is wrong with Richard Fairbrass sleeping with women is that he's not offering the gay scene the clear-cut media image it feels it needs for promotional purposes.

As part of the launch for UK Pride 1993, a semi-erotic poster was released depicting two adults: one in make-up, dress and long black gloves, the other masculine in jeans and a Pride T-Shirt. A letter to *Capital Gay* snarled:

What exactly are we supposed to feel proud about? The erotic possibilities that exist between and man and woman? Oh right—yeah: let's hear it for the hetero-erotic love that dare not speak its name. OK, let's give them the benefit of the doubt. Let's assume that we can somehow tell that she's lesbian and he's gay. So what's this picture telling us then? Lesbians and gay men are proud because they enjoy sex with each other? ... Is this the beginning of the end for lesbian and gay affirmation?[5]

After the shouting, it was revealed that the person in the photograph who looked like a woman was a man in drag and everyone who had been disturbed by the image calmed down. But journalist Lisa Power commented:

...what if it had been a lesbian and a gay man? How much longer, in an age when only sexual honesty and self-respect will save our lives, are we going to keep on pretending that while heterosexuals constantly stray across the line, we all stick to the gay and narrow? Wasn't this year supposed to be lesbian, gay and bisexual Pride, too?[6]

When Greater London Radio launched the 'Lesbian and Gay London' magazine programme in 1993, some listeners disapproved of the presenter's bisexuality and wrote to the gay press to complain:

We were annoyed to hear that the lesbian voice of the programme was being presented by a newly out bisexual woman...a programme purporting to be lesbian and gay should, we strongly believe, have a lesbian identified voice i.e.: a woman who only fucks with other women. We also feel that having a bisexual presenter on a lesbian and gay-identified programme will prevent an honest discussion on how lesbians and gays feel about bisexuality at some future date on this programme.[7]

The main motives and reasonings behind lesbian and gay bi-phobia revolve around the essential importance of identity. The presence of bisexual people in what is perceived as 'gay space', what is mistakenly understood to be a 'gay haven', is felt as an intrusion. Bisexuals are seen to be having 'the best of both worlds', and denying their full commitment to the cause of gay liberation—which can only be fought for by pure and true gay cohorts.

The organisers of a bisexual conference in London in 1991 held a party at a well-known London gay club on the Saturday night over the conference weekend. The club manager told them that they would be allowed to party, so long as there was no 'heterosexual behaviour'. The organisers spent the evening watching the dance floor nervously, hoping that none of the conference participants would disgrace themselves and snog with someone of the other sex.

The commissioning editor of a series of lesbian and gay television programmes was approached about the possibility of making a programme about bisexuality. She declined on the grounds that the slot was 'lesbian and gay space'. The editor of a lesbian and gay newspaper neglected to report a national conference on bisexuality. His reason: 'this is a lesbian and gay paper'.[8] A gay history book, subtitled *The Making of the Lesbian and Gay Community in Britain*,[9] managed to 'document' the gay liberation movement in the UK and virtually ignore the existence of bisexual people. Power-brokers of lesbian and gay commercial identity are clearly interested in defining a 'pure' lesbian and gay culture, in keeping that culture 'clean' by holding any hint of bisexuality at arm's length.

Good Sex and Bad Sex

The delineation of homosexual *desire* as qualitatively different from homosexual sex is an idea which reaches across the left and right of gay political and cultural writing. It shores up the false ideas of identity politics by implying that there is a unique, shared sensibility which all gay people share. It provides cultural and sex activists with the political alibi that simply by having gay sex they are challenging homophobia. But everyone brought up in capitalist society is deeply affected and conditioned by ideas about gender stereotyping, whether heterosexual or homosexual. There are no gay people who are immune to this conditioning, although many people, both gay and straight, reject gender-roles on a personal level. The idea of a gay 'nation apart', though, reinforces the false political assumption that gays are separated *by their very gayness* from sex role stereotyping. It leads many radical gay activists into the trap of trying to define the difference between gay lifestyle and straight lifestyle, between gay sensibility and straight sensibility. These categories are particularly current in the reinvented gay identity politics of 'queer'.

Peter Tatchell, advocate of direct action and proponent of queer identity politics (often cast by conservative gays and straights as a rabid left-winger), argues that homophobia prevents heterosexual people from discovering their sexual potentials:

> *Hatred of lesbians and gay men screws up straights. By making heterosexuals afraid of lesbians and gay men, homophobia denies straights the joy of loving relationships with half of humanity. They deprive themselves of erotic and emotional involvement with other people solely on the ground of their gender.*[10]

Tatchell's arguments go some way to explaining the interests heterosexual people have in getting rid of homophobia. However, he does not refer to the divisiveness of anti-gay discrimination or react to the widespread nature of sexual repression under capitalism. He prefers to explain sexual politics solely in terms of interpersonal relationships and individual identities, without even attempting to look at the reasons why homophobia and sexism exist in the first place. He elaborates:

> *Some women avoid dressing too butch, or getting too physical with a woman friend... Others think twice about being overly assertive. The result is that many heterosexual women are pushed into a feminine passivity which limits their independence... Heterosexual men adopt a false exaggerated machismo... This distorts their whole personality, crushing sensitivity and tenderness and leaves many straight men emotionally frigid... Ultra machismo...is not unrelated to social problems such as rape and domestic violence as well as football hooliganism, racist attacks, vandalism and queerbashing.[11]*

Tatchell certainly pinpoints some of the devastating effects of homophobia on people's lives and relationships. However, by seeing homophobia as a cause rather than an effect of inequality, it appears that all that needs to happen is for heterosexuals to get in touch with the gay side of themselves. Then women will attain total independence and men will stop being violent. Clearly, however, this cannot happen. Women are denied independence through unequal and low pay, through having the burden of child care and housework thrust upon them by the privatisation of reproduction within the family. Men are weighed down with the imperative to earn a 'family wage', to be in control at all times and to protect and provide for their partners and children. Encouraging homophobia is one of the most vicious and repressive ways that the state maintains this ideological divide. Only through tackling the system which perpetuates and benefits from gender-roles will we really undermine the foundations of homophobia. Only in the process of struggling for a society free of sexual oppression can we dispel lesbians' and gay men's fears of bisexuality. This struggle will make redundant the survival strategy of creating a 'gay community' and of controlling that community with the ideology of lesbian and gay sexual orthodoxy.

Unsex Me Here![12]

Defensive gestures and tactics by those who run the gay media against including bisexuality within the gay community appear even more misguided and unconstructive when seen in the context of research into sexual practices and desire. Such research is showing more and more clearly that there are many lesbians and gay men who are not exclusively attracted to their own sex. Identifying as lesbian or gay is absolutely no guarantee that a person will not have, has not had or is not already having sex with someone of the other sex.

Project SIGMA, a research programme linked to South Bank University in London, produced a paper in 1990[13] which analysed through interviews the heterosexual practices of 930 homosexually active men. The paper concluded that over 60 per cent had had at least one sexual experience with a female. Of this number, 90 per cent had had vaginal intercourse. Twelve per cent of the whole group (111 men) had had sexual contacts with females in the past year and five per cent (47 men) had had sexual contacts with females in the month preceding the interview. The authors of the study commented, 'It is becoming clear that there is no straightforward relationship between self-proclaimed sexual identity and sexual behaviour.'[14]

SIGMA collaborated with *City Limits* magazine on a survey about the sexual attitudes and practices of people in London, with 472 respondents. 78 per cent of the women polled who said they were lesbian had had sex with a man at some time. Sixty-eight percent had had intercourse with a man and 12 per cent had done so in the past year. Eighteen per cent of women who said they were bisexual had not had sex with a woman compared with the 27 per cent of bisexual men who had not yet

259

had a sexual relationship with a man. Five per cent of bisexual men had not had sex with a woman. Seventeen per cent of gay men admitted to having had sex with a woman during their current gay relationship.[15]

Similar conclusions were reached in 1993 by researchers on the National Survey of Sexual Attitudes and Lifestyles, a massive study of 19,000 people in the UK. As one researcher put it:

> ...we did not ask people if they identified with particular labels such as gay, straight or bisexual—we just asked them about their sexual history. The findings really blow the whole idea of having separate homosexual and heterosexual boxes apart—from our results that is clearly not the case.[16]

Peer pressure from inside the gay community may prevent them from speaking about it, may make them feel ashamed and guilty about it, but many lesbians and gays have fantasies about sex with one another. Some of them—an unknown number because no research has been carried out—act on these fantasies. Occasionally, research carried out to gather data on safer sex reveals the reality behind the myths of sexual orthodoxy. The *Rouge* Sex Survey, for instance, carried out by the magazine in 1993, found that a significant number of the lesbians who replied had had or were still having sexual relationships with men. The results of a survey by the Harvard Medical School and Maryland's Centre of Public Health Policies published in 1994 discovered that less than one per cent of men had exclusively gay relationships. Bisexual writers and activists have gathered substantial anecdotal evidence to show that whilst it is a taboo subject, there are many lesbians and gays who covertly fantasise about and pursue sexual relationships with each other. Jo Eadie, a bisexual writer and academic, relates some examples he has found of people whose sexuality has changed over time:

> It was 1989 and she was the university lesbian and gay officer, but she and a gay man had just fallen in love with

each other and were trying to decide what this meant. It wasn't something they could ask their friends for help with. It was 1990 and he was giving a workshop for bisexual men: 'I was going to talk to you about how we in the gay community feel about you and what our complaints are. But since I offered this workshop I've fallen in love with a woman so now I'm a bit confused.'

He comments:

For me, these ambiguities speak clearly of the inadequacy of existing categories for sexuality. The assumption that people will settle as either gay or straight—will one day come down off the fence and pitch their tent on one side or the other—simply doesn't fit the reality of most people's lives.[17]

Jan Clausen, for many years a prominent lesbian writer and acivist, describes in the US gay magazine *OUT/LOOK* her own unexpected relationship with a man and the effect this had on her honed 'lesbian identity' and her friendships within the lesbian and gay community. She admits to having previously used her lesbian sexuality as a defence against unity and her words attest to a dangerous link between right-wing essentialist moralism and the irrational belief in lesbian and gay sensibility:

...I believed, along with most of my friends, that our lesbian way of life was superior to even the best of heterosexual arrangements. Although I'd never been a separatist, and had long been critical of essentialist thinking, I also harboured what I would have admitted to be the rationally untenable conviction that lesbians themselves were politically and even morally superior to other people—more 'evolved', if you will... Why would I ever choose a man, when the world is full of women?[18]

261

Clausen goes on to describe how, after a 12-year relationship with a woman, on a trip to Central America and away from the codes and ethics of her usual lesbian milieu, she fell in love with a man. Shocked by this turn of events, she realises that the lifestyle-based identity politics of the lesbian-feminist coterie she inhabited simply cannot cope with or tolerate this development:

> *I felt the need of a zone of experience off-limits to instant political critique...unequivocally in the realm of private life, an exquisite relief to me after years of feeling like a walking revolutionary project.*[19]

In a community where it is essential to live your politics through the sexual rejection of men, her sex with a man is a profound taboo. Thinking it through on her return she anticipates ostracism from other lesbians, but she also finds that her own experience is far from isolated:

> *Reactions from other lesbians run the gamut from a curiosity that seems to border on mild envy of my daring to the rigid rejection of my nightmares... Overnight I seem to have become the repository of heterosexual confessions, the occasion for articulating thoughts about areas of their lives that lesbians don't frequently discuss with one another.*[20]

Clausen's article encourages the diehards of identity politics to stop the internal moralising and look outwards at the real threats from homophobia. The letters page in the following issue of *OUT/LOOK* was full of reaction to Clausen's article—almost equally divided between 'for' and 'against'. Those supporting the publication of the controversial article range from genuine relief ('...it was obviously designed with me in mind...I feel much less alone now') and reaffirmation against 'political correctitude' to an appreciation of how 'it...is a powerful statement against the oppressions placed upon us by others, and those we place on ourselves'. By contrast, those who dislike the article express nothing less than heterophobic attitudes towards other-sex relationships: 'I do not get *OUT/LOOK* to read about how wonderful heterosexual fucking is', 'Jan Clausen can rationalise her "interesting condition" until she is blue in the cunt', 'women like Jan Clausen...present a danger to the lesbian community far greater than any threat by a homophobe'. One letter prescribes complete separatism for such dysfunction and advises the lesbians working on *OUT/LOOK* to leave and form another magazine away from men, threatening: 'Betrayal of faith is costly. It will be costly to you.' The writer of this letter signs off chillingly with the phrase: 'I'm your conscience.'

Three women who contributed to an article on lesbians who are 'erotically involved with gay men' in British sex-culture journal *Body Politic*, spoke freely but only under the guise of pseudonyms. Their stories and fantasies attest to the absolute constraint of lesbian and gay 'purity' and the need that many lesbians and gays feel to experiment, to express their love, affection and friendship for one another in a way that is not 'socially acceptable' on the gay scene or in the gay community:

> *I think the majority of men friends see me as a lesbian which increases the gulf between us... maybe they prefer to think of me as a lesbian because it's safer—Anna;*
> *Recently I was out with Bill, a close gay friend. He kept pointing out women and saying 'Oh what about her for you, she's really attractive'. He was really excited. Why was he so anxious that I get off with these women he fancied?'—Sandy[21]*

Discussion in the article clearly marks out the inward effects of women's sexual oppression as being crucial to the sexual divisions between lesbians and gay men. It appears that the potential for a communicative chasm between women and men continues whatever sexual enclave we find ourselves in.

Describing her sexual fantasies, 'Hilary's' interest in gay men's sex is less a form of envy than a recognition of the boundaries forced on women by the rigid divisions of sexism and an attempt to express a need to break those boundaries:

> I've had sex with men who are having relationships with other men, who go to gay places... Gay male sex is really exciting. The taboo areas that a lot of straight people and women have around the body, like the anus or certain acts, don't exist. I'd like to be a gay man, just for a little while, to have sex as a gay man... Lesbians and gay men sleep together but it's still very underground... I suppose occasionally barriers between individuals are being broken down but certainly not women's oppression...there could be a sexual environment there which sees sex in terms of emotional, sexual or physical attraction rather than gender.

The narrative voice in the article articulates the deep sense of dislocation between the conventions of gay protocol and the suppressed energies of transgender gay sexual desire:

> How can I break through his fear when I can't break through my own? Are the lessons of liberation we have learnt with our own sex to become another wall of silence to prevent us from loving each other? What are our (homo) sexualities while we love one another?—Narrator[22]

These examples and extracts point to the very real dangers of identity politics. If political and social change is dependent upon building identities around which to organise then we are in serious trouble. *Identity is not fixed*—but identity politics seek to make it so. This does not just mean that many people hide their sexualities, but that a whole movement for change is based upon dishonesty and has built into it a constitutional inability to recognise that desire cannot be subject to any form of orthodoxy, be it mainstream or 'alternative'. Identity politics are a result of radicalism being bought up by consumerism. They do not present a threat to the state or the status quo and serve to divide rather than unite.

Sex in Capitalism

Not only are people's sexual identities unfixed in the sense that they are often not as exclusive as they appear, they are also variable in terms of time and personal development. Preferences and tendencies change during a person's lifetime. Someone may live a heterosexual life while all their sexual fantasies are homosexual. Another may be an out gay person but fantasise secretly about 'straight' sex. Many more will change their behaviour, their desires, fantasies and sexual tastes as they grow, change and develop. Emotional ties may be tightly or loosely connected with sexual desires. A person's sexual life may be completely divorced from their social life. Circumstances may open up new possibilities or close down potential experiences. Changes in society's ideas will affect people's expectations and aspirations.

In the 1950s, the American sexologist Alfred Kinsey produced two reports—one on male sexuality and one on female sexuality. One of his major contributions was to devise a scale from 0 (exclusively heterosexual) to 6 (exclusively homosexual) and note that the majority of people—whatever their beliefs or lifestyles, class, gender, race or social background, fitted somewhere in the middle. In other words, more people are potentially or actually *bisexual* (with tendencies towards or away from heterosexuality/ homosexuality) than *monosexual*. Although it was a radical challenge to conservative sexology, which collected all theories around the supposition that homosexuality was a minority disorder, the Kinsey model still contained elements of fixity. Kinsey calculated sexuality as something inherent and more or less unchanging. In other words, sexual orientation and identity came before sexual practice. This remained the most flexible and liberal analysis in science until the 1980s. Then, in 1985, American psychiatrist Fritz Klein developed a 'Sexual Orientation Grid' which measures sexual preference on a scale of 1 to 7.[23] His interviewees and questionnaire respondents describe various aspects of their lives, such as sexual fantasies, sexual attraction, sexual behaviour, emotional preference and self-identification, in terms of this scale. The scale ranges through the following variations:

1. - heterosexual only
2. - heterosexual mostly
3. - heterosexual somewhat
4. - heterosexual/homosexual equally
5. - homosexual somewhat
6. - homosexual mostly
7. - homosexual only

This grid model enables researchers to document the many different ways that people respond sexually. It can also be applied to different stages in life, such as childhood, adolescence, middle age, old age etc. to create a changing picture of dynamic sexuality in every individual. It goes some way to explaining how sexuality has different meanings and functions in different aspects of people's lives. However, it remains for socialists and sexual liberationists to face the political challenge of these findings and fuse the theory with real action.

People do not always act on their fantasies. Neither do they always find that their sexual partners are the people they love the best. They may embrace a fixed sexual identity (straight, lesbian, gay, bisexual) but this may not correspond to their actual behaviour. They may live in a recognised heterosexual family unit and score 1 on 'lifestyle' but emotionally and sexually they may rate a consistent scale 6. The Klein grid throws the question of sexual identity onto a more complex and challenging level. It certainly throws out a radical challenge to conservative moralists who seek to censor and crush discussion about sexuality which makes heterosexuality 'good' and homosexuality 'bad'. It also makes a nonsense of lesbian and gay activism which refuses to acknowledge as a political priority the reality of bisexuality across all sections of society and all cultures.

Capitalism rests upon the foundations of a rigid and exploitative class society where the majority create wealth for a minority and where the driving motive for all production is the drive for profit. This system breeds sexual repression and distortion. Even those of us who have resisted and survived the barrage of anti-gay propaganda to the extent that we come out as lesbian, gay or bisexual, are subject to the insidious effects of sexual repression. Censorship, discrimination, guilt (through religion, sexual orthodoxy and morality), commercialisation and advertising reach into our relationships, our minds and our beds, shaping and conditioning the quality of our sexual expression. Realising our sexual potential is often not a priority because we have other, more pressing things to do like paying the rent and buying food. Even when we do want to explore our sexual potentials the fact that this is a struggle is proof of the repression and limitations around us. One thing is sure. The pressures of poverty, of working long hours, of child care, of debt, the claustrophobia of poor housing, the restless exhaustion of homelessness, the fears of pregnancy and the debilitation of occupational ill-health make it much more difficult for working-class people to even begin to explore, investigate and experiment with their sexual potentials.

The Bisexual Movement: Where Now?

Bisexual identity is not universally surrounded in secrecy, silence and fear. There is in Europe, and more prominently in the United

States, a growing bisexual civil rights and cultural movement. Appropriately enough, this movement's main tenet is 'diversity'. Recognising the fluidity of sexual practice and desire is at the core of bisexual politics. Jo Eadie comments ironically on this political principle.

> *A gay SM leatherman who fantasises about vanila sex with straight women—where's he going to feel at home? Well, he might just feel at home in the bisexual community where, as if all postmodernism's dreams had come true, pagan transsexual lesbians share coffee with married businessmen who haven't yet come out to their wives... The bisexual community is so extensively made up of exiles from other worlds, scarred by lesbian, gay and straight intolerance, that respect for diversity has become almost, so predictably, an orthodoxy.*[24]

Clearly the danger is a clustering of commercial values around the notion of 'diversity' as the basis of bisexuality identity. This will leave the way open for marketing to a perceived, shared 'bisexual identity' which will inevitably make a doomed attempt to cut across class divisions.

Whilst many bisexual activists participate in the struggle for gay liberation, there is a distinct separation between what are considered 'gay issues' and what are considered 'bisexual issues'. Leaders of the bisexual contingent are preoccupied by the exposure of bi-phobia—both within and outside of the lesbian and gay communities. The bisexual movement aims to provide an organisational base for bisexual people who have been sidelined in lesbian and gay reform work. Most valuably, the bisexual movement goes some way to pulling bisexuality out of the purely private space of the family—or the 'pretended family'. It relocates the notion and experience of polysexuality out of the home and the bedroom, the cottage and the cruising-ground, to the outside world through political organisation, conferences and meetings. Some bisexual activists are openly participating in the direct action wings of the gay reform movement, taking part in demonstrations and 'zaps' organised by ACT UP, Outrage!, the Lesbian Avengers and Queer Nation. Others are concentrating on creating a culture of bisexual visibility, especially through publishing and the media. Jo Eadie identifies four main areas of bisexual political activism which form the basis of the international movement: 'autonomous resource development, visibility, reunification with lesbian and gay communities and anti-oppressive practice'.[25] Examining these four specified sites of activism leads to some fundamental questions about the real route to sexual liberation for everyone.

'Autonomous resource development' means creating spaces where bisexual politics can develop. Scheduling conferences, starting up local support groups, publishing books and magazines and opening community centres all constitute 'resource development'. Though scant, these resources operate locally, nationally and internationally as a network linking bisexual individuals. The 12th National Bisexual Conference in the UK reflected this emphasis on mutual personal support.

The political agenda of the international bisexual conference network, whilst still heavily weighted in favour of New-Ageism and the creation of alternative lifestyles, does display an increasing awareness of the fact that pressing issues like racism, health care and attacks on workers' rights are relevant to bisexual people. On a smaller scale than lesbian and gay organisation, the bisexual community is becoming visibly polarised over questions about fighting back. This polarisation is rooted in a dilemma over the crucial question of sexual liberation and how best to achieve it. A press release from the 1994 UK conference in Edinburgh, headed 'Bisexual Conference Hears Calls for Greater Co-operation with Lesbian and Gay Movement', led with a statement of unity: lesbian, gay and bisexual people would march together against the draconian Criminal Justice Bill.[26] At both the Edinburgh conference, and one in New York

Celebrating Bisexuality, isolated attempts to engage the bisexual agenda with the primary concerns of workers in the 1990s were seen in discussions on racism, the workplace, the fight against AIDS and domestic violence. For the most part, though, these issues were swamped by abstractions and ever-more distilled identity politics. Intellectuals and academics found theoretical solace in sessions on 'Polymorphus Perversity', 'Ethical Principles of Bisexuality' and 'Desire and Embodiment: Encouraging the Core Meanings of Bisexuality'. Those seeking deeper political fragmentation found it in 'Being Jewish and Bisexual', 'Black Bisexuality (Without Politics)' and 'Bi and Large'.

Jo Eadie's second category, 'visibility', is closely connected to the process of resource development. The bisexual movement aims to promote a level of public awareness of 'bisexual issues'. On one level, this can be no bad thing. Forcing bisexuality out into the public arena and the gay media is clearly essential in the fight against the spread of HIV and the development of sexual politics. However, the limitations of single issue campaigning are evident in attempts to create public awareness around specifically bisexual issues. Putting up posters and stickers and writing letters to the press have their place, and it's an important one, in the building of political organisation. However, they cannot be effective outside of a programme of activity which ties in with people's fundamental experiences of alienation, of isolation, oppression and exploitation. The aim of visibility campaigning is to make bisexuals visible 'to those who don't know we exist, or think we don't matter'.[27] Like the protagonists of gay identity politics, bisexual activists are whole-heartedly embracing the language of 'them and us', effectively bypassing the real challenge of bisexuality to the state and the status quo. Slogans like 'bisexual pride' celebrate bisexuality but do little to uncover the hidden aspects of human sexuality needs and desires which are repressed by life under capitalism.

'Reunification with the lesbian and gay communities' means reframing the term 'lesbian and gay' to include the word 'bisexual'. This would not only unify lesbians, gays and bisexuals, but it would also be a step towards admitting that bisexual people are within the lesbian and gay community anyway. In that limited sense, merging 'bisexual' and 'gay' is a blow against separatism and can only be welcomed. However, without bringing with it a revolutionary agenda, the bisexual movement has *little to offer a lesbian and gay movement already entrenched in reformism and commercial identities*. The point is not whether the two should or could work together, but that no one, outside of the ruling class, benefits from gay oppression and discrimination. The sexual liberation movement needs to move in the direction of the interests of the entire working class, whatever its sexualities—actual or potential.

'Anti-oppressive practices' like Equal Opportunities Policies (EOPs), represent the defeats of the 1980s when rank and file activists temporarily lost the confidence to fight for sexual liberation as part of a broad class agenda resisting exploitation and oppression. Radical ideas about women's liberation, the fight against racism and homophobia were not completely lost. Instead they went upstairs to executive level. It was now up to union executives and managers in local authorities to resist prejudice by formulating and implementing anti-discrimination policies. Tragically, these measures hid the continuing use of racism, sexism and homophobia to divide and rule workers. Complicated statements about 'privilege' and 'heterosexism', 'ethnocentrism' and 'pluralism' were issued to pacify the activists, some of whom moved into managerial or supervisory positions. Wide open to ridicule from the right and accusations of 'loony leftism' and 'political correctness', these developments also left women, gays and black people still vulnerable to victimisation and harassment. The anti-oppressive practices of EOPs did nothing to alter the fundamental strategic divisions of low pay, job insecurity and deteriorating working conditions.

The bisexual movement contains many activists who are determined to change society and eliminate the hypocrisy

271

surrounding all expressions of sexuality. The majority consider themselves to be left-wing and will have no truck with moralists or conservatives. They may find themselves worrying over the internal divisions which are coming to the surface and the high turnover of committed activists. Even the eternal debates over language reform and terminology signal an underlying divergence of political opinion about priorities and vested interests. The danger is that these activists will begin to form a radical reformist wing without considering the need for a revolutionary approach to sexual liberation. They may join forces with the gay direct-action cliques and dissipate their energy in stunts which grab the headlines but do little to expose the causes of oppression and discrimination.

The problem with creating a bisexual community is that it by its very nature it will exclude those who need it most. The challenge is to link issues surrounding bisexuality to broader questions of sex, class and social change. By doing this, we will transform the fight for sexual liberation. The sense of marginalisation will disappear and the real potentials of human sexuality will be made visible. The need for real freedom at work, at home, on the streets and in our relationships will then be revealed. This need is at the heart of our common aims and our common struggle.

Notes

1   *Pink Paper*, 23 July 1993.
2   Sue George, *Women and Bisexuality*, Scarlet Press, London, 1993, p. 21.
3   Kate Fearnley, 'Bisexuality' in *Bisexual Lives*, Off Pink Publishing, London, 1988.
4   *Gay Times*, May 1993.
5   Letter to *Capital Gay* from P. Scott, 18 June 1993.
6   Lisa Power, 'Diary', *Pink Paper*, 2 July 1993.

7 Letter from 'lesbian-identified Joan and Dee', *Pink Paper*, 30 July 1993.

8 Anecdotes given in confidence by bisexual activists.

9 *Stonewall 25: The Making of the Lesbian and Gay Community in Britain*, eds Emma Healey and Angela Mason, Virago Press, London, 1994.

10 Peter Tatchell, 'Realising Your Potential', *Pink Paper*, 18 February 1994.

11 Ibid.

12 Lady Macbeth:
> *Come, you spirits*
> *That tend on mortal thoughts, unsex me here*
> *And fill me from the crown to the toe topful*
> *Of direst cruelty!*

Macbeth I.v. 40-3.

13 "Heterosexual behaviour in a large cohort of homosexually active men in England and Wales', P. Weatherburn et al., *AIDS Care*, vol. 2, no. 4, 1990.

14 Ibid.

15 Published in *City Limits*, no. 508, 1991.

16 Kaye Wellings of the National Survey of Sexual Attitudes and Lifestyles interviewed in *Pink Paper*, 19 November 1993.

17 Jo Eadie, "We should be there bi now', *Rouge* 12,1993.

18 Jan Clausen, 'My Interesting Condition', in *Out/Look,* winter 1990, New York.

19 Ibid.

20 Ibid.

21 Nicola Field, 'Basic Instincts', in *Body Politic*, 3, London, 1993.

22 Ibid.

23 F Klein and T Wolf, *Two Lives to Lead: Bisexuality in Men and Women*, Harrington Park Press, New York, 1985.

24 Jo Eadie, 'We should be there bi now'.

25 Ibid.

26 Roberta Wedge, September 1994.
27 Jo Eadie, 'We should be there bi now'.

10. Class Struggle: Breaking Barriers

Imagine a mass demonstration of working people against lesbian and gay oppression. Nurses marching down Whitehall or up to the White House, their caps gleaming in the sun. Building workers carrying hammers, hods and gay banners. Firefighters and ambulance workers donning their uniforms out of hours to demand an end to homophobic and racist immigration laws. Bank clerks and cashiers, carrying placards blaring: Equal Rights Now! Shop workers and fast-food counter assistants using their one day off at the weekend to shout their contempt for a state which intervenes in consensual sexual relationships. Painters and decorators, milk van drivers, posties, teachers, cleaners—all chanting in unison for an immediate end to the AIDS crisis and increased universal benefits for those already sick. Miners in crash hats, their arms around car manufacturing workers covered in oil and furious about government sexual hypocrisy. A mass of white coats mingling together: doctors, laboratory workers, kitchen staff and dental assistants. Everyone yelling their derision at police who stand on the sidelines protecting the interests of the bosses, the politicians and the financiers.

It all sounds too good to ever be possible. It sounds like a revolution, a dream. But anyone who has ever taken part in a lesbian and gay rights march has indeed walked alongside those nurses, builders, teachers, shop assistants, bank workers and the rest. This is because the vast majority of lesbian and gay people fighting and resisting gay oppression are ordinary working people. They have one fundamental and important thing in common—regardless of sexual preference, gender, racial or cultural background. This is that they collectively create wealth through the work they do. This wealth goes straight into the pockets of those who employ us, own our homes, cut funding for our schools and hospitals and run society for their own benefit. Working people—whatever their lifestyle or sexuality—share an overriding common interest in resisting, fighting and ultimately overthrowing this elite. Every time a hospital is saved, a sacked worker reinstated or a racist or homophobic law defied, it is one more victory for our side, one more blow against regulation, oppression and exploitation. Every time a nursery is kept open, an estate launderette is won or a subsidised canteen is saved, people trapped in the privatised nightmare of the family are able to break out a bit further. This is why the ongoing war between those who have to work and those who reap the rewards is inseparable from the fight for gay liberation. Class struggle and gay resistance are part of the same battle.

Separation

Demonstrating as lesbians and gay men, many of us would not dare to wear our working clothes. We may be afraid of being recognised, of facing repercussions at work where we are isolated and alone. Many of us also feel that the clothes we have to wear to work are a far cry from the clothes we like to wear to express ourselves. The fact that most lesbians and gays wear their party clothes when they march for gay rights illustrates the sharp separation of our working life from our sexual identity. Indeed, when we go on gay pride celebrations, we are often able to do little more than consume and display. We are visible in a crowd but we remain largely invisible in our daily lives. The sense of strength and solidarity that comes with marching and mingling as part of a mass of gay people is therefore a welcome relief from the isolation of everyday life. When we march we say that this is the one day of the year that belongs to 'us'. However, it is impossible to sustain this sense of political power once the carnival is over. Re-aligning gay resistance and recognising its crucial role within the wider struggle against exploitation and poverty means being a lot more radical. It means demanding our rights to be ourselves, everyday and everywhere: at home, in the street and in the workplace.

Lesbian and gay oppression is one of the most powerful weapons used by the ruling class against workers. Its power is twofold. Firstly, sexual regulation is an essential part of class control. Capitalism requires the maintenance of the family at the heart of working class life. Neither men nor women can be permitted full expression of their sexuality or any other aspect of their creativity as this will detract from their primary roles as carers, providers and workers. Although the realities of mass unemployment and women's work outside the home mean that gender roles rarely match people's real experience, such is the power of the 'heterosexual norm' in society that any other relationship is regarded as 'alternative', unconventional, undesirable or downright dangerous. This leads to the second warhead of gay oppression: prejudice. Sexual regulation imposes restrictions, taboos and punishments. It also fosters prejudice and ignorance. It makes homosexuality something to be pitied, loathed, feared or denied. The curse of 'abnormality' is evidence that working-class homosexuality is a direct threat to the political order. Not only are lesbian and gay rights first and foremost political issues, but they are integral to the international politics of class.

The scenario described at the beginning of this chapter seems idealistic because it is widely believed that the working class is incorrigibly sexist, racist and homophobic. The working class has been written off as powerless in the fight against oppression. Instead, we have all been divided off into identity boxes, ostensibly to fight the oppression we know most about. Class is not dismissed as completely irrelevant but reduced in importance. Those who wish to unite on the basis of identity believe that women, black people, lesbians and gays have common interests which stretch across barriers of class. They believe that gay oppression is experienced in common by homosexuals

277

from all strata of society. But it is the very structure of class society that lies at the root of our oppression. All the theories of identity and all the posturings of post-Marxism cannot bypass this simple but crucial fact. Those of us experiencing first-hand the brutal and insidious effects of homophobia desperately seek respite from victimisation and oppression. Unfortunately we will never attain this peace whilst the underlying conflict—class conflict—rages on.

Workers and oppressed people are under attack around the world. These attacks have given bosses and rulers a sense of advantage. Our side has been on the defensive. However, the tide is now turning. More and more groups of workers are being forced to take action. Those of us fighting for sexual liberation must seize this opportunity. Identity politics may have fragmented the resistance but the willingness to fight is still there. It needs to be strengthened.

The very use of the term 'class struggle' is a real stumbling block to many gay activists who want to change society. They see homophobia as insurmountable and regard class organisation as being dominated by macho white men with no commitment to equality. They have seen many strikes ending in defeat for workers. They may even see industrial action as brave but doomed, a defiant gesture of confrontation. All these misgivings result from the defeats of the 1980s when organised resistance seemed to fall apart. In addition, what if working people turn out to be just as oppressive and prejudiced as the ruling class is now? Won't we have jumped out of the frying pan into the fire?

Division And Unity

The ideological compulsion surrounding the family and heterosexuality mean that most of us never get the chance fully to explore our sexualities. Gender roles cause us to harbour feelings of inadequacy and to try to prove ourselves through our behaviour or our appearance. Long working hours mean that we are prevented from really expressing or even discovering our potential skills and talents. The skills and abilities that we do develop in this society are never valued or respected by the people who employ us, so we battle every day against feelings of inferiority and worthlessness. Our parents and teachers are so overworked and underpaid that they frequently overlook our needs and feelings. As children we are systematically trained to recognise and never challenge authority. Morality, ever present through the institutions of class control, teaches us to feel disgust at our own thoughts and fantasies. We are often on the look-out for ways of attaining worth. In spite of all these setbacks we still explore, resist, fight and defy. But such acts are characteristics of the working class as it is at the moment. What will we be able to achieve when we have freed ourselves from the economic and social slavery which imprisons us now? What will be our major concerns when we no longer have to graft every day just to pay the bills? If we look closely at what happens to workers' consciousness and confidence when they do fight back, we can get some hint of the potential within us all to participate in the building of a new and better kind of society.

Workers may not necessarily be the most oppressed people. The unemployed, poor drug users, prisoners, students, the old, the disabled, those in psychiatric institutions and many others are on the real sharp end of the despair which characterises class society. They can fight, and frequently do. But they can be vulnerable, especially when fighting alone. Workers, however, have real power. Without their labour, capitalism cannot function. When workers act, the system comes to a grinding halt. Trains don't run, banks stay closed, schools are shut, electricity is cut off, offices lie dormant. A campaign to stop the building of a new motorway, for instance, can result in a confrontation between groups of protesters and the police. However, the campaign is much more effective when the road builders, firefighters and engineering workers involved in the construction of the motorway are involved. They can stop the road being built. They can prevent the police from removing the protesters. Workers' action is the powerful key to success. This is when the bosses lose money, big money. This is when the balance is shifted in our favour—and it often happens overnight. Workers suddenly become aware of their power and potential. They look way beyond the narrow horizons of a day's pay and are open to a whole new set of ideas. The challenge of uniting, of persuading other workers to show solidarity, throws up all kinds of issues. For sexual liberationists this is the most incredible opportunity. We need to be there, arguing for a completely different kind of society.

Class struggle isn't just about going on strike and standing on picket lines although these remain two of the most powerful weapons that workers hold. The struggle is about defending working-class interests. This means protesting against hospital closures and cuts in health care. It means demanding more and better HIV services. It means defending schools and nurseries against 'rationalisation' and 'market forces'. It means opposing privatisation whenever we can. It has to include rejecting cuts in education and nursery provision and demanding decent housing for everyone. It includes opposition to anti-gay legislation which seeks to inhibit the sexual freedom of ordinary people. It means opposing all immigration controls and laws which prevent workers from seeking refuge and asylum and stop people who love one another from being together. Class struggle almost always brings with it a confrontation with the police and other agents of the state. Throughout these struggles and campaigns, it is possible to identify a common enemy and a common ally. The common enemy is the politician, the manager, the factory owner, the police officer. The common ally is the person standing next to us who is threatened by the cuts, the laws and the sackings. When workers recognise this, they can overcome seemingly insurmountable obstacles.

When the Media Isn't So Powerful ...

The power of the mass media to whip up anti-gay hatred and homophobia is formidable. Newspapers which 'out' people—famous or not—invariably attempt to use the homosexual tag as a form of humiliation and a means of discredit. This treatment of homosexuality in the media underlines the fear of disclosure and repercussions, especially at work. However, a closer look at cases of media homophobia reveals that its power to form public opinion is not as sweeping as some believe. In reality, the media tends to try to reflect and reinforce prejudice rather than invent bigotry. And sometimes they get it wrong.

The Jane Brown Affair

In January 1994 a story broke in the British media. Jane Brown, head teacher at Kingsmead primary school in Hackney, east London, was reported as having turned down free theatre tickets for a performance of Shakespeare's *Romeo and Juliet,* thereby preventing pupils from attending the theatre. The story went that she had done this on the grounds that the play was 'a heterosexual love story'. The media exploded in an orgy of homophobia and self-righteous invective against 'political correctness'. Jane Brown's sexuality and relationships were seized upon and scrutinised. There were calls for her to be sacked. Questions were asked about her appointment and it was alleged that she had only got the job because she was sleeping with the chair of the school governors, Nikki Thorogood. Labour-run Hackney council's education department, led by 'left-wing' Director Gus John, responded by saying it would suspend Jane Brown pending an inquiry. She issued a public apology and did not speak to the media again.

On the surface, it appeared that this was indeed a case of political correctness gone mad. Who in their right mind would prevent underprivileged children from visiting a theatre to see Shakespeare unless they had perverse personal motives? How could anyone dismiss a literary classic as 'heterosexist'? It looked as though the homophobes had a point and that the media had struck gold.

Jane Brown had indeed called the play 'heterosexual' but this was during a private telephone conversation. She had turned down not free but subsidised tickets. Not all pupils would have been able to afford to go. Taking up the offer would have intensified problems of poverty in a school already starved of resources by Tory education cuts. Jane Brown was indeed having a relationship with Nikki Thorogood, but this had developed after she had started work at the school, not prior to her interview. It also transpired that it had been the council press office which had given the story to the London *Evening Standard* newspaper in the first place. This happened several weeks after the council first knew about the alleged 'heterosexual' remarks. None of these aspects of the case received the coverage given to the original story. It looked as though this was a successful case of lesbian-assassination. But neither Hackney education department, the media nor anti-gay critics had counted on the power of working-class people to defend themselves.

First of all, teachers and pupils at the school united behind Jane Brown and voiced their unanimous support for her as an excellent head teacher. Then parents and school governors refused to carry out the suspension. Whilst the Director of Education petitioned the Tory education minister John Patten to force the board of governors to get rid of Brown, Hackney Teacher's Association coordinated a campaign to defend her and formed the Kingsmead Support Group. Teachers, pupils and parents across London joined this campaign. Lesbians and gays recognised the fight as a focus for their anger over the isolation experienced by lesbians and gays in schools, and the homophobia of the media. All this time Brown continued to work at the school. Demonstrations, meetings, lobbies and benefits were organised. Supporters of Jane Brown all agreed that a person's sexuality had nothing whatsoever to do with their ability to teach. Lesbian, gay, bisexual, heterosexual, black and white united in Jane Brown's defence. Teachers, pupils and parents together proved that the media ultimately has no power to delude ordinary people about the facts of their own experiences. The campaign against Jane Brown backfired a hundredfold. The support she received was far more powerful than the accusations and attacks made against her. In the end it was overworked teachers, poor parents and deprived kids who overcame the might of the 'all powerful' national mass media.

Saving the Children

Sandi Toksvig, a comedian working in British broadcasting, was interviewed in the *Sunday Times* in September 1994. The popular performer, who had long lent active support to the international charity Save the Children Fund (SCF), whose president is Princess Anne, discussed her work and told the interviewer that she lived with her long-time woman partner and their three children. Other newspapers picked up on Toksvig's statements and followed up with further stories which were decidedly more negative and salacious. The comedian was due to host the SCF's 75th anniversary conference in early October and had telephoned the charity in advance of publication of the *Sunday Times* interview to forewarn the SCF Council. She had been told that since the charity operated an equal opportunities policy there was no problem. However, following the tabloid press reports, SCF decided 'with considerable regret' to drop Toksvig as host. The reaction of workers at the Fund, however, ensured that this hypocrisy rebounded on the council running the charity.

Outside the conference from which Toksvig had been dropped, direct action group the Lesbian Avengers staged a noisy demonstration disrupting the event. At the same time, angry and unwilling to accept the Fund's decision, staff decided to organise and 259 workers agreed to sign a letter of complaint to the charity's council upbraiding their bosses for double standards. In a letter to the press, they wrote:

> We were appalled to learn of this decision... [which] contradicts our stated principles and values as an organisation committed to equal rights and to fighting discrimination. We regret the damaging effects this could have on our work. We are required to uphold these values in our work and are motivated to work for Save the Children because it holds such values dear.[1]

If a well-known media figure could be treated like this what chance would a clerical worker or information officer have? The charity was known for its community work with young people of all sexualities—was this work now under question? The Toksvig episode made SCF look bigoted and hypocritical. The tactic of trying to appease the homophobic media had massively backfired—the staff used their power and held out for a full climb-down. A full and unqualified apology was issued by SCF's council to Toksvig who read out the letter at London's Royal Albert Hall during a celebrity gay rights extravaganza—'she won a louder cheer than any of the other all-star performers'.[2]

Soon after this episode came the revelation that another major UK based charity, The Children's Society, had decided to ban lesbians and gay men from fostering children in its care, despite a commitment on paper to full equal opportunities. The reason given was the charity's strong links to the Church of England. Inspired by the success of the Save the Children campaign, workers at The Children's Society leaked internal documents to the gay press which showed that the issue had been the subject of intense debate for nearly two years. They were quick to organise a campaign and, as trade unionists, recognised that the ban was a direct threat upon their own conditions and rights. The Manufacturing, Science and Finance Union responded by issuing a statement deploring the ban and throwing its weight behind the staff campaign. The charity then put a media gag on its employees. This served to fuel the campaign further. Outside support for the protesting staff poured in. As events unfolded, the Children's Society bosses found themselves more and more isolated.

Workers at The Children's Society recognised that an attack on lesbian and gay carers was an attack on the children in care. It was an attack on lesbians and gay men generally. It was an attack on lesbian and gay staff and most of all it was an attack on all workers in the organisation. This was clearly a case for coordinated industrial action in response to vicious divide-and-rule tactics.

Sexual Politics on the Buses

It's often claimed, mistakenly, that the working class, particularly manual workers, are far too homophobic, racist and sexist to fight for liberation and equality. The experiences of Roger Barton, a bus driver in Brighton and south London, shows how the workplace can and will be a primary site for changing people's attitudes about a whole range of issues, including sexual politics. In 1979 Susan Shell, a member of the national Union of Public Employees, was sacked from her job as a care assistant in east London for being a lesbian. Roger recalls:

> *I brought the subject up and said, speaking as a straight bus driver, that it was really out of order that this woman should lose her job because of her sexuality. There were some gay people who had a go at me later saying I shouldn't bring this sort of thing up at union meetings. But we talked about it over the next few weeks and sent a motion off from our*

branch to support her. There was a national trade union campaign set up called Gay Rights at Work which our branch then affiliated to.[3]

Creating an atmosphere at work where all kinds of things could be discussed meant that bus workers developed a more political outlook on many issues. The experience of fighting over pay and conditions was also a catalyst for changing people's attitudes. Lesbian and gay people were able to take a leading role in rank and file organisation:

I got the sack from Brighton buses, after a very long-drawn out strike, for being one of the main picket organisers. During that time it struck me how people's sexuality became really quite an unremarkable part of their life. There was one gay bloke who was into Citizen's Band (CB) radio which had only just become legal. He was very much instrumental in organising the flying pickets over his CB and it was wonderful to see him, really quite camp, giving instructions to groups of 30 and 40 bus workers to go flying off to Horsham or Uckfield or wherever. Nobody gave a moment's thought to what his sexuality was. On the pickets you talked about all kinds of things. The women were so open about their sexuality, it didn't really bother them. They'd talk about how they'd been washing a dildo when the insurance man came round and how he couldn't take his eyes off the washing-up! So they were quite funny with it as well.[4]

During the strike, Roger and his workmates travelled to south London to rally support and make collections.

We were taken round the garages by a member of the Socialist Workers Party who was gay. We went to Camberwell Bus Garage first and didn't really get a good response from the union officials who said 'You don't want to go over to Walworth, they're all queers over there'. At which point the comrade who was taking us round said 'Oh yes, I must renew my subscription to Gay News*.' All the Brighton bus workers started laughing at this and said 'That's not a problem for us, we'll take money off anyone!' So we went over to Walworth and they immediately gave us £50 out of union funds for our strike.*[5]

Roger later got a job, ironically, at Walworth Bus Garage:

Very quickly I discovered that as in Brighton there were quite a few gay and lesbian workers. Anyway, Walworth was earmarked for closure and within a few months we were transferred over to Camberwell. There was quite lot of hostility from the Camberwell crews and the idea that we were all gays was used as a stick to beat us with. There was a big union meeting in the games room where all kinds of stupid arguments came up about whether someone who had done twelve years at Walworth should be treated as new staff. It was not very well handled by the union and at the end a couple of us went round with Socialist Worker*. There was a very horrible group of Camberwell rightwingers who sort of dominated the atmosphere. They picked up the pool cues and started shouting 'You're not selling that fucking paper around this garage!' We said 'Well, who's going to stop us?' and a group of Walworth drivers appeared around us and took our side. I remember we picked up the snooker balls from the tables and said 'You haven't got the balls to stop us' which made a lot of people laugh, made them look really stupid and they just put the cues down and we carried on selling the paper. Things changed very much from that moment because there was a group of us who were socialists and we had around us people who were quite interested in the things we were saying, particularly about gay liberation.*[6]

A number of women and men came out as gay at Camberwell and became active in the union and in defending gay rights. By 1987 Camberwell bus garage sent a contingent, with a union banner from the branch, on the Lesbian and Gay Pride March.

Roger and his workmates showed in practice that the main division in society is not between gay and straight, between black and white, or men and women, but between classes.

> *When it came down to any kind of struggle a person's sexuality became almost meaningless. During a strike in Camberwell we had trouble with a whole number of scabs and when they came along people literally did link arms and join together to have a go at the scabs and stop them getting through. That's the key thing—when people are fighting together the differences in sexuality, or anything else, are relatively meaningless.*[7]

Connections

There are dozens of examples of workers linking the fight for sexual liberation to class struggle against oppression and exploitation. They illustrate over and over again the crucial role of class struggle in fighting gay oppression and the vital importance of arguing for lesbian and gay rights in the context of any fightback in the workplace or in the streets. For instance, the UK Pride march and carnival in 1993 coincided with a long-running strike at the Timex factory in Dundee where workers were taking action against massive job and wage cuts. On the same day, lesbians and gay men travelled to the Dundee picket line to join a mass demonstration in support of the Timex workers. Hundreds of others at the picket joined in the rallying cry: We're here, we're queer—and we won't scab at Timex!' Some demonstrators recalled how reminiscent this was of the massive Anti-Nazi League Carnival in 1978 when the whole crowd sang along with gay performer Tom Robinson the words: 'Sing if you're glad to be gay! Sing if you're happy that way!'

The 1970s were a time of powerful resistance. Under the influence of the Gay Liberation Front (GLF), gay trade unionists gained the confidence to force the issue of gay rights to the surface. Unlike GLF in the US, the UK organisation actively engaged with workers' struggles. In this spirit, lesbians and gays began to organise within their trade unions to get gay issues recognised as workers' rights issues. One example was of rank-and-file gay activists in the college lecturers union ATTI (later renamed NATFHE) who succeeded in getting the union to adopt a gay rights resolution in 1976.

In November 1978 voters in California were asked to decide whether or not they supported Proposition 6, which demanded that teachers who openly declared their homosexuality should be dismissed.[8] A campaign was waged which united trade unionists, gay activists, feminists and civil rights groups. The official teaching unions accepted that Proposition 6 was a threat to all teachers and resolved to defend any teacher threatened with dismissal if the ruling became law. In the end, after demonstrations and public debates about gay rights at work, Californians voted no to Proposition 6 by 59 per cent to 41 per cent.[9]

In England and Wales, Section 28 of the Local Government Act, banning any attempt by local authorities to 'intentionally promote homosexuality', became law in June 1988. In the run up to the law change, several local authorities, including those run by Labour, attempted to head off potential prosecutions through a series of sackings and by removing teaching materials which were positive towards gay rights. Councillors in several authorities took the opportunity to launch public attacks on local lesbian and gay groups and initiatives. Austin Allen, a gay teacher in Labour-controlled Bradford, was sacked for responding to pupils' questions about homosexuality. The local National Union of Teachers met to condemn the sacking and called for a half-day strike. Several schools voted to back the strike and teachers lobbied the district Labour Party. Taken aback by the speed of workers' reaction and the high level of support, the education authority did a complete U-turn and reinstated Austin Allen.

This dramatic action showed the gay community how best to fight the implications of Section 28. Already violent attacks on gays and gay venues were increasing, fuelled by the prejudice stirred up by the new law. Unfortunately, gay community leaders made no attempt to build on the cross-sexuality solidarity which had been demonstrated during the Stop the Clause Campaign and which was so in evidence during the Austin Allen affair. They did not even point out that Section 28 was a government tactic to off-load the blame for draconian public spending cuts. The defence of teachers and librarians who were targeted under the provisions of the Act could only really effectively be coordinated through enlisting the support of predominantly straight union members in these workers' branches. Lobbyists and community spokespeople did nothing to push for this solidarity and as a result the energy of the campaign was largely thrown away.

Resistance and Revolution

Sexual liberationists often point to times of repression as illustrations of how shifts to the right are always linked to the tightening up of sexual regulation. The Thatcher/Reagan years were times of deep reaction. Working-class gains, such as welfare and public housing, were viciously attacked. Trade union organisation was assaulted. Lesbian and gay people were vilified and their campaigns for justice ridiculed or ignored. The family as an institution was resuscitated as a model for moral rectitude. But what happens when our side is more confident? How do lesbians and gays benefit when collective action against the ruling class is successful?

The Tangible Proof

The 1984-5 British miners' strike against pit closures was a time when the real potential of the working class became a visible inspiration. Striking miners and their families endured extreme physical hardship during the 12-month dispute. Government tactics to break the strike included the use of force hitherto only seen on the war-torn streets of Northern Ireland. Bosses, government, the media, and all weapons of the state were coordinated to break the miners struggle. Mass pickets organised to defend the strike were attacked by armies of riot police equipped with batons, shields, armoured vans and horses. Whole villages were put under siege and sealed off by riot police. The Department of Health and Social Security stopped benefits to striking miners, even those with children. The Labour Party and the Trade Union Congress (TUC), managed to avoid making any real commitment to organising the solidarity desperately needed to win the strike. It would have taken solidarity action by transport workers, electricians and others to prevent the movement of coal and the supply of power stations. On the other hand, working people responded magnificently with widespread and sustained support. Regular collections on the street and in workplaces kept the miners going.

Soon after the beginning of the strike, a group of lesbian and gay socialists in London called a public meeting in support of the miners in a room above a gay pub. Lesbians and Gays Support the Miners (LGSM) was born—an organisation which changed the course of gay history and remains to this day part of the tangible proof that when people unite on the basis of class, barriers of prejudice and ignorance simply crumble and collapse. Soon after the group was established, further chapters of LGSM began to emerge in other cities. LGSM London linked up with mining communities in Neath and Dulais, South Wales. The group grew fast as lesbian and gay people seized the opportunity to support the strike in a way which linked with their fight against homophobia. They started to make regular collections around gay clubs and pubs, winning new support and opening up discussions and debates as they went. Soon, common experiences began to emerge. Kay, a miner's wife, pointed out the need for unity at a public meeting:

> *Over the last year we've not had things easy and it's only over the last year that we've come to know lesbian and gay people. Their struggle is something similar to ours. We've suffered over the last year with the police what they've been suffering all their lives and are likely to continue to suffer unless we do something about it.[10]*

Men and women in mining communities took their chance to discuss issues of sexuality. Some came out as lesbian or gay. Everyone joined in vigorous discussion about the family, marriage, unions, socialism, the Tories, the betrayals of Labour, the kind of society they wanted. Between July 1984 and January 1985 LGSM collected £15,000 for the South Wales mining communities. Ben, a member of LGSM, talked during a visit to Dulais about the links that had been made and their amazing consequences:

> *A few months ago if anyone had asked us if this kind of alliance was possible we would never have believed it. I don't think the miners in the Welsh valley that we went to two months ago would have imagined that they would have entertained in their community the largest single donating group as a gay group. I think they would have laughed— and we would as well to imagine that we would have been welcomed so warmly. All the myths and all the barriers of prejudice were just broken down. It makes me feel quite moved by the possibilities. You can unite and fight!*

Lesbians and gays organised and demonstrated openly and proudly in support of the miners' struggle. They were attacked by police, along with miners and their families during a mass demonstration in support of the miners in central London. LGSM also organised a benefit concert of lesbian and gay performers at the Electric Ballroom in North London. Over 1500 people attended and heard Dave, a striking miner, announce amidst cheers: 'Victory to the miners! Victory to lesbians and gays! Victory to the old! Victory to the young! And victory to the working class!' He was closely followed by LGSM member Nigel who declaimed:

All lesbians and gay men who are attacked by the police, attacked by the media, attacked by the state, know what it's like to be attacked. That's why we're here openly as lesbians and gays and as socialists. A victory for the miners is a victory for us all!

It wasn't just the mining communities who learned lessons from the strike. Gay activists themselves had an opportunity to find out that alliances and unity against the common enemy are a far more effective way of fighting homophobia than single-issue identity groupings. LGSM member Mark pointed out an important lesson for the gay movement:

It's not just about defending the miners, it's about defending the right to organise. It's quite illogical to say 'I'm gay and I'm into defending the gay community but I don't care about anything else.' It's ludicrous. It's important that if you're defending communities that you defend all communities.

The strike ended in defeat in March 1985. Nevertheless, the gains of the struggle were not lost. Hundreds of men, women and children from mining communities travelled to London to demonstrate their support for gay rights on the 1985 Lesbian and Gay Pride March. LGSM member Derek identified a key shift in the politics of the march as a result of gay support for the strike:

On the gay pride march this year it was more than what it normally is, that is an expression of lesbians and gays marching through central London saying 'This is our sexuality.' This year the miners, miners' wives and their families came, as well as friends, fellow students, people from work. It became a political march of people wanting to say something about lesbian and gay rights and the attacks on our community.

At the TUC Conference that year, the NUM led the campaign to incorporate lesbian and gay rights into the Congress equality policy. Sexual liberation has been recognised as having an unbreakable link to the politics of class. Sian, a miner's wife and political activist, describes the lasting meaning of class solidarity:

Lesbians and Gays Support the Miners came to our aid when we really really needed help... It wasn't just financial help. We gained an insight into a different way of life... In our community one of the things that captures people's attention immediately is the van. [A bright red transit van bearing the message 'Donated by LGSM London' and bearing a gay pink triangle which was bought from money collected by LGSM.] That van is the tangible proof of the support and the friendships that were made. It's there, it's active and being used by the community. It's marvellous when I see the van going down the road! I see people doing double-takes but I don't mind that because it means they've got to think about lesbian and gay issues and ask: 'What does that mean? What is the story behind that van?' And that sets off a chain of thought and reaction.

The Russian Revolution

In the period between the establishment of a workers' state in 1917 and the rise of Stalinism in 1924, Russian society underwent a genuine, though unfinished, sexual revolution. Socialists committed to building a just and fair society can look to that era as a pointer towards the gains that can be won for sexual freedom through the class struggle.

The Bolsheviks who led the revolution were not interested in changing the existing order to make it a bit fairer to those who had been marginalised or discriminated against. They knew that they had to sweep away, in Marx's words, 'the muck of ages' and get rid of the family completely. Thus 'homosexuality' was not simply a question of 'rights'. It was a discriminatory definition which would eventually cease to have any meaning.

Two months after the October revolution, in December 1917, the Bolsheviks abolished all laws against homosexuality. Subsequently, safe abortion and contraception were made available on demand and divorce was granted on request. Legal distinctions between legitimacy and illegitimacy were removed. The laws on the age of consent were repealed. In order to undermine the basis of women's oppression—the family—communal laundries, nurseries and restaurants were opened to set individuals free from the drudgery of housework. No longer was the home seen as separate from work, but part and parcel of the *collective* human environment. Workplace meetings included discussions on a whole range of experiences, including domestic violence and the problems of parenting. Relationships between women and men began to be transformed and open to a whole new set of ideas about equality, consent and sexual freedom. Alexandra Kollontai, a leading Bolshevik organiser and writer, wrote eloquently about the damaging effects of capitalism upon people's personal relationships. She asserted that socially sanctioned sexual relationships—marriages—were established on the basis of protecting property and had nothing to do with people's underlying needs:

... it is only by becoming aware of the creative process that is going on within society, and of the new demands, new ideals and new norms that are being formed...that we can possibly make sense of the chaos and contradictions of sexual relationships, and find the thread that will make it possible to undo the tightly rolled up tangle of sexual problems.

We must remember that only a code of sexual morality that is in harmony with the problems of the working class can serve as an important weapon in strengthening the working class's fighting position.[11]

These first measures were taken despite horrific civil war. The new workers' state was being attacked on all sides. Sixteen capitalist armies invaded the country on a mission to destroy the new socialist society. The working class was decimated. On the back of this devastation Stalin broke through with his disastrous theory of 'socialism in one country', effectively paving the way for a state which called itself socialist but was in fact a form of state capitalism. Stalin's solution to the crisis of child care and the demands of women workers for a decent level of service provision was the reintroduction of family values. He and his ministers reasserted the conservative idea that a woman's primary role should be that of wife and mother, carrying out privatised work within the home. The promise of sexual freedom was lost with the degeneration of the revolution.

A Gay Issue or a Class Issue?

Many prominent reformist lesbian and gay leaders see it as their duty constantly to rework the agenda for sexual political action on *behalf* of the mass of lesbian and gay people in society. In Europe and the US, noted radicals and liberals endlessly reinvent a set of priorities for lobbying, campaigning and direct action. New terms are coined in the reformist effort to recast the 'lesbian and gay movement'. It is as though if we reframe our oppression in a new vocabulary, we will find the key to bringing about the revolutionary change that everyone yearns for. In the US concepts like 'oppression sickness', 'internalised homophobia' and 'diversity awareness'[12] are whisked up in an effort to explain the fragmentation of the gay movement and the problems of corporate organisation. Peter Tatchell of UK direct action group Outrage! took a double-page spread in a gay newspaper in 1994 to ask: 'Which way now?' The article claimed that there were 16 points of law which embody most of the legal discrimination against lesbians and gays in the UK. The (apparently) crucial question was: 'what kind of legal changes should we be aiming for?'

The factor which holds all reformist strategies back is the way that they define and ringfence supposedly 'lesbian and gay issues' as though lesbian and gay oppression simply affects those who have same-sex relationships. The reality is that gay oppression is a weapon of social control. We cannot hope to bring about real change for gay people whilst the system which causes gay oppression remains in place. It would be misguided to dismiss any legal changes which improve lesbian and gay people's rights. Any gain is worthwhile and should be welcomed. But real change can only come from understanding and fighting gay oppression in a wider context.

In comparing these two approaches I shall concentrate on five of the main areas where gay and lesbian people face discrimination in the UK, by drawing on briefings produced by the Stonewall Group. However, most of the categories of discrimination apply to other countries and many of the examples have their counter-parts elsewhere.

1. The Age of Consent

Sexual contact between men in England and Wales is still criminalised. Consensual sex between men over 18 is only legal 'in private', that is, in a place where no one else could possibly come across them. This means not in hotel rooms or other people's homes. The age of consent for heterosexual and lesbian sex is 16, with a far less stringent definition of privacy.

The imposition of an age of consent is widely regarded as a way of protecting young people against predatory older people. This is particularly the case with gay men who are suspected by homophobes of being congenital paedophiles. But how can any society decide when a person is old enough to consent to sex with another person? It would be ridiculous to suggest that all young people suddenly achieve the maturity and self-knowledge necessary to have safe and consensual sex on their sixteenth, eighteenth, twelfth, tenth or fourteenth birthdays. Yet this is what a law on the age of consent suggests. The reality is that underage teenagers find ways to have sex all the time, no matter how repressive their parents, teachers or guardians are. There is simply no way that this can be stopped or prevented. The problem is that in denying the sexuality of young people, the law and social institutions deny young women and men information. An age of consent prevents young people below the designated age from getting advice about contraception, sexual health and safer sex. It shrouds early sexual experiences in an atmosphere of secrecy and fear. Rather than protecting young people it criminalises them and puts them at risk of disease and unwanted pregnancy.

The concept of consent is far more complex and delicate than simply being a matter of age. It is fundamentally linked to the way that capitalist society treats the body and sexual relationships. Because we live in a society where profit is the driving motive, all aspects of human relationships, including sexuality, are intensively commodified and commercialised. Women's bodies are continually defined as the property of men. Until very recently, it was impossible in the UK for a man to be accused of raping his wife. Her body was simply seen as his property—he had the right to force sex upon her.

More generally, female and male sexualities are subject to all kinds of social conditioning. The notion of a sexual relationship is couched in the disinfectant of romance so that the reality of sexual contact is submerged in a hotch-potch of sentiment and false hopes. The law on an 'age of consent' is simply a clumsy irrelevance. What we need is the space and the opportunity to understand and explore our emerging sexualities openly and without shame—at any age. If that means lessons on same-scx love for seven-year-olds, or condom-practice play sessions for fourteen-year-olds—then so be it. In a society which depends on the codes of morality and the strictures of sexual regulation, real sexual freedom and genuine consent are simply not possible.[13]

2. Immigration

Gay reformists base their criticisms of immigration law on a perceived 'singling-out' of lesbian and gay people for discrimination. If a host country recognises a heterosexual partnership/marriage as grounds for granting a person permission to stay, but makes no provision for allowing lesbian or gay couples to stay together, then gay rights activists point to this as an inconsistency. For instance, Stonewall, in its 'Briefing on Lesbian and Gay Partnerships and the Law', says:

> *The immigration rules for the UK recognise and accommodate emotional relationships between individuals of the opposite sex. By comparison a gay man or lesbian who falls in love with a non-EC citizen cannot get permission for that person to enter the country, or remain in the country, on the basis of their relationship.*[14]

There is a certain perversity about this kind of analysis. It represents the logical conclusion of a single-minded pursuit of identity politics and reveals the middle-class preoccupations of gay community leaders. The whole concept of immigration law has to be seen in an international class context—only then will the significance of anti-gay discrimination have its full impact.

Strict immigration legislation is a response by capitalism to its own inherent crises. It is used to control the movement of the working class around the world and to prevent poor people from escaping the disastrous effects of competition between sections of the ruling class: famine, partition, imperialism and war. It provides a convenient scapegoat for people's suffering. So when cuts are made in welfare, housing, education and health care, governments can put the blame on immigrants by saying there are simply too many people in the country.

Black people are most often the victims of this kind of scapegoating. Detention centres in the UK, where asylum seekers are imprisoned for up to 17 months without being accused of any crime whatsoever, are overwhelmingly full of people from Africa and the Middle East. People have been deported when Home Office officials have judged that the suffering they would undergo if they were sent back is not sufficiently great. They have also been sent back when, after invasive investigation, it has been 'proved' that their marriage is not 'genuine'. The rich and powerful are not subject to these kinds of controls and regulation. They can buy their way around the world, bypassing stringent entry rules and easily producing evidence of financial independence.

The main purpose of immigration law, then, is to divide workers by creating the illusion that redundancies, homelessness and hospital closures are the fault of refugees, visitors and settlers. Racism is the cornerstone upon which this elaborate web of lies is built. But this racism works hand in hand with that tried-and-tested conservative weapon: morality. This is why evidence of a lesbian or gay relationship is rarely accepted as grounds for allowing a person to stay. In the few countries where this is possible, in Denmark or New Zealand for instance, would-be settlers or refugees are still subject to racist regulation.

The gay reformist agenda on immigration rights barely scratches the surface of how deeply damaging immigration laws really are. A radical response needs to confront racism and homophobia as indivisible parts of a whole system of oppression and blame. It is important to initiate and support campaigns which defend the rights of gay and lesbian people to visit, stay and live in the country of their choice. But such campaigns need to be linked to the wider fight against all immigration regulation.

3. Partnership Rights

When reformists complain that gay couples cannot avail themselves of the same benefits as heterosexual couples because their partnerships are not recognised, they are implicitly asking for lesbian and gay relationships to be sanctioned by law. This is a very dangerous and short-sighted strategy. It is true that married partners do sometimes benefit from superannuation schemes and compassionate leave. Transport workers have also won benefits such as concessionary travel passes for their partners. Where these benefits are won for same-sex partners this is a great victory for all workers; it boosts confidence and asserts the principle of equal pay for equal work. But it is important not to use this as an argument in favour of 'gay marriages'. The marital contract is a legally regulated social institution which is primarily concerned with the apportioning of property. The family is important to capitalism because it saves the state money. As a result of this, parents are forced to take legal responsibility for and ownership of their children. They also find themselves forced to participate in the petty private property system whereby, in order to have a home and a measure of independence, they are forced to take out mortgages, buy consumer durables like cars and invest in taxable savings accounts.

Monogamy is an essential component of marital status because in a multiple partner relationship, it would be impossible to apportion property rights either during a relationship or at a time of divorce. Lesbian and gay couples are discriminated against in this system because they do not fit the model of reproductive family life. It can be argued that getting recognition of same-sex relationships would be a step forward. However, in those countries where homosexual relationships have been recognised, this recognition falls far short of full marriage rights. In Denmark for instance, same-sex couples may not marry in a church, nor may they apply jointly to adopt a child.

Laws on divorce illustrate most clearly the drawbacks of state intervention in people's relationships. At times of conflict the law is permitted to decide on levels of blame and entitlements to property. It also judges individuals' moral standing and ability to have custody or 'care and control' of children. For the majority of working-class people who divorce, the process is agonising, long-drawn-out and expensive. Nobody wins. The real basis of a long-term partnership—love, commitment, companionship—is fundamentally irrelevant to the use of marriage to regulate private property.

A socialist response is to argue for the eventual abolition of private property and marriage altogether. Such an argument is part and parcel of changing the world so that sexual relationships are no longer subject to the regulation, restriction and moral restraint which governs them under capitalism. Lesbians and gays cannot be and will not be accommodated into capitalism. In order to achieve lesbian and gay liberation we need to get rid of the system which breeds and feeds discrimination and homophobia.

4. Housing, Transport, Education and Welfare

The needs for shelter, safe passage, education, food, clothing and child and health care are common to all workers. Servicing these basic human needs is perennially resented by the ruling class and its institutions because they resent paying out for workers' welfare. Thus provision of these services is always inadequate and frequently chronically ill-resourced. There is also a deeper political motive for making welfare and service provision insufficient for people's needs. When people, through their own efforts, are relieved of the worry of homelessness, hunger, preventable illness and death, illiteracy and transport difficulties, they become confident. They start to develop creatively. They believe they can change their situation and are not willing to endure high levels of hardship. When workers in Britain won a National Health Service after the Second World War, they began to demand a comprehensive non-selective education system which would be free for everyone. They fought for and gained a welfare benefits system which, to a great extent, relieved the fear of hunger. Although these institutions and services had many faults, they represented a massive achievement for working people. For lesbians and gays, this principle of universal, free welfare is crucial. Most of us have no real housing rights. If our partner is a tenant and she or he dies, we get evicted. We travel a lot at night to the pubs and clubs where we can relax and be ourselves with our friends and lovers. For this we need regular and accessible public transport. Like everyone else, we need to be educated but educators are hindered from teaching about sexuality. We need free, comprehensive education to be broadened and developed, not cut and censored. As with all other humans, we need health care and disease prevention. When hospitals close we all suffer. We need nurses and doctors to have the time and resources to learn how to treat us equally and sensitively. Real equality of opportunity, therefore, can only come through building upon a basis of collective control. This will happen when those who produce and provide, together with those who consume and use, decide together how to structure society so that it can meet *all* the people's needs.

5. The Military

Campaigns to gain equal rights for lesbians and gays in the military have gained momentum on the lesbian and gay reformist agenda, especially since Bill Clinton was elected US president in 1992. Discrimination is rife in the military. Lesbians and gays are frequently investigated and dismissed because of their sexuality. It is important to oppose this inhuman and degrading treatment. However, we cannot simply ask for equal treatment and equal rights to 'serve our country'. In criticising the military we need to expose its international role in the defence of ruling class interests. Soldiers, sailors and air crews are deployed to protect the political and economic interests of capitalism. Military personnel may indeed be won to fighting on the side of the working class—this has happened many times in history in many countries, including Britain. But whilst they serve the capitalist state, even as national or international 'peace-keepers', they are used against the poor. Individual soldiers will disagree with the tasks they are forced to do. But the discipline of capitalist military forces means that even if they allow lesbians and gays to serve, they cannot suddenly become a force for freedom, equality and liberation. In opposing unjust treatment of gay people in the military, we need to ensure that our campaign addresses the underlying role of military forces in the world.

Revolutionising the Agenda for Gay Liberation

All 'lesbian and gay issues' are rooted in the politics of class struggle. When ambitious, bourgeois 'community leaders' seek to divorce these issues from wider social and political concerns the lesbian and gay movement becomes atrophied. Being able to rework and reassess the reformist gay rights programme in the context of defending working-class interests is a vital step in breaking away from the frustrations and divisions of identity politics. It enables us to see how the issues which are so close to gay people are of equal importance to the rest of society. Far from losing our identity in this process, we can begin to recognise actual and potential allies all around us.

Do we just want the same poverty traps and institutions? Seeking assimilation into what is perceived as 'straight privilege' has led many gay activists to confuse *equal rights* with *equal oppression*. This can lead to obscure and isolated campaigns against some of the most innocuous sides of homophobia. It can also mean that gay activists may, in defending their 'own corner', actually work against workers' struggle.

The Lesbian Avengers are a good example of the type of identity grouping around which left-wing gays and lesbians are congregating, often in frustration at the softly-softly approach of lobbyists in the corridors of power. Rightly they want to take politics onto the street. But they mistakenly believe that direct action—making a big noise and getting into the media—will bring about real change. They are unable to summon up large numbers for demonstrations and this makes such organisations appear like coteries and identity clubs. In their obsession with singling out examples of lesbo- and homophobia, they jump on obscure targets to make bland points. One target was a museum of a deceased lesbian in New York where the curators had ignored the artist's sexuality. Demonstrators gatecrashed a museum party, 'spoke to' guests at the reception and sang bawdy lesbian songs. At no point could such an action engage with wider issues of privilege and censorship. The effect of this type of action is often to make sexual politics cryptic and irrelevant.

Direct action groupings reinforce their exclusivity by setting themselves as experts and specialists. ACT-UP New York showed its colours after a successful demonstration on Brooklyn Bridge against cuts proposed by the Department of AIDS Services. Protesters included health workers, people with AIDS, lesbian and gay activists, socialists and members of ACT-UP. The proposed cuts were reversed. Tragically however, ACT-UP's analysis of the event concentrated on the lack of experience of those many demonstrators who were protesting on the streets for the first time:

> The problem is that ACT-UP does not see it as a victory that can lead to further struggles. The fact that new people took part led some to deride them as 'Johnnie-Come-Latelies' to the cause. The tactic of mass action is used sporadically and without a broader strategic goal of involving greater numbers and linking the battle for AIDS funding and research to other struggles for health care taking place within the working class. Over 80 per cent of all strikes over the last few years have dealt with health care issues.[15]

There is a danger that single-issue identity politics can undermine workers' action in some circumstances.

For example, Watney's, a brewery which supplied major London gay pubs, tried to impose redundancies and drastic changes in working patterns on workers in 1982. A strike was called which was very successful in blocking deliveries of beer to pubs in London. However, landlords of gay pubs took pride in reporting that they had successfully broken the strike and indefatigably obtained beer for their gay customers.[16]

The same year there was a London Transport strike over fare increases and job losses at the time when the annual Gay Pride demonstration was scheduled to take place. This was an opportunity to link the strike and the march in a common fight against the Thatcher government. Gay contingents could have gone to local picket lines to offer solidarity. Speakers from the strike could have been invited to address the rally. Instead, Pride organisers saw the strike as an obstacle to be overcome in order to get the numbers at the demonstration. Good attendance levels on the march were reported in the gay press as being the result of determined gay and lesbian people 'beating' the strike to exercise their civil liberties.

A day of action over National Health Service cuts and attacks on health workers' pay was called in September of 1982. Thanks to rank-and-file organisation throughout the country, the day was a resounding success. Schools were shut down and transport and construction was stopped in many towns and cities. Hundreds of thousands of workers struck in sympathy with the nurses, including transport and council workers, teachers, Post Office workers, factory workers, miners and television technicians. Again, this was an opportunity to link the fight for sexual liberation to the fight for workers' rights. Instead, members of the National Graphical Association (a print workers' union) working on *Gay News* broke their union's instruction to stop production in support of the hospital workers, claiming that gay people had to get their paper at all costs.[17]

Cutting off the struggle for sexual liberation from wider struggles means that opportunities for building support are continually lost. By insisting on separate organisation and by disdaining potential solidarity from heterosexuals, lesbian and gay community leaders preserve the middle-class and essentially isolated character of the struggle for gay rights. Indeed, they transform a universal fight for sexual liberation into an exclusive campaign, conducted by a select few for the benefit of an artificially constructed 'minority'. Most workers see in this approach no relevance to them or the issues they are forced to deal with every day at work and in the street.

Where Will the Class Struggle Lead Us?

Of all the groups of people ranged in opposition to injustice, inequality and oppression, it is workers who are the most organised and the most potentially powerful. They can unite with connected groups, such as the unemployed, gays and black people, to lead a forceful movement for social transformation. How can class struggle lead us to the fundamental social and political change we want and need?

Marxism is about turning small, everyday struggles into the big historical revolt. Small battles, conflicts and skirmishes can lead to a genuine mass class confrontation on the scale seen in Russia in 1917 and which almost occurred in several European countries at that time. The key to this transformation is organisation.

The ruling class controls the means of production, education and communication. It has a strategic grip on what workers are allowed to know. However, it is inherently weakened by its own fierce internal competition and lack of cohesion. Moreover, it cannot control the experiences workers gain from contact and organisation with one another. Because of these weaknesses, the potential power of the working class is much much greater than that of the ruling class. If the working class refuses to work, to produce, then the ruling class immediately loses its advantage. Meanwhile workers increase their power and confidence. Change can happen very fast and we need to be ready for it. The events of the past two decades have ensured that when the working class is next in revolt, issues like sexual liberation and AIDS will be at the forefront of our demands.

Marxism, with its emphasis on resistance and struggle as the key to building revolution, is crucial to the development of our organisations now. Moreover, the lesson of previous revolts and revolutions is that a necessary component of building and sustaining revolutionary change is the existence of a revolutionary organisation. The role of this organisation is to connect struggles, to draw the fights together and to put forward a revolutionary socialist perspective. At times of revolt this organisation is in the vanguard, drawing the mass of workers into a revolutionary focus and uniting them in a battle for a new and liberated society. A collective society, run by workers, far from sacrificing the choices, needs and potentials of the individual, would set people free to live, study, work and love in ways that they cannot possibly do under capitalism.

For me and thousands of other workers, lesbians and gays,

black people, women, students, children and unemployed people, the Socialist Workers Party in Britain is such an organisation. It is the means by which we coordinate our struggles and activities. It is the place where we can unite, learn lessons from the past and build for the future. As part of an international organisation, the Socialist Workers Party plays a crucial role in leading the resistance now and in preparing the ground for revolution.

When the next revolt comes, the vision described at the beginning of this chapter will begin to take shape in reality. Workers will fight for sexual liberation openly *as workers*. Millions of lesbians, gays and bisexuals will come out on the strength of the solidarity and support around them. We have already seen this happen in microcosm and can only guess at the potential of a revolutionary mass movement for universal sexual liberation. But this glorious outcome is not a foregone conclusion. Liberation is not inevitable. Workers' militancy is a response to the pressures of class oppression. There is a nightmare alternative which also appears at times of crisis in capitalism: fascism. People turn to Nazi ideas and the politics of blame when they see no way out of their own troubles. They seize upon easy targets—gays, disabled people, black people, minorities— in their despair. Socialists have to be there, in the workplaces, communities, schools, colleges and on the estates, showing that there is an alternative. We need to be strong and visible so that when people have had enough they turn to the left and not to the right. We are all part of the class struggle. It carries on and we exist within it. The challenge is to recognise its power and harness its energy to the struggle for sexual liberation—now.

Notes

1   Letter to the *Guardian*, 8 October 1994.

2   *Capital Gay*, 28 October 1994.

3   Roger Barton, interviewed by the author, 1994.

4   Ibid.

5   Ibid.

6   Ibid.

7   Ibid.

8   *Tech Teacher*, no. 23, autumn 1978.

9   *Tech Teacher*, no. 24, spring 1979.

10 All direct quotations from the LGSM story taken from the video *All Out! Dancing in Dulais,* Lesbians and Gays Support the Miners/Converse Pictures, 1986.

11 Alexandra Kollontai, *Sexual Relations and the Class Struggle,* reprinted 1984 as a Socialist Workers Party pamphlet, p. 16.

12 'Eating Our Own', *the Advocate*, August 1992.

13 See Regan Kilpin, 'They Try to Tell Us We're Too Young', *Socialist Review,* March 1994.

14 Stonewall, 1993.

15 Sherry Wolf, Midwest Organiser, International Socialist Organisation, in a letter to the author, 1994.

16 John Lindsay, 'Pink but not red' *Socialist Review*, January 1983.

17 Ibid.

Index

Mineshaft Club, Manchester 222
modernism, and post-modernism 147, 239-41, 244, 268
'moral majority' 105
Mort, Frank 153
Murphy, Tony, gay policeman 213, 221-2
Muslims, as scapegoats 30

National Front 213
National Gallery, workers on strike for Pride in London 2015 40
National Graphical Association 307
National Lesbian and Gay Task Force (US) 60, 122
National Society for the Prevention of Cruelty to Children 71
National Union of Miners (NUM) 20-1, 23, 25, 28-9, 294
National Union of Teachers 289
Naughton, John, TV critic 203
New Realism 242
New York Celebrating Bisexuality 269-70
New Zealand 300

oppression 9, 18-20, 23-4, 26, 33-40, 42, 43-6, 48-9, 57, 59-62, 75-7, 83, 99-101, 104, 108, 110, 115-6, 118, 120, 122-35, 130-143, 146, 148-50, 155-8, 161-2, 178-9, 183-4, 186-8, 191, 195, 197, 205, 214, 227-8, 232, 235, 244, 246-8, 250-1, 258, 262-4, 270-2, 275-8, 288, 295, 297, 301, 305, 307, 309
OUT magazine 121, 167
OUT/LOOK magazine 261-3
Outrage! 60, 119, 129, 185, 196, 198, 205, 206, 219, 222, 224, 242, 244, 269, 297
Outweek, US magazine 243
Owen, Wilfred 107

parents 10, 37, 39, 58, 65-8, 71, 73, 76, 80-1, 84, 92, 104-5, 119, 187, 246, 279, 282-3, 298, 301
partnership rights 299, 301-2
patriotism 104-8, 116

Socialist Workers Party 32, 39, 286, 309
Soho 34, 129, 163, 169, 180, 191, 206; Pink Weekends 129
South Bank University 259
South Wales, LGSM in 20, 25-6, 291-2
Southwark, London Borough of 91
Spy, Capital Gay critic 180
Stalin, Joseph 151, 295-6
Starbucks, as sponsors of Pride in London 2015 40
Starkey, David 190
Stonewall bar (Greenwich Village) 12, 35, 224-5, 234
Stonewall group 60, 166, 183, 185, 187, 189-91, 195-6, 199, 207-8, 210, 297, 299
Stopes, Marie 78, 80-1, 88
strikes 22, 24, 34, 201, 215, 278, 306; see also industrial action
Strong, Alan, police harassment 221
Surrealism 240

Tatchell, Peter, of Outrage! 119, 135-7, 139-41, 143, 196, 198, 257-8, 297
teachers 9, 38, 40-2, 47, 78, 89, 113, 135, 275, 279, 282-3, 289-90, 298, 307
Terrence Higgins Trust 23
Thatcher, Margaret 9, 13, 20, 25-9, 31, 33, 37, 47, 93, 217, 290, 306
'third sex', theories of 116-8
Thorogood, Nikki, and Jane Brown affair 281-2
Timex factory, Dundee, strike 288
Toksvig, Sandy, media treatment of 283-4
TORCHE (Tory Campaign for Homosexual Equality 166, 190-1
totalitarianism 111
Tower Hamlets, BNP in 226
Trade Union Congress (TUC) 21, 25-6, 28, 33, 41, 291, 294
trade unions 13, 23-4, 41, 113, 289
transport 40, 63, 69, 176, 187, 239, 291, 301-3, 306-7; bus workers 38, 286-7
Tredegar Town Band, marching at Pride in London 2015 40

Tress, Arthur 235
Turner, J.M.W. 236
Tyndall, John, BNP leader 113

Ulrichs, Karl Heinrich 116-7
United Kingdom; see also Great Britain
United States 12-3, 84, 108, 122, 138, 147, 185, 199, 208, 210, 240, 243-4, 249, 262, 265-6; see also California

Valentine's Carnival (1993) 129, 206
violence 43-4, 67, 71, 73, 196, 207, 214, 216-7, 219-20, 226, 244, 246
Virgin company 166-7
Vittorini, Polly 32
voluntary organisations 66, 166

wages 22, 41, 45, 74-6, 79, 85, 87, 91, 104, 114, 141, 165, 173-4, 176-7, 189, 198, 200, 202, 214, 253, 258, 288-9
Walker, Kenneth 81, 84
Walker, Peter 27
Warhol, Andy 234
Watney's brewery strike 306
Watson, Kim 166-8
Watson, Oscar 123-4
Weeks, Jeffrey 154-6
welfare 14, 23, 27, 43, 63, 68-9, 74, 76-7, 80, 86, 92-3, 97, 113, 123, 149, 177, 290, 300, 302-3
'What's Wrong with Angry', film 245-6
Whitehouse, Mary 31, 106, 112
Wilde, Oscar 30
Willetts, David 35, 89-90
Williams, Frances 146
Williams, Tennessee 30
Williamson, Dugald 148
Wistrich, Harriet 124